TO KEEP
THE BRITISH ISLES
AFLOAT

ALSO BY THOMAS PARRISH

The Ultra Americans

Roosevelt and Marshall: Partners in Politics and War

The Cold War Encyclopedia

Berlin in the Balance

The Submarine: A History

The Simon & Schuster Encyclopedia of World War II (editor)

The Grouchy Grammarian

Restoring Shakertown

Smithsonian Books

COLLINS
An Imprint of HarperCollins Publishers

TO KEEP THE BRITISH ISLES AFLOAT

FDR's Men in Churchill's London, 1941

THOMAS PARRISH

Picture Acknowledgments

Bettmann/Corbis: 3, top. Churchill Archives Centre, Cambridge: 4 (both). Franklin D. Roosevelt Library: 1 bottom; 2; 5; 6 (both); 7; 8 (both). Margaret Suckley/Franklin D. Roosevelt Library: 1, top. Stephen Simpson: 3, bottom.

TO KEEP THE BRITISH ISLES AFLOAT. Copyright © 2009 by Thomas Parrish. All rights reserved. Printed in the United States of America. No part of this book may be used or reproduced in any manner whatsoever without written permission except in the case of brief quotations embodied in critical articles and reviews. For information, address HarperCollins Publishers, 10 East 53rd Street, New York, NY 10022.

HarperCollins books may be purchased for educational, business, or sales promotional use. For information, please write: Special Markets Department, HarperCollins Publishers, 10 East 53rd Street, New York, NY 10022.

FIRST EDITION

Designed by Mary Austin Speaker

Library of Congress Cataloging-in-Publication Data

Parrish, Thomas (Thomas D.)

To keep the British Isles afloat : FDR's men in Churchill's London, 1941 / Thomas Parrish. — 1st ed.

p. cm.

Includes bibliographical references and index.

ISBN 978-0-06-135793-0

1. World War, 1939-1945—Diplomatic history. 2. United States—Foreign relations—Great Britain. 3. Great Britain—Foreign relations—United States. 4. Roosevelt, Franklin D. (Franklin Delano), 1882-1945. 5. Churchill, Winston, Sir, 1874-1965. 6. Hopkins, Harry L. (Harry Lloyd), 1890-1946. 7. Harriman, W. Averell (William Averell), 1891-1986. I. Title.

D753.P27 2009

940.53'1—dc22   2008046206

09 10 11 12 13   OV/RRD   10 9 8 7 6 5 4 3 2 1

"I want you to go over to London and recommend everything we can do, short of war, to keep the British Isles afloat."

President Roosevelt to Averell Harriman—
February 18, 1941

CONTENTS

PREFACE

This account seeks to capture times and places that have become strangely distant and in many ways mythical. It tells the story of the troubled gestation and difficult birth of the Anglo-American alliance, which has been a central fact in the world since World War II, and at the same time it tells the story of Harry Hopkins and Averell Harriman, two remarkable men who played vital roles in the development of this unique international partnership in its early, fragile days. Behind these special presidential representatives we see the figure of Franklin D. Roosevelt, the pragmatic designer and director of this unprecedented alliance, as he patiently persevered from small beginnings despite all the traditional (notably including the strong isolationist outlook in the United States) and political obstacles standing in the way.

When urgency came in June 1940 with the dramatic escape of British forces at Dunkirk and the unexpected surrender of France, the president made an unprecedented and pivotal move toward alliance—the "destroyers-bases deal," seen here from the inside. For Roosevelt, this decidedly unneutral exchange represented a step not toward war but toward national security by helping to sustain Britain in the fight.

But could, and would, Britain hold out? FDR took an extraordinary direct step to find out by dispatching a "personal representative," Harry Hopkins, to see and report. These moves in 1940 and 1941 involved new kinds of thinking, as did lend-lease, the material manifestation of the alliance, which was being debated in Congress while Hopkins made his varied investigations in Britain. His favorable reports on Winston Churchill and British prospects undergirded lend-lease, though controversies and lesser disputes had to be thrashed out. Then, with the passage of lend-lease, came the final complement—the dispatch of Averell Harriman, the second of FDR's special envoys, to England to oversee the relationship at the receiving end and to act as the British terminal of the link between Roosevelt and Churchill, through Hopkins and Harriman. The adventures of Hopkins and Harriman and the many sides of their relationship to the prime minister dramatize the creation of the working alliance. Could the United States keep Britain in the war against Germany? It was their task to provide a positive answer to the question.

The narrative shows how even the president's closest associates failed to understand his purposes—that when he spoke of "all aid short of war" he meant exactly that, though most commentators, friendly and otherwise, presumed he was simply dissembling to minimize opposition. The story is told through the eyes of the participants at the time, showing how in their different ways they tried to deal with the issues they faced with the knowledge they had. Here, as I have done previously, I acknowledge Robert K. Massie's formulation of three golden principles for narrative: importance, immediacy, and suspense. The importance of the story speaks for itself, I believe, in its own day and still in ours, and immediacy and suspense come when we see and feel what the characters saw and felt at the time of the story, or what others knew and our principals could have known. What is discussed and dramatized in the book is, of course, chosen on the basis of what we know today, or think we know, but that is quite different from interference in the story by forecasting ("little did he know"), or hindsight, or condescension. Guided by today, we can live in the world of yesterday and perhaps even learn something from it.

THOMAS PARRISH

TO KEEP
THE BRITISH ISLES
AFLOAT

PROLOGUE: CRISIS, 1940

F or Americans, Europe has become the place where horrible and unaccountable things happen," a refugee Czech journalist wrote in early 1941, looking back across the Atlantic at the continent he had fled. "The pleasant dream of a United States of Europe has become a cruel reality. War, terror, slavery, and hunger have fused most of the Old Continent into a unit. Frontiers have been washed away by waves of common suffering. Since the same Gestapo presides over their single, tragic fate, what difference can there be now between Frenchmen, Dutchmen, Czechs, Serbs, or Norwegians? Never before in history have so few brought so much suffering to so many."

The tragedy that befell Europe had struck with quick violence. During the first half-year of the war that began in September 1939, Americans and their leaders had felt little sense of urgency about the outcome, since the British and French were comfortably presumed to be capable of standing off Nazi Germany just as they had, though barely, stood off imperial Germany in the Great War of 1914–18. Indeed, *Life* magazine declared, "as fighters the French are tops," and these tough *poilus* were led by "the largest and best-trained officer corps in the world." A French journalist noted that half of the people might have confidence in the premier, but "four Frenchmen out of four believe in the French Army." But in the early spring of 1940 the *poilus* and their British allies had yet to engage in much actual fighting with Adolf Hitler's Wehrmacht; seven months earlier, while the Germans were demolishing Poland, the Allies had stood quietly on the border of the Reich, with many of the French troops manning the great frontier defensive cordon, the Maginot Line. So uneventful had been the whole scene, for month after month, that it acquired various derogatory nicknames; the Bore War was one, but the lasting tag came from America: the Phony War.

What did this strange departure from normal wartime protocol really portend? One American, a private citizen, not only asked such questions but possessed the connections that would enable her to turn her curiosity into a quest. In February 1940 Clare Boothe, a playwright and fashion editor, arrived in Europe to make her own assessment of the Phony War. (At the time of her sailing, the current Gallup poll showed that 68 percent of the U.S. public believed the country would stay out of the war—a hardly surprising finding, if only because there did not appear to be much war to get into.) Though not a reporter by trade, Boothe came to Europe as an accredited correspondent for *Life*, a status she had readily acquired as the wife of the magazine's publisher, Henry R. Luce. Even if she seemed unlikely in the role of political and military investigator, the elegant and witty Boothe enjoyed certain advantages beyond her connection with *Life*, in particular a wide acquaintanceship in the social and diplomatic worlds; one way or another, she had access to everybody.

In Paris, among the many and strident clashes of political opinion she encountered, Clare Boothe heard much confidence expressed in the state of French morale and much talk about the idea that once again, as in 1918, the Germans would run out of time: a long war favored the Allies. And this time, said the voices in the salons as social life whirled on, *il faut en finir*—we must finish the job! Another reporter noted the refrain: "We're sick of all this blackmail and these crises coming up every six months." The eminent British military critic B. H. Liddell Hart declared in an article widely read in France, Britain, and the United States (and, no doubt, in Germany) that he saw little likelihood of a successful German offensive, because "their margin of superiority in numbers is not enough"; however, "extraordinarily bad generalship on the Allies' side" could give the enemy at least the chance of success.

At the Maginot Line, where the army had made Boothe the *marraine* (godmother) of one of the forts in that incredible spine of steel and concrete stretching through the hills of Lorraine and Alsace, the officers all assured their distinguished visitor that these fortifications could repel any attack the Germans might launch. But, though she had no training in such matters, Boothe wondered whether—since the Germans had conquered Poland with deadly new techniques of mobile war—the enemy, instead of flinging its forces against such a great static obstacle, might decide to take advantage of the possibilities offered by movement. The Maginot Line, after all, did not run all the way from the Rhine to the English Channel but stopped at Luxembourg, halted there by French budget stringencies and by Belgian protests at the possibility of being left on the exposed side of the French defensive system. (Some French leaders, including Premier Edouard Daladier, observed that farther north the terrain and the nature of the soil made it necessary to consider fortifications of a different type.) The Belgians of course had their own forts, which were said to be strong. On April 9, while lunching as guest of honor at a divisional officers' mess, Boothe heard the surprising news that the Germans had swept into Denmark and had sent an expeditionary force to Norway. Her hosts seemed to have only limited ideas about the location of Oslo, from which the Norwegian government was reported to have fled, and in general looked on the whole affair as naval in nature, and therefore a British concern. Never mind Denmark, it seemed.

Back in Paris, the American observer found excitement and even joy. The Germans, people said, had blundered; they had grown reckless, extending the conflict into the sea, where the Allies enjoyed marked superiority. They were cracking! A talk with the U.S. military and air attachés in Paris, however, quickly set Boothe straight on this point. The German invasion of Norway represented a serious strategic setback for the Allies, said these officers (one of them a lieutenant colonel named George C. Kenney), but of far greater portent would be the "real offensive," which they said was coming "sure as death" through the Low Countries in May or June.

Just a month later, on the evening of May 9, Clare Boothe arrived in Brussels, where she was to stay at the U.S. embassy. A staff member suggested that the next day she might like to go out to see the battlefield of Waterloo, but that promising plan had to be abandoned. At 5:20 in the morning, as the visitor slept in her room on the top floor of the house, a maid shook her awake, exclaiming, "The Germans are coming again!" Then antiaircraft guns began to fire and bombs to fall.

The Germans had indeed come. The great blow in the West had fallen; the "real offensive"—anticipated, pooh-poohed, feared—had begun. Showing that the blitzkrieg combination of armor and tactical air could work as well against the forces of established powers as it had against the brave but helpless Poles, the Germans slashed across northern France to the English Channel, squeezing the British and French forces that rushed into Belgium between two powerful army groups. Far from proving to be the anticipated replay of 1914, the campaign of 1940 lasted a mere six weeks. With much of the British Expeditionary Force having evacuated from the Continent at Dunkirk, the French signed an armistice—actually a document of capitulation—on June 22. Though failing to realize the role armor would play and hence wrong in his overall forecast, Liddell Hart turned out to be right in two respects: the Germans had won by the way they employed their resources, not by great superiority in numbers, and the Allies had suffered from bad generalship indeed.

Having amazed themselves as much as they had everybody else, the Germans now stood as the masters of Europe. The only possible countervailing power, the Soviet Union, tied to the Reich by treaties of friendship, continued scrupulously to serve its mighty friend as an important supplier of food, oil, and raw materials.

With the German conquest of France and the Low Countries—as earlier in Poland, Denmark, and Norway—came the kind of nightmarish oppression described by the refugee Czech journalist: control not only by the secret police, the Gestapo, but by an array of other security agencies, summed up by Winston Churchill as "all the odious apparatus of Nazis rule." In time would come one of the most chilling forms of such control, the Night and Fog Decree (*Nacht und Nebel Erlass*), under which people in occupied countries would not be openly executed but would simply disappear like ghosts into the "night and fog" in Germany.

British operations in Norway during April had turned into a total fiasco, with the result that a revolt in his own Conservative Party forced the unwarlike Prime Minister Neville Chamberlain from office. This event occurred, coincidentally, just as the Germans began their lightning invasion of the Netherlands and Belgium. Winston Churchill, the new prime minister, declared to the House of Commons, "I have nothing to offer but blood, toil, tears, and sweat." His policy, he said with superb defiance, was simply to "wage war against a monstrous tyranny, never surpassed in the dark, lamentable catalogue of human crime." In a later speech Churchill spoke for another country as well, as he looked to the day when the "New World, with all its power and might, sets forth to the rescue and the liberation of the Old." Just how and when would this happy event occur? No one knew. It would happen, the prime minister said, "in God's good time."

Clare Boothe had gone to Europe as an observer; in early June she returned to America as an impassioned advocate, bearing a great challenge. Britain and France had failed democracy, she believed; Hitler had declared it to be a decadent system, and he seemed to have made his point in Europe. Inertia, ignorance, jealousies—everything had come together to cause France to fall and to leave England naked to invasion. Her picture of Europe, said Boothe, was also a mirror held up to America. Would her fellow Americans recognize themselves and acknowledge their failings, renounce their detachment and their aloofness, and gird themselves to prevent the worst of all imaginable disasters, the death of democracy in the world? How many of them would share her sense of urgency? What, demanded Clare Boothe, would the United States do?

She had asked a good question about the America of 1940. She was returning from blitzkrieg and catastrophe to a country in which, on Sundays, the telephone switchboard at the executive mansion did not open until one o'clock in the afternoon. If you wanted to reach the president of the United States in the morning, you had to send a messenger.

1

MONEY FLIES

Franklin D. Roosevelt possessed a temperament that had always allowed him to enjoy a laugh—a golden trait with which to meet "one of the darkest moments in American life," as a commentator of the day characterized the spring of 1933, three-and-a-half years after the Wall Street crash had turned into the Great Depression. When FDR took the oath as president on March 4, "the banking system was in collapse, agriculture was prostrate, factories were chill and smokeless, fourteen million workers were unemployed."

In their fright and paralysis the people had turned to Roosevelt, and the new president, as he had promised during his campaign, set out to create a "New Deal" for the American people, launching, in concert with Congress, a series of vigorous attacks on the Depression; this inaugural period of intense activity would be known as the First Hundred Days. Just a few of these days after his inauguration, in the minutes before going on the air in his first radio "fireside chat"—the first presidential speech ever addressed directly to the public rather than to an audience physically present—Roosevelt impressed a broadcast reporter by his "cheerfulness and wit and tremendous love of banter."

Some of the New Deal programs took forms new to American policy, since the traditional methods and limited innovations employed by FDR's predecessor, Herbert Hoover, the celebrated humanitarian and "great engineer," had singularly failed to stop the downward business spiral. Though Roosevelt did not come into office with any certified remedies for a sick economy, he brought with him a willingness to cast aside failed formulas and engage in experiments, even if some of them actually contradicted each other. After making basic efforts aimed at the foundations of the economy, industry and agriculture, the administration turned to the situation of the millions of unemployed workers. Previously in the deeply conservative United States, questions relating to employment and relief had been considered primarily local problems to be solved by local people, with the help of an occasional few dollars sent over from the state capital, and by a large dependence on voluntary agencies and private philanthropy, with no involvement on the part of Washington. President Hoover subscribed to these principles, though in a period of drought he departed from them far enough to make funds available to farmers for feeding livestock, a gesture that led a congressman to charge the president with favoring "jackasses" over starving babies.

Two years earlier, as governor of New York, Roosevelt had struck out on his own, challenging the prevailing social and fiscal orthodoxy by declaring to his legislature that it was "time for the State itself" to respond to the widespread suffering through providing direct help to the jobless—"not as a matter of charity, but as a matter of social duty." In response, the governor received funding to set up a new kind of state agency, the Temporary Emergency Relief Administration; to chair his creation he chose Jesse Straus, a prominent philanthropist and president of Macy's department store. The agency would need, under Straus, a director who would actually manage the operation—a capable executive with relevant experience who, at the same time, would not shy from running all the risks involved in taking on a strikingly unpromising job. Roosevelt's and Straus's first choice for the position, though declining what insiders regarded as at best a career-threatening honor, was a friend and colleague who just might be willing to take up the challenge. Roosevelt even went so far on his own as to telephone the friend to ask him directly; Harry Hopkins responded instantly: "I would love it." The appointment quickly followed.

A quarter of a century earlier, as a gangling, long-jawed youngster in the Congregationalist-Methodist-flavored town of Grinnell, Iowa, Harry Hopkins had acquired something of a reputation as a hell-raiser; this boy, some of the local people decided, would never amount to much. But others were not so sure. Aside from the time he spent in hot water, they said, Harry was a good lad, and anyone could see how bright he was. He also gave the high school, and the town, a striking if blatantly irregular demonstration of political skill and determination. Rebelling against the teachers who fixed class elections to favor the best students, Harry organized an effort to stuff the ballot box on behalf of one Sam O'Brien, a presidential candidate whose good points did not include much in the way of academic achievement. Though Sam won this particular election, the teachers, realizing the tainted nature of his victory, reacted by refusing to accept it and instead set up a new vote. In turn, Hopkins responded by mounting a vigorous campaign on behalf of O'Brien; in the second balloting, this time honest on both sides, Sam won again, and with a bigger margin than he had received earlier.

Harry's reputation as a talented politician followed him into Grinnell College, where he immediately became prominent, winning election—honestly, it appears—as the freshman representative on the student council; moving up from class to class, he remained on the council throughout his college career. He also, as a freshman, was taken into The Institute, a society normally open only to upperclassmen. But more striking evidence of the popularity his "restless, electric personality" won him and of the respect with which he was regarded—and also of his readiness to look at situations in his own idiosyncratic way—came from his role in one of the annual freshman–sophomore battles. This particular epic struggle rose to a crescendo when the freshmen, having besieged the sophomores in a barn, dropped potent stink bombs through a hole in the roof. An unpleasant tactic of this magnitude brought tight-lipped intervention by the dean ("unworthy of Grinnell's traditions of sportsmanship and fair play"), with consequent penalties for all concerned—except Harry Hopkins. Neither the freshmen nor the sophomores nor anyone else had any idea that Harry had served as chief strategist for both sides.

The son of a harness maker—a salty, irreligious, contrary but intermittently amiable sort of fellow and notable local character—and of a zealous Methodist mother who served for a time as president of the Methodist Home Missionary Society of Iowa, Harry Hopkins could attend Grinnell partly because his mother had seen to it that the family settled in a college town. In his freshman year, he proved himself not only a shrewd campus politician but also a first-class basketball player.

That summer his mother treated him to what proved a fateful trip to New York. "I've liked New York since the first day I saw it," he said years later, and after graduating, in 1912, he eagerly accepted an offer to serve as a program director at a New Jersey summer camp operated by a Manhattan settlement house. "You'd go on hikes and picnics, plan baseball games, and struggle to discipline the boys," he said. "I'd never disciplined anyone and they made a sucker out of me." But he claimed, at least, to have taken up social work in order to get to New York, and his planning paid off at the end of the summer when the settlement house took him on as a caseworker.

Though the bustle and the bright lights played their part in drawing Hopkins to the city, and his personal style had nothing of the do-gooder about it, he also had higher motives for his choice of profession. At Grinnell, while concentrating on history and political science, he had become imbued with the ideas of the Social Gospel movement, a turn-of-the-century Protestant approach to the problems of working-class people caught up in the stresses and inequities of industrialization. The Social Gospelers took an optimistic view of human developments generally and, in practice, advocated the adoption of specific measures like the abolition of child labor and the improvement of working conditions for women. But the Lower East Side of Manhattan represented a new kind of world for the boy from Iowa; he had seen poverty in the Middle West, but now he encountered squalor on an intensity and scale he had never imagined, as he climbed tenement stairs, mixed with gangsters (Gyp the Blood, Dago Frank, Lefty Louie), and "really got exposed to the whole business of how the working class lived and to their poverty and joviality."

Looking for a way to increase his tiny income (he was working just for room and board and pocket money), Hopkins managed to get himself taken on as a kind of trainee, at $45 a month, by one of the city's leading charitable organizations, the Association for Improving the Condition of the Poor. Continuing to work at the settlement house during the day, he spent his evenings going out on assignments for the AICP to try as a "friendly visitor" to solve problems in trouble spots, particularly on the waterfront. "An easygoing, wisecracking, sympathetic, conversational individual with a liking for nearly everyone who isn't a stuffed shirt," Hopkins, some workers felt, spread some of his own joviality to his clients simply through "pure contagion." Within a few months he was seeking out the director, John A. Kingsbury, to ask for a raise in pay. Since he had been hired not to fill any vacancy but simply because Kingsbury had found him likable and promising, the boss responded with amusement as well as surprise. "On what possible grounds would I be justified in giving you a raise?" he asked. Shyly, for once, Hopkins explained that he had fallen in love and wanted to get married. Struck by the young man's audacity, even if it had come cloaked in some diffidence, Kingsbury agreed to increase his stipend to $60 a month.

Hopkins had presented his case awkwardly because his courtship of a part-time co-worker had, by mutual agreement, been kept secret. His fiancée, Ethel Gross, came from a background about as different from Grinnell, Iowa, and Grinnell College as could be imagined. Her mother, recently widowed, had brought the five-year-old Ethel and her four siblings from Hungary to New York in 1891, settling in the ghetto of the Lower East Side—the area to which her daughter's suitor, and the daughter herself, would later devote their professional attention. When Ethel met Harry, she was, though engaging in social work, devoting much of her time to the suffragist cause, to which she was fervently dedicated; her drive in a cause matched Harry's own. In one of their almost daily courtship letter exchanges (some of which were actually delivered by messenger), Hopkins, making one of his many humorous efforts to accommodate himself to his fiancée's militancy, commented: "I can hardly picture myself as a dutiful 'hubby' and I'm not so sure that I will always obey, and I know that you won't."

In a time when intermarriage of any variety won little favor in any quarter, "given their differences in age, ethnicity, and class, the two had sufficient reason to keep their relationship quiet"—though in one of their love notes Ethel said, plaintively, "Sweetheart, I wish your family at home knew about us. I find myself wishing that every once in so often." The secrecy simply did not seem right, but, Ethel added, "I only think about it sometimes."

Later, looking back, Ethel remembered Harry as a "charming, sociable, even light-hearted figure"; for this first-generation Jewish immigrant, their granddaughter and great-granddaughter felt, Hopkins in his person had embodied the American dream, and, for his part, Harry had found Ethel equally exotic. Whether this classic attraction of opposites provided a sound-enough basis for a lasting marriage perhaps posed a serious question, but the two showed no qualms. The wedding took place in October 1913, and by the end of 1914 the couple had become the parents of a son (the first of four children Harry had with Ethel).

In 1915, Hopkins went to work with the just-created New York City Board of Child Welfare as executive secretary—a fitting posting, since the organization had in part been established in response to findings he had made in a city-wide economic survey of the conditions of widows and their children. Rejected for an eye problem by all the armed services, Hopkins spent the World War years as a Red Cross executive in the South, where he proved an efficient and often inspiring leader, acquiring a reputation that led to his being sought out by other agencies and, after the war, even by the League of Nations.

One of the pioneers in the movement to professionalize social work, Hopkins played a leading part in the establishment of the American Association of Social Workers, of which he became president in 1923. The next year, with the support of John Kingsbury, he took over the active leadership of the New York Tuberculosis Association as executive director. This position gave him a wide platform for the display of his talents, and he proceeded to expand the organization's programs, enlarge its income—partly through his merchandising of the association's famous Christmas seals—and greatly increase its spending. During his stewardship Hopkins built the association into a major force by merging it with several other organizations, and it acquired a fitting new, broad-scope name: the New York Tuberculosis and Health Association. To achieve his purposes, Hopkins was evolving his own kind of management style, far more collegial than top-down, seeking opinions from everyone involved in a particular situation and often needling his colleagues to see what reactions he could evoke. A later associate would credit him with "a three-hundred-and-sixty-degree point of view."

During this period, in a particularly notable instance of his marked ability to develop a working mastery of a subject he knew nothing about, Hopkins took the lead in finding methods to protect subway diggers against the ravages of silicosis. He began his quest by asking a medical colleague, "Say, Jack—what *is* silicosis?" and went on from there. "He was intense," said this doctor, "seeming to be in a perpetual nervous ferment—a chain smoker and black coffee drinker." As for his appearance, "most of the time he would show up in the office looking as though he had spent the previous night sleeping in a hayloft." Presciently, the doctor felt that "you could mark him down as an ulcerous type."

Despite Hopkins's ability to win financial support, the expenses involved in his imaginative expansion of the association's activities tended to keep the organization scrambling for cash. Such problems caused him no concern; for him, the possession of a fat bank account merely demonstrated the failure of a philanthropic organization to do as much as it could and should be doing. The association's president noted, benignly, "Harry never had the faintest conception of the value of money." (Even so, when he left the association, the board commended him for his financial management—partly, to be sure, because he not only spent money but attracted it.) "He is a man of good will with a sense of responsibility," said a board member. "He created an atmosphere in which other men of good will could work."

Then, in 1931, Hopkins moved into government, with his appointment as executive director of FDR's Temporary Emergency Relief Administration. He had first met Roosevelt in 1928, as a fellow admirer of Al Smith, the Democratic presidential nominee. FDR had worked with and supported Smith for years, and now Hopkins was campaigning for both men—Smith for president and Roosevelt for governor of New York. For Roosevelt the encounter amounted to nothing more than an ordinary incident in a political setting, but it left Hopkins extremely impressed; during the campaign, other meetings would follow, but the acquaintanceship grew slowly, and as TERA administrator Hopkins did not belong to FDR's inner circle; however, he also had the great merit of causing no problems for the governor.

Along with his excellence as an administrator, Hopkins at TERA displayed an almost amusing personal reformist streak. "He was indefatigable in promoting sound living," writing hundreds of letters on lifestyle topics to newspapers: on safety rules for swimmers, controlling flies, dealing with tuberculosis, scolding women who spent more on makeup than on toothbrushes and praising girls who led healthy outdoor lives. When Jesse Straus resigned the chairmanship of TERA the following year, the devotion, energy, and efficiency Hopkins had displayed as director ensured that Straus would recommend him and that Governor Roosevelt would choose him to be the new chairman.

Though a marked idealist in his profession, Hopkins had a sardonic touch, and, as his career had abundantly shown, his incisive mind gave him a penetrating approach to problems and an impatience with woolliness and evasion. He would need all his positive traits for the task he took up in May 1933; as Federal Emergency Relief Administrator he would be starting from absolute scratch to create a national organization, one that would replace the patchwork and exhausted local efforts (while working through state organizations) and would have higher aspirations than simply expanding the soul-eating relief payments—the dole. In short, much ingenuity and improvisation would be required; the magnitude of the Depression had "rendered utterly obsolete every private charity for which Mr. Hopkins had worked and threatened every theory of private charity that he had ever considered."

Perhaps curiously, FDR had not moved on his own to establish the new federal agency, even though he had created the precedent of the New York TERA; the impetus actually came from Hopkins himself, who, with an associate, drafted a plan that won the support of Secretary of Labor Frances Perkins, who got it to the president's attention. However much FDR sought innovation, he had not in his thinking parted company with all the old dogmas and formulas. Having, bizarrely enough, criticized the Hoover administration for its spendthrift ways, FDR, though in office less than a hundred days, tried to economize where he could and felt an initial spasm of fiscal guilt at the thought of accepting Hopkins's proposal, but with the desperate situation of the unemployed carrying the day, the president put Hopkins to work.

This appointment represented an extraordinary opportunity for an old Social Gospeler, and he did not waste a minute: during his first two hours at the desk (actually, beginning in the corridor before the desk was moved into his bare, shabby office), he spent nine million dollars. The press, and the nation, quickly discovered that Washington now had a new type of high official, "rarely tactful or tactical," who snarled back at the press—the reporters loved it—and "looked as though he belonged on the other side of the desk with his tormentors." No nattier than he had been in New York, Hopkins, said one reporter, gave off "a suggestion of quick cigarettes, thinning hair, brief sarcasm, fraying suits of clothes."

Scorning red tape, Hopkins rushed cash to where it was needed; on the day after he began his work, the *Washington Post* headlined the story "MONEY FLIES." It would continue to fly as fast as Hopkins could make it move; he soon became, officially, the biggest spender in the history of the United States. No one who had seen him in New York could have felt much surprise that he was making the most of his great new opportunity to put cash to work. When told about objections to the idea of spending the unheard-of sum of $2 billion on relief, Hopkins snapped: "Some people just can't stand seeing others make a decent living."

Hopkins would soon move toward providing work relief—actual jobs that would pay wages—through a new agency called the Civil Works Administration. Established in early November, by January, under the lash of this unbureaucratic driving force, the CWA had created jobs for more than four million people. A useful job (and even, sometimes, a job without much value) rather than the handout and the voucher represented for Hopkins the functional goal of a relief program. Not everyone agreed. Al Smith, who had lost the 1928 presidential election to Hoover and had been supplanted in Albany by Roosevelt, never seemed able to accept either of these realities. Having turned conservative as well as crabby, he launched a baroque attack on the CWA as "a grapefruit halfway between the lemon of public works and the orange of relief." Hopkins, who showed little verbal restraint with politicians, fired right back: "Al Smith taught me the word 'baloney' and now he has taught me sour grapefruit juice." Statements that the economic situation would sort itself out in the long run evoked a legendary reply from Hopkins: "People don't eat in the long run, they eat every day."

Despite the work of the CWA, however, national recovery, the overall aim of the New Deal, was proving hard to achieve. In the early months of Roosevelt's presidency, this imperative for recovery encountered a basic and inescapable question of definition: should the Depression be fought in cooperation with other countries, or would the United States do better to wage the battle on its own? Meeting in London, the portentously named and lengthy World Monetary and Economic Conference produced a proposed declaration affirming that "maintenance of existing gold parities is in the interest of world recovery." The American president, the world quickly learned, regarded this embrace of the gold standard as the donning of a monetary straitjacket; desiring to exercise discretionary control over U.S. financial policy, Roosevelt rejected the declaration, thus, as the subsequent accusation would go, "torpedoing" the conference. Indeed, the president by his action had made it plain that the United States, in this realm, was choosing to isolate itself in order to create its New Deal policies and carry out its programs. Amid all the criticism, John Maynard Keynes, who would prove to be the most influential economic thinker of the twentieth century, declared that "President Roosevelt is magnificently right." Why should a country bind itself by "gold fetters" to a static standard? But many of the disappointed Europeans saw the picture as the United States going its own way with a cold lack of concern for others.

A close observer of the situation might not have felt total surprise at FDR's detachment, since the group the president had sent to London to represent the United States consisted largely of mediocrities, some of them almost odd enough to have been plucked from the funny papers. Europeans who had paid attention to Roosevelt's inaugural address on March 4 would also have noted that, while acknowledging the importance of "international economic readjustment," the new president had said straight out that "the emergency at home cannot wait on that accomplishment." Disappointed at the outcome of the big party, and displeased by the style of some of the American actions, the host, Prime Minister Ramsay MacDonald, added a footnote to the proceedings: "How on earth," he asked one American, "did Roosevelt send such a delegation to the conference?"

In his inaugural speech Roosevelt had also declared that, if the emergency lingered, he would ask for "broad executive power to wage a war" against it, even if such an action involved a temporary departure from the "normal balance of public procedure." The very next day, in Germany—like the United States, especially hard hit by the Depression—Adolf Hitler's Nazis, with the help of an associated party, squeezed out an electoral victory that would enable them to create a legal basis for all the violent and repressive actions they had already taken in the five weeks since their Führer had been appointed chancellor of the Reich. In language sounding almost like Roosevelt's, Hitler asked the Reichstag to give him extraordinary powers, which he would use "only to the extent required to carry out vitally necessary measures." But when the Reichstag passed this "Enabling Act," it thereby committed institutional suicide as a legislative body; already, American correspondents in Berlin had realized what a profound disaster the coming of the new regime represented for Germany, one of them declaring that "only Hitler's death or the armed intervention of a foreign power could prevent the worst." Back home, no comparable changes would occur in the face of crisis; Roosevelt, Hopkins, and the other members of the New Deal administration, seeking no enabling act, would simply do their best to grapple with the great range of problems presented by the suffering U.S. economy.

2

FRIENDSHIPS

President Roosevelt's style and his early actions seized the imagination of the country. "It was an emotional, psychological thing," remembered a visiting young Englishman, Alistair Cooke. "You could not speak a word against Roosevelt, and there were pictures of him every place. I mean in igloos and hotels, barbershops . . ." A desperate Congress had given the president the funds to support Hopkins's drive to put people to work, and the veteran social worker had produced remarkable results: On December 1, two weeks after the creation of the CWA was announced, two million people had gotten jobs; two weeks later, another two million had joined them. But that still left many millions jobless and unemployment as the number-one challenge for the administration.

Washington had never seen a public official like Harry Hopkins. Not at all sure what to make of him, analysts and reporters took various approaches. One observer impressionistically pondered the face of the man who quickly became the New Deal's symbolic figure:

Small, sensible, quiet forehead, deepset lugubrious eyes cocked cagily under little sardonic eyebrows. (Can't-put-that-over-on-me.) Long ruminating nose, hitched to two deep dissimilar grooves, struggling from nostrils around lips to chin. Mouth twisted, wary, speculative, expressing distrust and dubiety—strain and seriousness battling profound indifference. Attitude shrinkingly solitary, secretively sucking in cheeks and chewing his lips—neutrality crouched on the fence, feline style, glancing circumspectly to the right and left. Drab coloring and an air of dismal youth. Pale urban-American type, emanating an aura of chilly cynicism and defeatist irony like a moony, melancholy newsboy selling papers on a cold night.

Profound indifference? A strange misreading.

"On first glance," said another commentator, "Hopkins looks young and delicate, a high, white, bookish forehead, long, narrow, restless eyes, extremely thin, mobile lips. When he speaks, however, he has a trick of twisting his thin lips to the left, and talking out of the side of his mouth, that makes him seem not delicate, but tough." This writer concluded that Hopkins was, in fact, tough.

A third writer saw Hopkins simply as "a lanky, good-humored New York social worker" who "marched to the White House, spent five minutes with the President, and marched out again—as Federal Relief Administrator."

Reporters would continually turn to Hopkins, speculating and probing, and he would just as often provide material for them simply by his actions, each instance contributing to the creation of a legend. Speaking to a worshipful convention of social workers in the Midwest, he began his remarks by complaining about his losses at the local racetrack. He surprised another and very important audience—mayors and high state and city relief officials—by acknowledging his boredom at his own address. Interrupting his delivery of bureaucratic boilerplate, he said with some feeling: "You know, I can hear my voice bouncing back at me like a preacher's. I don't feel that way about this thing. This thing is very serious business to me, and I know it is to you. I know that there are a lot of things about it that many of you have misgivings about. Well, I have them too. However, I have no misgivings about the fundamental fact that we have got to get these fellows to work, and I know we can do it on decent projects and do it right away." "This thing" was nothing less than the Civil Works Administration, which Hopkins was launching with this speech. He was as "busy as a nurse at an earthquake."

Though he had not been especially close to Roosevelt in Albany, Hopkins in Washington displayed a marked loyalty and even devotion to him. If the president's surges of conservatism sometimes dismayed him, he did not show it, nor did he allow his associates to complain; he had come to the capital as a professional, not as a politician. Looked at closely, the relationship between the two men reveals highly pragmatic underpinnings, with great benefits for each: Hopkins did his work with imagination and great efficiency—"almost faultlessly," said a reporter—and hence did not require anxious supervision or intervention by the president; in return, FDR gave Hopkins great freedom of action and always backed him up.

Hopkins also began developing other friendships in the White House, notably with Eleanor Roosevelt, whose voluntary social-work activities had given her an outlook on poverty and social pathology similar to his own. "The appeals for help which had poured in during the early years of the depression," she said later, "had brought me in close contact with the people administering the relief programs." Hopkins she "not only admired but came to have a deep trust and confidence in." An interviewer observed of Hopkins: "All his working life it has been necessary for him to be intimate with those aspects of our civilization that most people find it very convenient to be able to eliminate from their minds."

For his part, the president adapted for Hopkins a practice he had, as governor, devised for Eleanor. Perhaps her greatest value to her husband in Albany had been as a set of legs that could go where, because of his handicap, he could not. He even gave her an informal course in inspecting state institutions; at a hospital, for instance, she could not content herself with reading the menus but had to go into the kitchen and look into the cooking pots. FDR now at times employed Hopkins as a similar surrogate on a national scale, giving him the mission of looking at cities and states close up: What were the people doing? Did they seem sullen or despondent? What was the state of the washing hung out to dry on the clotheslines? Were the buildings cared for or neglected?

In background, Hopkins and Roosevelt differed in almost every way—Roosevelt the product of the establishment East, an aristocratic Episcopalian; Hopkins the son of small-town Methodists and Social Gospelers in the distant Midwest of a century ago: Harvard versus Grinnell. But one striking parallel marked their lives: each man showed the influence of a strong and much-involved mother (though Anna Hopkins as a controlling influence could hardly compare to the dominating Sara Delano Roosevelt). And as the two worked together, it began to become evident that they shared a remarkable number of traits. Each had "a mixture of idealism and political shrewdness, and a relish for fairly ribald anecdote and the exercise of irony," Hopkins's irony finding expression with perhaps a sharper edge. They also shared "a concern for the average man and a preference for the society of the rich, the gay, the talented, and wellborn." Such social relationships came naturally to the Hudson Valley squire, who never in speech or act made any effort to appear anything but patrician and in the darkest days of the Depression could, with no concern at all, move effortlessly from grappling with the problems of the economy to enjoying an interlude on his friend Vincent Astor's yacht in the company of the multimillionaire *"Nourmahal* gang."(Astor was, at least, one of the few millionaires who had voted for him.) Naturalness was the key for FDR, the reason people in all walks of life could feel close to him. He "simply behaved like himself," a commentator noted. "He didn't give it a thought."

For Hopkins, these glittering associations represented an extension of the bright lights that had originally lured him to the city, and they could shine in elegant suburbs as well as in midtown Manhattan. He would weekend sometimes at Hyde Park, and the Roosevelts would often josh him (occasionally putting an edge on it) for spending time in such other spots as the croquet-playing circuit on Long Island, with luminaries like the editor-publicist Herbert Bayard Swope and the Broadway producer and play doctor George Abbott.

Out of Hopkins's activities in this circle came an important new friendship with an unusual kind of businessman, Averell Harriman— a lean, handsome entrepreneur, financier, and, indeed, croquet champion, whose particular strength in this realm lay in his mastery of the game's strategy; this was an intense, expertly played, take-no-prisoners game, far removed from the ordinary quiet, clack-clack backyard pastime. Averell "was like a giant spider," said Herbert Swope, Jr. "He would wait and wait until somebody made a mistake, and then he would pounce." Part of his approach also consisted of consummate gamesmanship, pretending not to know which ball was his, carefully studying the grass blade by blade, and altogether proceeding so deliberately that the name "Averell" became generic for a dawdler. Opponents frequently boiled with frustration, but he won games, time and time again. "I just kept at it," he once said. "Persistence is the key." Young Swope thought Averell played life the way he played croquet.

Like Franklin Roosevelt, though in a different style and on a different scale, Averell Harriman had grown up in the circles of privilege. His father, E. H. Harriman, neither lean nor handsome, was the son of a chronically down-on-his-uppers Episcopal clergyman—an economic condition that would not long be endured by his ambitious son Henry, as young E. H. was known. Going to Wall Street as an office boy when he was fourteen, in the expanding post–Civil War financial world he rode his tremendous drive to the establishment of his own broker-age firm when only twenty-two. From building up this firm he moved into the anarchic realm of railroads, the symbolic big business of the day, taking over the Illinois Central and various feeder lines and in the 1890s the Union Pacific, which he revived and expanded. Unlike most of the financial kings, for whom winning control of an industry repre-sented only a game for money and power, E. H. paid close attention to the substance of his conquests, making himself into a think-of-every-thing railroader, keeping an eye on every detail of operations no mat-ter how small and coming forth with imaginative innovations. He also showed himself a relentless bare-knuckle fighter in the financial ring who could best even J. P. Morgan. "When he started on course, nobody could swerve him from it," said a Union Pacific official. "He would go right through despite all opposition and carry the situation alone."

Harboring no small ambition, E. H. aimed at extending his Chi-cago-to-California railroad domain into a rail-and-ship web around the world. Armed with credits from the Rockefellers, who admired his monopolistic schemes and his boldness in executing them, this "human dynamo" "climbed swiftly over the heads of other railroad captains during the closing years of the century, to reign as a 'Napo-leon' of the national railway system during a brief, dazzling career."

In the era of the famous robber barons, men who behaved as though they believed they had a God-given right to run things exactly as they pleased—regardless of the financial panics and depressions their activities might produce—E. H. Harriman shone as a star, car-tooned and lampooned as one of the chief national symbols of greed. This man with his legend stood as the role model for his son William

Averell, born in November 1891 (and thus Harry Hopkins's junior by just a year).

Though a man of many preoccupations, the elder Harriman paid close attention to the education—both intellectual and, interestingly, moral—of his children. When Averell, as he was usual known, was learning to drive and, broke the clutch in the car, his father expressed anger not because of the damage to the car but because he had learned about the incident from a servant, not from the boy himself. E. H.'s intimidating supervision probably lay behind the permanent stammer Averell acquired. (Touchingly, he once wrote from school: "I think I am doing better in my stammering because last night when I spoke to the Rector, I did not stammer once.") Strong moral instruction also came from the school—Groton, the elite institution founded in the 1880s by the formidable Reverend Endicott Peabody, who seemed to incarnate morality in his own person and preached an incessant gospel of public service, and who proved as demanding a mentor as Averell's own father.

Averell's circle of friends at Groton included Hall Roosevelt, younger brother of Eleanor, who with her husband Franklin (a Groton alumnus) assumed some responsibility for Hall's welfare after the death of his parents. In further connections, Eleanor worked with Averell's independent-minded older sister Mary in charity enterprises (Mary, reacting to the pointlessness of the debutante life, had also devised the Junior League), and Averell's mother and Sara Delano Roosevelt had an old friendship. The most public connection of the two families, the friendship between E. H. Harriman and Eleanor's Uncle Teddy, had produced some notable benefits for the country, particularly in a California flood in which Harriman had found himself spending his own funds as a kind of one-man federal emergency management agency (the government never repaid him). But the friendship had ended in a spectacular exchange of accusations concerning politics and money. Once, admonished by Roosevelt to use care on one of the high-speed train runs he enjoyed, E. H. could jauntily wire his friend in the White House: "You run the country, I'll run the railroads." But those days had gone.

In September 1909, shortly after Averell returned from a summer of rugged field work on one of E. H.'s lesser railroads, ready to go off to Yale, his father died at Arden, the great hilltop house he had built in Orange County, northwest of New York City. An obituary of E. H. declared that "the secret of his victorious career was his utter lack of moral scruples," but this judgment told only part of the story. A man of supreme self-confidence, as many people noted, "a bold and gifted administrator" with a remarkable imagination and limitless drive, E. H. had every gift he needed to achieve success in his particular world, quite apart from any moral considerations.

"All my father's life was an influence on me, a tremendous influence—his character and personality and his objectives and ideals," Averell later said. "He was a tremendously decisive and dedicated man, and I was devoted to his memory." And now, suddenly, the son of this remarkable figure, only a college freshman-to-be, had become titular head of the family. (In choosing Yale, Averell revealed himself, in a peculiarly rarefied way, as a kind of rebel, leading a number of his classmates away from Harvard, the standard college for Grotonians, toward the supposedly more democratic Yale—though how the young man could have cherished such an idea about the citadel of Skull and Bones remains thoroughly puzzling. The choice, however, pleased his father. A Groton contemporary of Averell's said that most of the "bright boys" went to Harvard and then into the professions, and "the ones who weren't quite as bright became stockbrokers," though some of the "key people" went to Yale "and it sort of split the class.") Led into corporate and other adult activities by his mother, Averell began to grow out of his shyness and to lose some, at least, of his stammer.

He enjoyed notable popularity in college, particularly because of his contributions to Yale rowing during a period of the school's "lackluster reputation on the river." With his father's strong support he had participated in the sport at Groton, but detection of a heart murmur meant that he had to drop out of varsity competition in college. As a junior, however, he coached the freshman team, and, determined to make a go of it, he went off to Oxford to master the long stroke that had made the university's rowing team the world's most admired. Carefully noting and studying every measurement, every technical detail—just as his father would have done—Harriman stayed in England six weeks, paying attention to the activities of the suffragettes and to other aspects of the lively political scene as well as to the methods of the Oxford crew. Though wishing to extend his stay by several days in order to witness the Oxford–Cambridge race, Averell felt obliged to stick to the schedule agreed upon with the Yale authorities, and thereby forewent his chance to return to America on the celebrated new liner, the *Titanic*.

In that spring's regatta, using the Oxford stroke, Harriman's freshman crew (including a fellow Groton boy, one Dean Acheson) did unusually well against Harvard, losing this time only by inches instead of the customary lengths. This success brought him an invitation to coach the varsity team in his senior year, but, unlike the freshmen, these veterans did not absorb his instruction in the Oxford stroke, their reluctance producing the usual dismal result the following spring. Even so, Yale asked him to stay on after graduation; he accepted, but continued failure caused him to resign "before he could be fired." Harriman's coaching experience with a squad of as many as eighty men held particular importance for him, he said later; he "learned a great deal about handling men—teaching, selecting, criticizing and yet encouraging them." As he put it another time, "I got most of my college education on the water."

Harriman's lack of coaching success, despite his ingenuity and his hard work, came in good part from the pull of his business responsibilities, which frequently kept him away from New Haven; unfortunately, one devout and vocal Old Blue raised objections to Acheson as substitute coach—after all, that young man had never pulled an oar in varsity competition! The year 1913 found Harriman far away, indeed, out in Omaha working in all departments of the Union Pacific to learn the business in a thorough way befitting its future head. Moving from here to there on a handcar, he served for a time as a section hand as part of the curriculum arranged for him by Judge Robert Lovett, who had become chairman after E. H. Harriman's death and whose son Bob was a good friend. Out in the field, noted a newspaper, "Harriman's dinner is taken from a tin bucket, and he eats it in company with his fellow laborers. To them he is simply 'Bill' and a cub engineer, who doesn't know much about the business but is learning."

In 1916 Averell, who during his western apprenticeship had proved himself a good cost-cutter with an eye for inefficiency and dishonesty, found himself back in New York as a vice president of the Union Pacific. With the Great War raging in Europe, he responded to the government's call for an expanded merchant marine by resigning his railroad position and entering the first of a number of ventures in shipping that involved both construction and operation of passenger and cargo vessels. In these enterprises Harriman had many of the same kinds of adventures and found himself involved in some of the same conflicts as his father's in the realm of railroads. Though the World War period and the 1920s had some similarities with the America of fifty years earlier, the primordial license and unlimited scope enjoyed by the robber-baron generation had not quite returned to the U.S. economy.

The end of the war, the recession that soon followed, the unpopularity of German interests with which Harriman had established a postwar partnership, the chilling impact of Prohibition on American ships' passenger lists (no drinks, at least legal ones, for the travelers)—all these and various other factors combined to induce Harriman, in the mid-1920s, to sell out and seek other fields; though he had wheeled and dealt in America and Europe, he had not managed to create a lasting empire.

He turned now to a new frontier and a new group of associates, commissars of the new Soviet Union, including Leon Trotsky; he had as his target the former republic of Georgia, recently and violently annexed by the Russians, which had the greatest manganese deposits in the world. Since the deoxidizing and other properties of this mineral make its use essential in the production of steel, a project to mine these beds at something like the prewar rate seemed to Harriman first a doubtful but then an attractive idea. Against the advice of colleagues and of Secretary of Commerce Herbert Hoover, Harriman entered into another complex, costly, and frustrating adventure, in which he proceeded impulsively and without adequate safeguards. Fortunately, he had other successful business activities in hand (including his investment-banking firm, W. A. Harriman & Co., founded in 1920), since the exotic manganese project, after showing some signs of life, was fated to die a lingering death. Harriman managed to work out a liquidation deal that saved something; the worst sufferers proved to be local people who had worked with Harriman's company. After having misled and cheated the American entrepreneur every way they could think up, the Soviet authorities arrested these wretched locals and dispatched some of them to Siberia.

On his way home from Russia in 1927, Harriman, always seeking to "take every occasion to meet the important men of the day," tried without much success to talk about international finance with Benito Mussolini, but, moving on to the Riviera, sought out Winston Churchill, chancellor of the Exchequer in the government of Prime

Minister Stanley Baldwin. Churchill advised him to terminate his concession in the Soviet Union—he saw no point in trying to do business with the Bolsheviks. The Russian experience, Harriman later said, "led me to conclude that the Bolshevik Revolution, in fact, was a reactionary development."

Averell's sister Mary Harriman Rumsey, ten years older, not only led in the founding of the Junior League but worked in other organizations such as the Women's Trade Union League. High-strung, a natural leader—not to say a dominating one—and a mile-a-minute talker, Mary attracted other young women into social work, including Eleanor Roosevelt; one friend called her "the first really modern woman that I ever knew." Though a Harriman Republican, Mary did not view the 1920s as an inspiring era for her party and began to interest Averell in the progressive programs of New York governor Al Smith, whom Averell liked; he also disapproved of the Republicans' high-tariff policies. No longer "a good, hard-shelled Republican," brother joined sister in moving over to the Democrats in 1928. Though Smith lost the presidential election in the Hoover landslide and even failed to carry New York State, Franklin D. Roosevelt won the governorship by 25,000 votes—not many out of more than four million, but enough not only for the present but for the future.

3

"BRILLIANCE AND GLITTER"

A
s his business career developed, Averell Harriman showed himself to be a compulsive sportsman, matching his commercial exploits with the mastery of any game or activity he took up—including harness racing (one of his father's enthusiasms) and polo, at which he truly excelled and which became his favorite, as well as croquet. In every area he seemed to display all the characteristics of manic behavior except the mania itself. For a time, horses had seemed likely to determine his destiny. A skilled driver, he had an amazing escape from serious injury in a 1915 amateur race in Cleveland when his trotter panicked and broke into a gallop, crashing through barriers and ending his run only with a fall into a ditch, with Averell still in the sulky, hanging on to the reins. Remarkably, both driver and horse survived unscathed. "I pulled him back," Harriman said of the incident, "and evidently pulled him back too tightly."

But the next year, fortune did not prove so kind. Averell and his fiancée, Kitty Lawrance, a banker's daughter who had been raised by her grandfather, an old friend of E. H. Harriman, took their horses out in Manhattan on an April afternoon. As they rode on a bridle path uptown, near Riverside Drive, a speeding train passing over a trestle frightened Kitty's mount, which reared and fell backward on top of her; she suffered a broken pelvis and for some time seemed unlikely to walk again. Some friends believed that Averell's feelings for her had cooled but that, feeling guilty because of the accident, he nevertheless moved ahead with the wedding, which took place in September, not long after Kitty had regained the ability to walk. The couple would live in Manhattan and at Arden, which they received as a most impressive wedding present from Averell's mother.

The marriage soon took a strange turn. Though weakened by the accident, Kitty presented her husband with two baby girls born within the same year, and shortly afterward she contracted tuberculosis. From then on, she spent much of her time out of the city in search of fresh air, and by the mid-1920s Averell had become involved in a relationship with one Teddy Gerard, a "rather spectacular-looking" cabaret singer who also, paradoxically, performed in silent films—bankrolled behind the scenes by her young tycoon lover. The tabloids spoke of an impending marriage.

What happened was, indeed, a divorce and a marriage, but not to Teddy Gerard. By the summer of 1928, Averell had fallen in love with the wife of a younger friend, another super-rich polo-playing Yale man, C. V. (Sonny) Whitney. But Harriman could not be accused of breaking up a happy marriage, since Sonny, a playboy who made headlines, had the true aristocrat's disdain of fidelity and had already suggested to his wife that they seek a divorce. Kitty Harriman had been very attractive, slim and dark-haired, but Marie Whitney was a beauty and as shapely as the notable Teddy Gerard. A true original as well, Marie came from a background unusual in Whitney-Harriman circles. The daughter of Sheridan Norton, a minor Democratic politician and professional dog-show judge, and "a wonderful old character of a mother who was part Jewish and part Irish," said Peter Duchin, her de facto stepson, Marie had "the mongrel's love of the unconventional." She spoke out of the side of her mouth "in a sort of drawl through clenched teeth"; she "swore like a trooper" and "loved talking about sex." Marie "was pretty rough," said one of their circle of friends at Sands Point, Long Island. "One time she said, 'Let's take our dresses off and see who has the best breasts,' and she dropped her dress, and *she* did."

Friends would soon credit Marie with softening some of Averell's stodginess, bringing him "out of his starched collars," although she proved unable to graft anything resembling a funny bone onto him. (A friend once noted Harriman's only known foray into the realm of humor: "My French is excellent, except for the verbs.")

The divorces of the Harrimans and the Whitneys both came through in the summer of 1929; the divorce, upper-class style, of Averell and Kitty called for each of them to establish legal (if pseudo) residence in Paris, far from the restrictive New York law. Averell and Marie then were married in New York on February 21, 1930. After honeymooning in Paris, they returned home bearing a stock of Cézannes, Renoirs, and Picassos for Marie's great new interest, the art gallery she soon opened on 57th Street. The project embodied her own studies, Averell's interest in art, and her response to his view that everybody should engage in useful work. She was soon "buying Matisses right off the brush," a friend said, "and made a great success of it."

Averell and Kitty remained friends, although she would live only six more years; for him, their fourteen-year-marriage stood as one of the games he had played but not won. Later, he would rarely speak of her.

Though in a far less spectacular fashion, the winds of marital change were also blowing through the life of Harry Hopkins in the late twenties. He had achieved real eminence in his profession, which in fact he had helped to define and enhance, and had proved himself an outstanding administrator. On Ethel's urging, but fittingly enough for a flourishing executive, he installed his family in the suburbs, first near Mount Vernon and then fifteen miles farther north, in Scarborough on the Hudson, commuting to the city like any businessman while his wife stayed at home with, after 1925, their three sons.

The story that would now develop could have come from any one of a hundred novels and dramas. Harry always worked long hours, he traveled, and Ethel—herself a dynamic, driving social worker—told him early in their marriage, "I am going to make an effort to be of some use—outside—if only for a few hours a week." At the same time she hoped her husband would arrange his work so as to be more involved with the family, including giving her the emotional support she openly sought. In the days of their exciting secret courtship, neither had imagined this kind of problem, much less that within a decade they would find themselves enduring the standard stresses of exurban living. For a while Harry played his part reasonably well, entertaining the boys, playing bridge and tennis, and getting in some golf. He had chosen Scarborough because John Kingsbury had a house there, and he spent a great deal of time with his old boss and now close friend, often roaming fields in the area engaging in Kingsbury's hobby of collecting and classifying mushrooms (and learning the possibly useful skill of distinguishing between the poisonous and the benign). Harry also discovered and became passionately devoted to John Keats, reading every word of every poem and also a number of biographies of the poet.

Into this situation innocently stepped, one day in 1927, Barbara Duncan, an attractive young woman from Michigan and a graduate of Bellevue Hospital's nursing program. Having developed some symptoms of tuberculosis, she was, appropriately enough, given a job at the Tuberculosis Association, presumably while the doctors dealt with her problem. This meant that she would often see Harry Hopkins, and it did not take long for the boss to fall in love with this comely, appealing, easygoing new associate, who was as unlike Ethel as Harry was himself; it also did not take long for Barbara to return Harry's feelings.

But here Hopkins departed from the classic scenario. Instead of declaring his marriage at an end and seeking his release from Ethel, he turned to psychiatry. He did not believe it right to abandon his wife, and he therefore sought the help of science, in the person of the prominent Dr. Frankwood Williams, former editor of *Mental Hygiene*, to help him do the proper thing. Hopkins, very much in character, also decided to contribute directly to his redemption—redemption being called for because resorting to divorce, except among the very rich, represented the acknowledgment of moral failings—by studying the writings of Freud and Jung so that he could psychoanalyze himself. In accordance with Dr. Williams's advice, Harry and Barbara decided to stop seeing each other, and to help in that direction Hopkins followed the doctor's suggestion that he join Kingsbury on the latter's trip to Europe to study social conditions and to attend the first International Conference of Social Work in Paris. He even secured a foundation grant to look at health-care systems in France and England.

Writing regularly, and encouragingly, to Ethel, the traveling Hopkins told her, "I can understand why you raved over Paris. It is all true." Primly enough, he also informed her that he had gone to the Folies-Bergère but had walked out after the first act; he enjoined Barbara to tell nobody about it, because he didn't "want to appear blasé." The Louvre definitely lived up to expectations: the Venus de Milo was "perfectly exquisite." In London, Hopkins became more serious, reporting the cooperativeness of the authorities, speaking of "dirty-rotten slums but magnificent school health work," and declaring that "we are amateurs indeed!"

But perhaps the high point of the trip came when an English doctor took him for a tramp across Hampstead Heath, north of London. "We suddenly came on a lonely path," Hopkins wrote, "upon which was a very impersonal sign called 'Keats Walk'!" Transfixed, Hopkins then realized that nearby he would find Keats's house, "where the 'Ode to the Nightingale' was written and other heavenly music." He summed it up as "the most exalting experience." But his joy was limited by the realization that he was experiencing it in the company of perhaps the only educated person in England who knew nothing about one of the greatest of all lyric poets; the amiable doctor proved unable to share his guest's enthusiasm.

Interesting and exciting as the psychiatric sessions and the geographical cure proved to be, however, these measures failed to accomplish their explicit purpose. While they left Hopkins with "a good psychiatrist's tolerance toward personality types," though he surely entered the game with a slant in that direction, and the experience perhaps increased "his reluctance to accept convenient theories on human conduct and affairs," he could not mend his marriage. The Hopkinses separated in September 1929, with unglamorous, middle-class legal procedures following. In 1931 Ethel won a divorce on the only permissible ground in New York: adultery. This break led to a further separation; highly disapproving of Harry's treatment of his wife, John Kingsbury ended their friendship.

Hopkins and Barbara Duncan were married in 1931, and a year later they became the parents of a daughter, Diana.

In 1932, a Harriman vote for Roosevelt for president represented no surprise. When the new administration came in, Mary Rumsey moved to Washington, where she shared a house with the new secretary of labor, Frances Perkins, and became chairman of the Consumers Advisory Board, an arm of the New Deal's complex superagency, the much-heralded National Recovery Administration (NRA). Mary encouraged her brother to take part as well, but Averell had his own reasons for involvement with Washington. (Continuing the family saga of tragic involvement with horses, Mary, one of the most important persons in Averell's life, would die the next year as the result of a hunting accident.)

In April 1933, Averell came down from New York to the capital to keep an eye on the swirl of evolving New Deal plans and proposals concerning reform of Wall Street to prevent another catastrophe like that of October 1929. Not at all a typical denizen of the Street, as he had shown earlier, Harriman did not question the need for change in the financial culture, but he feared that zealous amateurs might in their dismantling and rebuilding do more harm than good. Quickly, with his "fine, discriminating intelligence," he became a consultant to the administration and Congress and succeeded in softening some of the proposed strictures. But such was the virulence infecting some Wall Streeters that Harriman's contributions to their welfare did not prevent many an old acquaintance back in New York from quickly stepping across one of the financial district's narrow streets to spare himself the indignity of shaking the hand of a traitor.

In Washington, Harriman had seen the New Deal's bright lights as signifying the rise of the capital as the actual—as well as the formal—center of national power. Here, in the midst of the real action with all its dash, improvisation, and excitement, he knew he must find a place. He agreed to serve on a Roosevelt creation, the Business Advisory Council of the Department of Commerce, set up, optimistically, as a bridge between the administration and the business world. He arranged to organize activities as a deputy administrator for the NRA, later moving up to administrator. Though the Supreme Court would declare this misbegotten organization unconstitutional, the effort to mobilize industry against the Depression gave Harriman a new kind of experience he could draw on in the future. His experiences were also providing the basis for an observation he liked to make: "I've had a lot more fun out of life since I've been a Democrat."

Soon would come the beginning of his friendship with Harry Hopkins. A friend of Harriman's recalled his once saying that he wanted to get into the government and, to be on the safe side, was contributing to both parties, and then he got to know Hopkins. "I think he liked Harry all right," the friend said, but "Harry's situation made him especially attractive." Averell "didn't get full satisfaction out of his commercial activities," the friend believed. "He was not recognized as a great figure," but government offered another realm of possibilities, including that of power. The friend also pointed to Harriman's great capacity for work.

Not gregarious like Hopkins, Averell struck most persons who met him as remote and detached, and he would sometimes concentrate so intensely on his work or his thoughts that he failed to recognize a close friend. Yet as unlike Hopkins as he was, he shared two important traits with his new acquaintance: though not in the least intellectual ("he might read three or four pages of a book, but he had a genius for plucking things out of other people"), he was shrewd and hardheaded, and he had to be at the center of the action, whatever and wherever the action was. And much of the time in FDR's Washington, that action involved Harry Hopkins. While tending to his variegated commercial activities, Harriman kept his eyes on the capital, maintaining his ties with the administration, and in 1937 he became chairman of the Business Advisory Council, a development that would shortly bring him into an enhanced relationship with Hopkins.

Operating from a bare office in "a secondhand building which had been fumigated and painted over," Hopkins remained the New Dealer *par excellence*, "as zestful, as eager and as hopeful" as when he had arrived in Washington to create federal relief. As one of the capital's probers and analysts observed, "Hopkins attracts attention and fame effortlessly; whatever he does has brilliance and glitter about it. He will be worth watching for a long time."

Contrary to FDR's hopes, the need for the Civil Works Administration did not prove to be temporary. In its attempts to cope with the serious continuing problems, the New Deal, in one of its aspects most delightful to young people and most annoying or perplexing to many of their elders, went on to establish an array of alphabetically labeled agencies that took over much of the turf formerly owned by staid administrative departments or staked out new territories not previously the subjects of federal action. In 1935, most provocatively of all, perhaps, FDR created a successor agency to the CWA—the Works Progress Administration (WPA), with Hopkins as director; this newcomer immediately began to take hostile fire from Harold Ickes's Public Works Administration (PWA). It was all very confusing, people said. Which was which, and why were there two of them? Like the CWA, the WPA would preside over thousands of projects, tangible and intangible, the pouring of sidewalks and the writing of songs and sonnets, hurrying cash into circulation while Ickes laboriously planned dams and bridges. In one of his most famous comments, Hopkins snapped back at a critic by declaring that poets, just like any other workers, had to eat. His "caustic good nature is seemingly unchangeable," a reporter noted, "and is the best proof of the appeal of his work."

Not one for niceties, however, Hopkins also went toe-to-toe with reporters questioning projects employing white-collar workers, particularly a study researching safety pins in the ancient world. Did Hopkins plan to investigate this scandalous activity? "Why should I?" Hopkins retorted. "They are damn good projects—excellent projects."

Not content with that answer, he added that "dumb people criticize something they do not understand, and that is what is going on up there—God damn it!" (A distorted version of this remark was picked up by the newspapers and in some circles became identified with Hopkins: "People are too damned dumb.")

Only slowly did the administration realize the significance of the contribution that work programs were making to the recovery of the economy as a whole as well as to the individual worker; when Hopkins put $5 in a ditchdigger's pocket, which he did with commendable efficiency, the money went immediately into circulation. Hopkins "took all the heat for the boondoggles of the WPA," one of Roosevelt's sons observed. "But he put a hell of a lot of people to work and saved their self-respect and did a remarkable job in a very short time."

Whether Hopkins contributed the initials "WPA" for the new agency as a sardonic joke on Ickes remained a provocative question; Ickes convinced at least himself that his rival hijacked the initials in order to steal some of the credit for airports and other large and permanent projects. On their own, however, WPA workers would build thousands of miles of highways, thousands of bridges, and thousands of buildings.

Serious as the country's economic problems remained, President Roosevelt fully recognized that the United States belonged to the world and that the state of the world was giving cause for serious alarm. But not all of his countrymen agreed with him.

As the 1930s heated up, with strident continental dictators becoming the symbols of the time, the European democracies, as Britain and France were known, constantly faced fresh challenges. The Italian attack on Ethiopia in 1935, the Spanish Civil War, which began in 1936, and the Japanese invasion of China in 1937 all seemed to put the democracies on continual trial; people on both sides of the Atlantic criticized the inaction of the British and French governments—a resolution or two from the League of Nations in Geneva represented their chief efforts to affect events—but how indeed could the Americans complain?

Americans tended to look on political Europe as a kind of zoo housing a bizarre mixture of creatures wearing odd uniforms and given to strange gestures—creatures that seemed devoted to making constant trouble for themselves. What, one could wonder every day, are they up to now? Whether their families had been in America for one generation or ten, people felt themselves fortunate to be out of the European mess, separated by thousands of miles of open salt water. Since we're lucky enough not to be involved with the troubles of "the other country," as one old lady called Europe, why should we change that? We did it once, and now look! Indeed, the dismal results of American participation in the World War had led to a general determination not to make that ghastly mistake again. "It was utter social insanity," declared Washington's unlikely senator Homer T. Bone, and "we had no business in it at all." Thus came the rise of isolationism, the belief that the United States could live and flourish as an island, staying aloof from any involvement in Europe's quarrels.

Persuaded that the country had been bamboozled into war in 1917 by fiendishly ingenious British propaganda, that cabals of arms manufacturers and dealers had manipulated the great powers, and that financial ties to the Allies had forced the government to save Wall Street's stake in an Allied victory by sending an American army to France, the U.S. Congress counterattacked. With the heavy involvement of traditional populists and other agrarians from the heartland, the legislators passed a series of Neutrality Acts aimed at curbing what had long been known as the Money Trust in its commercial and financial dealings with countries at war. These acts had as their central feature the prohibition of arms sales to any country at war. Though in early sympathy with the aim of the legislation, Roosevelt, characteristically, felt less kindly toward the inflexible nature of this arms embargo, which left nothing to his discretion.

4

DARK AUTUMN

One day in late September 1937, President Roosevelt saw a newspaper account of a meeting between Adolf Hitler and Benito Mussolini, with their "bombastic utterances, their fond embraces, the military pomp that was marshaled in the stage setting of the meeting." FDR "fairly glowered at the pictures of the two little men" amid their swastika banners and glittering Fascist medals. Even though domestic problems demanded most of his attention, the president kept up with the steady flow of foreign reports from the State Department. The rapprochement between the two dictators represented an increasing concern, and, as FDR's secretary put it, "the Spanish Civil War was going on, Japan and China were in a shooting war, the French and British Governments were feuding with Mussolini over conditions in the Mediterranean, Hitler and his stooges were ranting about living space and Moscow was mad at almost everybody."

Though he disliked the limits the Neutrality Acts imposed on any possible actions, FDR always had the pulpit of the presidency at hand, and now he determined to give public expression to his concern about the alarming spread of international lawlessness. On October 5, in Chicago, he delivered to a huge outdoor crowd an address in which he declared, with the kind of familiar figure of speech he liked to use, "When an epidemic of physical disease starts to spread, the community approves and joins in a quarantine of the patients in order to protect the health of the community against the spread of the disease." And, make no mistake, "war is a contagion, whether it be declared or undeclared."

Even if the "quarantine speech," as this address became known, did not commit FDR to the pursuit of any specific line of action, it served as a personal catharsis and a step along the road toward a future policy, and it gave the world an insight into the president's general outlook: "There is a solidarity and interdependence about the modern world, both technically and morally, which makes it impossible for any nation completely to isolate itself from economic and political upheavals in the rest of the world, especially when such upheavals appear to be spreading and not declining."

Roosevelt had read the newspaper story about Hitler and Mussolini as he sat in his train, which was looping across the country on a "look-see" trip, undertaken to give the president a firsthand view of what had become a troubling national economic picture. In November 1936 he had won a triumphal, record-breaking reelection, running up a huge margin in the popular vote and carrying all but two of the forty-eight states, and the nation's prospects had looked bright for 1937. But in August, after four years of advance, the stock market had begun a slide that appeared to be signaling the arrival of a bitter recession.

One evening FDR asked his wife why she thought the great business tycoons were sitting on their cash instead of putting it to work building the economy. Why did they hate the New Deal?

Eleanor had a ready answer: "They are afraid of you."

She was right. Indeed, declared a conservative columnist, Roosevelt after a heroic start in 1933 had by now "aroused in the financial and business communities a fear amounting almost to terror." A visiting British financial editor noted: "Roosevelt is blamed for everything. The majority of capitalists and industrialists think that he hates them and believe me there is no lack of reciprocity. Wall Street worthies gibber at his name."

The president had made his own unfortunate contribution to the situation. Feeling confident about the progress of economic recovery (the Dow Jones index hit a summer high of 194.40—still only about half the 1929 peak but a great advance from the appalling 1932 low of 41.22), he had yielded to the blandishments of Treasury Secretary Henry Morgenthau, Jr., and approved the creation of a balanced budget for the 1938 fiscal year. The ending of even the relatively moderate deficit spending then practiced had almost immediately brought on the downturn. This bad news, and the weakened political position that came along with it, threatened not only to hamper the president domestically, but to limit his ability to act with authority in the world of international diplomacy.

Even though the quarantine speech had contained no mention of policies or programs, it had suggested a direction, and the president quietly sought to make specific attempts to influence the deteriorating international scene. One move involved an approach to the new British prime minister, Neville Chamberlain. In succeeding Stanley Baldwin, a Midlands businessman with little interest in foreign affairs, Chamberlain brought a striking new emphasis to the conduct of Britain's relations with other powers. While appearing in every way to be a typical member of the prevailing generation of Conservative leaders—wing-collared, aging, and cautious—and in fact not much better informed about other countries than his predecessor, Chamberlain believed he had been given a great chance to lead the way to a fundamental settlement of Europe's political and territorial quar-rels. Having formed his political style as mayor of Birmingham, he had later, as a cabinet minister, carried this personal approach into greater realms, "treating a department in Whitehall as the affair of himself and one town clerk." Why should dealing with foreign leaders be much different?

The British had found the United States a troublesome and preachy associate in war, and in turn, with their imperial airs, though gravely weakened by the great struggle (more so than was apparent), the British rubbed many Americans the wrong way. In the postwar world, carping and discord had marked relations between the two countries in all realms—financial (as at the 1933 economic confer-ence and in the continuing disputes about the debts from the World War), naval (as in a long and serious wrangle over how many and what kind of cruisers each power should be allowed to have), and diplomatic. A symbolic representation of one strand of American anti-British feeling was provided in the late twenties by the mounte-bank mayor of Chicago, Big Bill Thompson, who sought support among his electorate by threatening to "punch King George in the snoot" if the monarch should ever dare to venture to the Windy City; the king, then in his sixties and not robust, did not choose to take up the challenge.

Though declaring his strong desire to improve Britain's relations with the United States, Chamberlain believed that "it is always best and safest to count on nothing from the Americans but words." And at the moment, American considerations seemed to him of small moment compared with what he saw as the chance to do direct political business with the dictators, in the man-to-man way he liked, through "appease-ment," the name he gave his conciliatory policy—a policy not illogical in the abstract but one that depended for any success on an accurate reading of the other parties involved.

So it was not surprising that the prime minister expressed sharp disapproval when, in January 1938, his ambassador in Washington forwarded a message in which President Roosevelt proposed an ambitious plan designed to lead, through a series of steps involving a variety of countries, to the creation of standards for the maintenance of world peace. Probably the greatest significance of the proposal lay in the fact that it would involve the United States in European affairs after a twenty-year hiatus, and thus would represent something of an emergence from the isolationism with which Roosevelt had been branded since he had fired the famous economic torpedo at the 1933 London conference. Contemplating the deterioration of the world situation and the growing shadow cast by Hitler's Germany over the small states of Central and Eastern Europe, the president felt that the influence of the democratic countries must be restored as soon as possible. But, given the political realities at the moment, FDR told the British ambassador, Sir Ronald Lindsay, this gesture represented the best he could do.

Lindsay urged his government to meet Roosevelt's initiative "with a very quick and cordial acceptance." But in recognition of Britain's worldwide responsibilities yet limited strength, Chamberlain was attempting in his own way to reduce the number of potential enemies for his country, and he felt that FDR's plan might interfere with the appeasement of Germany and Italy, including proposed recognition of Italy's conquest of Ethiopia. He dispatched to the president a reply "in the nature of a douche of cold water"; he did not bother to consult the foreign secretary, Anthony Eden, who was out of town but hardly beyond the reach of twentieth-century communications. Later, pressed by Eden, Chamberlain dispatched a more agreeable message to Washington, but Roosevelt, lacking wholehearted British cooperation and keenly disappointed, let the whole design fade away. Within a few weeks, Eden had resigned.

It had become clear that if the president wished to affect events in Europe, he would have to launch a different kind of effort—behind-the-scenes, more than words, practical.

President Roosevelt returned to Washington for a sad occasion in his official, and now personal, family. On October 9, the Roosevelts and an array of administration dignitaries took part in the funeral of Barbara Hopkins, who had lost a battle with breast cancer. She and Harry had in their six years together enjoyed a quiet and what was invariably described as happy marriage. On coming to Washington they had moved into a four-room apartment in the Kennedy-Warren building at 3133 Connecticut Avenue, called by an unkind reporter "an ornate example of the best Balaban & Katz type of modernism" (i.e., for him it called to mind a 1920s movie palace), but actually an Art Deco triumph. The couple, with their daughter, had lived quietly in these lively surroundings, with Hopkins generally preferring to spend any free evenings playing poker at home rather than going out. They accepted social invitations only on the understanding that he might not be able to appear.

As if grieving were not enough, Hopkins now had to face a serious illness of his own. Shortly after Barbara died, internal problems sent him to the Mayo Clinic, where he underwent an operation that removed not only a cancerous tumor but most of his stomach. (To protect his possible political future, the tumor, in public discussion, was referred to as ulcers.) At this point, Hopkins found the Roosevelts to be true friends at a time of need. Jimmy and Betsy, who had been friends of Barbara's, played a sort of uncle-and-aunt role, often taking Diana into their home; and then Mrs. Roosevelt herself, becoming almost a surrogate mother, brought the little girl into the White House, where she lived much of the time.

In view of the extremely long odds against it, Hopkins's recovery from the drastic surgery represented almost a miracle. And then, after being away for six months, mostly spent convalescing in Florida, he made an emphatic return to action. Responding to the disconcerting economic signal sent by a black March 25 on the stock exchange, Hopkins, data in hand, hurried to FDR's Little White House at Warm Springs, Georgia, to press his friend into undoing the balanced-budget move of the previous summer: the continuing recession, he insisted, had to be met by government spending.

On the same March 25, John Maynard Keynes dispatched another letter in his continuing correspondence with FDR. While regretting the president's naïveté concerning economics, Keynes nevertheless had earlier adopted him as the only vigorous, forward-looking leader the democracies could claim. Now he gave Roosevelt a pointed warning about "treading a very dangerous middle path. You must either give more encouragement to business or take over more of their functions yourself." And FDR also had to educate public opinion. Previously—and perhaps ineffectually—Keynes had suggested to the president that "businessmen have a different set of delusions from politicians; and need, therefore, different handling."

Roosevelt adopted Hopkins's proposed program calling for money for highways and other public works of all kinds, for the WPA and other agencies, and for slum clearance and flood control, and Congress (at this point still the one elected in 1936) gave the president essentially what he asked for. These moves, though not in reality drastic, horrified Henry Morgenthau, still firmly thinking inside the box of non-Keynesian fiscal convention. He had not, however, been able to sway the president—the slide since the previous summer had undone too much of the progress painfully achieved since the launching of the New Deal. But the administration had suffered heavy political damage. In the November elections the Republican

Party, which had seemed almost beyond resuscitation just two or three years earlier, made fateful gains, winning enough seats in the Senate and the House of Representatives to create, together with anti–New Deal Democrats, a formidable conservative coalition. This new potent force would bury the New Deal, damaging the president's prestige and indeed, so closely are presidential power and prestige entwined, cutting down his ability to act effectively in all spheres, foreign as well as domestic.

Unlike other railroad chiefs, who met the Depression by retrenching, and in particular by paying little attention to passenger traffic, Averell Harriman had boosted the Union Pacific with a combination of dazzling new streamliners and ingenious merchandising campaigns to promote them. Involving himself in his typical fashion in the details of design and development, he took a tape measure along on business trips on conventional trains, crawling here and there in an effort to determine the ideal dimensions for the new Union Pacific creations—just as he had done in England twenty years earlier with the Oxford shells.

The railroad soon offered all-coach as well as Pullman versions of the streamliners, and it also cut fares and improved service on regular trains, providing coach passengers with inexpensive meals and amenities like porter service and free pillows. The chairman proudly told his stockholders that "improved equipment resulted in improved passengers." People who boarded the train in unpressed clothes took a good look around and then withdrew to spiff themselves up. Some of the male passengers even went to the length of shaving each morning of the trip from Chicago to Los Angeles.

To improve the railroad's competitive position in relation to its rival, the southerly Santa Fe, Harriman also took the striking step of creating a special cold-weather destination for Union Pacific passengers in an Idaho valley 6,000 feet above sea level, sheltered from freezing winds by 12,000-foot peaks. Sun Valley quickly became the glamorous playground for Hollywood types and other celebrities—a spectacular ski resort Harriman saw as an American answer to St. Moritz. In a typical touch, the boss ordered the railroad shops to produce a new kind of facility for moving skiers; the engineers responded with the world's first chair lift. Until Harriman, perhaps inspired by the 1932 Winter Olympics at Lake Placid, New York, came up with the idea of Alpine skiing, nobody associated with the Union Pacific, it appears, had ever looked on snow as anything but very big trouble in the winter, and now the railroad's chairman, people said, had "put Americans on skis." Averell also realized, said his daughter Kathleen Mortimer, that "if you showed somebody a good time in Sun Valley, they were more apt to ship their potatoes on the Union Pacific."

For the Sun Valley project, Harriman not only visited various ski lodges, crawling through them with tape measure in hand, but engaged in a bit of outsourcing. "You wouldn't believe it," said his male secretary. "He had me measuring the size of the doors in Pullman car men's rooms, because he was wondering how small it was practical to make a door—they had some problems about hanging doors in Sun Valley bathrooms." Since Averell had never learned to ski, he also took effective steps to eliminate this personal deficiency. He liked to go into things, he told a friend, "as hard as I know how."

In late July 1937, Harriman extended an unusual invitation to his friend Harry Hopkins. Sun Valley may have been conceived as a ski resort, but on August 14 and 15, Averell wrote, it was going to be the scene of "a big rodeo," one "on a par with Cheyenne's 'Frontier Day' and Pendleton's 'Round Up.'" Could Harry and his wife come? "We will make you a Grand Mogul, guest of honor, etc., or anything else you want, even let you ride a bucking horse."

The Hopkinses were already vacationing in upstate New York, Hopkins's secretary replied, and hence could not accept. (In any case, as Averell had no way of knowing, Barbara was now in the last stages of her fatal cancer, and this stay at Saratoga Springs, she and Harry knew, represented their final good time together.) But Harriman and Hopkins had kept up a regular if not frequent correspondence, and their friendship had continued to develop. A few months earlier, Averell had written to thank Harry for an address to the Business Advisory Council, with its "frank and full discussion of the outlook and your own point of view." Those present "didn't all agree with everything you had to say," Harriman observed in an impressive bit of understatement, "but your approach to the problem and your willingness to talk to the point made many new friends for you."

In late 1938, when a White House aide asked Harriman, now in his second year as the Business Advisory Council's chairman, "What would you think about Harry as secretary of commerce?" Harriman had replied, as he recalled it, "You never had a better idea in your life." Increasingly close to Hopkins, Roosevelt had begun to reveal a new political purpose: Harry, if his health held up, would have the inside track for FDR's favor and support for the Democratic presidential nomination in 1940. But since Hopkins had no electoral experience and he held unquestioned status as the New Deal figure most reviled by conservatives, the plan obviously had its unrealistic aspects. The president nevertheless forged ahead, presenting his friend on December 23 with an impressive Christmas present, the nomination to be secretary of commerce. The gift came with one string attached: the secretary-designate would have to undergo the confirmation process in the new Senate just produced by the November elections.

After his visit from the White House aide, Harriman undertook to enlist the support of the members of the council, some of whom at first turned purple at the thought of the arch–New Dealer as secretary of commerce; they might not like Hopkins's point of view but Harriman assured them that his friend "had an open mind, was completely objective, and would listen to us." Harriman could also make the argument that by backing the president's closest associate, the council could attain real influence in the White House. After intensive lobbying by their chairman, carried out with his unvarying single-mindedness, Harriman's fellow millionaires agreed to give Hopkins the council's formal support.

Aside from an angry encounter in a Washington hotel between the nominee and North Carolina's Senator Josiah Bailey—which looked for a moment as if it might develop into a fistfight—the Senate Commerce Committee hearings had their ups and downs but did not prove unduly brutal. With matters already proceeding satisfactorily, the famous Mr. Harriman, flourishing the Business Advisory Council's unanimous resolution of support for FDR's nominee, appeared before the committee, where the expression of such sentiments by a Wall Street figure of the first rank—tycoon, railroad king, and glamorous Sun Valley host to Hollywood stars—astonished the chairman, Senator Walter F. George, who apparently had expected something else entirely. "This support," Harriman said later, speaking of Hopkins, "brought us together."

One exchange in the hearing showed the unalloyed nature of Hopkins's loyalty to Roosevelt and to Roosevelt's policies. When the combative Senator Bailey asked the nominee how he would react to the president's enunciation of some policy with which he did not agree, Hopkins replied with a clear statement of his simple credo: he belonged to a team, he said, and while he might try to influence a policy, once the policy was set he would immediately be fighting for it.

With the strong business support he received, Hopkins came through the hearings in good shape. He won confirmation by the full Senate on January 23, 1939, and a month later, now possessing a measure of independent political standing, he made his first public hometown-boy address in his native Iowa, chaperoned by his good friend Averell Harriman. But Hopkins would never run for the presidency or any other political office. His destiny would lie in an entirely unimagined direction.

5

TERROR IN THE AIR

Across the Atlantic, 1938 became the year in which the curtain was drawn back on the vision of a horrendous future, as Europeans began to take Adolf Hitler seriously. In March the Führer sent units of his army across the border into Austria, quickly proclaiming the union of his native country with the Third Reich. Within two months the German focus turned its glare onto Czechoslovakia; this baleful attention seemed likely to be followed by actual armed attack, although in May this war scare faded away—for the moment.

Two years earlier, Franklin Roosevelt had been among the small number of observers who sensed the sinister shape of the future from one decisive event. In March 1936, with an army only in the first stages of maturity, Hitler had boldly defied the World War Allies by sending troops to occupy the Rhineland (the German area west of the Rhine, toward the Low Countries and France, together with a strip of territory on the east bank) in contravention of the Treaty of Versailles, which prohibited the Germans from having any military installations or activities in the region. The treaty already lay in pieces, violated on all sides, but in practical terms Hitler's march had the deadly effect of removing the security shield Versailles had created for Germany's neighbors on the west, in effect transferring it from France to Germany, and thus of diminishing the importance of France in the overall European strategic calculus. The passivity of the French in passing up an ideal opportunity to stop Hitler easily sent a clear message to Central and Eastern Europe: if France would not defend her own interests, nobody else should look to Paris for help, whatever a treaty of alliance might say. But in London a prominent political figure, speaking for many of his fellows, dismissed any concerns about the Germans' move, saying calmly, "After all, they are only going into their own back-garden."

Watching from America, however, Roosevelt saw the picture more clearly. "The Tragedy—the deepest part of it," he said in a personal letter, "is that a nation's words and signatures are no longer good." But "if France had a leader whom the people would follow, their only course would be to occupy all Germany quickly up to the Rhine—no further." France could still do it, FDR commented, but time was running out.

The severity of the strategic blow Hitler had dealt the democracies in the Rhineland thus allowed him to annex Austria in March 1938 and to begin sounding a chorus of threats against the Czechs. These alarming developments led the British government to take a fresh look around and devise a plan for expanding the aircraft industry and also to send an air mission to the United States to investigate American production. The group, which included a tough-minded advocate of strategic bombing, Air Commodore Arthur Harris, found a skeletal scene, with companies moving slowly since existing U.S. laws limited the army to only 2,300 planes and the navy to one thousand; for the current fiscal year the two services had money to buy only nine hundred aircraft overall. The British mission, which dealt with private companies and not with the government, departed having placed just two orders—though one of these, for a reconnaissance bomber, showed what the U.S. industry could do when given an opening. Hungry for markets and working from scratch, Lockheed designers and engineers created in forty-eight hours a mock-up impressive enough to win an initial order for two hundred; the resulting plane would become known as the Lockheed Hudson.

The French, too, looked to the United States. Their young air minister, Guy La Chambre, spent four hours one May evening explaining France's needs to the American ambassador, William C. Bullitt. To be ready for war with Germany the following spring, said La Chambre, France needed some 1,100 new aircraft, particularly pursuit (fighter) planes; although the selection officers were extremely picky, the Air Ministry was close to signing a contract with Curtiss-Wright, though only for one hundred P-36s. "I was shocked to discover," wrote Bullitt to FDR, that La Chambre believed that "if Germany and France should go to war, you would certainly circumvent the Neutrality Act and would continue deliveries of planes to France." Not so, Bullitt told the minister—the president would apply the act as soon as war came. No matter how democratic a country might be, he would have no choice.

After a summer of rising tensions, increasing violence in the Czech border areas inhabited by "Sudeten" Germans, and diplomatic dabbling by the British, the Führer brought matters to a head on September 12 with a brutal speech, delivered to the Nazi party rally in Nuremberg, in which he demanded "justice" for the oppressed Sudetens. (Listening in Prague, William L. Shirer had "never heard the Adolf quite so full of hate, his audience quite so on the borders of bedlam," and his words so "dripping with venom.") This sound of generalized menace began a remarkable eighteen-day marathon featuring not only politicians and diplomats and newspaper reporters but voices of the still young electronic medium, radio, including Shirer's on the Columbia Broadcasting System. As a new and enthralling kind of media event for Americans, the Czech crisis would produce its performing star, a sixty-year-old gentleman named H. V. Kaltenborn. The broadcaster slept on a cot in his CBS studio for those eighteen days and through almost continuous news bulletins and analysis—delivered in his calm, clipped voice—brought European affairs directly into America, including the isolationist heartland, in a way never before imagined.

President Roosevelt, who had some knowledge of German, did not need his ear for nuance to catch the menace animating the Führer's words: a world crisis was threatening, isolationism or no isolationism. Listening to a later speech, on September 26, FDR noted that Hitler's audience did not applaud, "they made noises like animals." Roosevelt might have his plan to make Harry Hopkins secretary of commerce and perhaps to push his friend toward the presidential nomination, but now another kind of task demanded immediate attention. Though no military expert, Hopkins knew a great deal about the working of large-scale operations and he could always draw on his native ability to absorb information and put it to quick use; he was also a completely reliable keeper of presidential secrets. FDR quickly dispatched his friend to California to make a discreet survey of the aircraft industry to determine what the factories would need for major expansion; air power, the president said, expressing an increasingly popular view, would win the coming war.

In turning Hopkins into a confidential agent, Roosevelt was further adapting the old tradition he had begun in New York with Eleanor as his eyes and ears in the kitchens of state hospitals and in Washington, with Hopkins himself as the investigator of the national mood; the limitations on his personal mobility led FDR increasingly to rely on

surrogates to fill specific roles. The move also represented an impro-
vised solution to a besetting problem, the president's lack of anything
approaching adequate staff support; the structure of the executive
branch, created in an era of minimal government, had revealed its
inadequacy almost as soon as he moved into his office. Steps he had
taken toward reorganization were progressing, despite some congressional allegations of a presidential drive toward dictatorship—but
had not yet resulted in legislation.

Now FDR was not only dispatching Hopkins on a mission but,
in making it militarily related, was starting a process that would
change his friend's outlook. The more politically active isolationist
population, an extremely mixed group, was composed of straight
conservatives, some Anglophobes, bitter émigré groups of various
nationalities, and liberals who feared the effect that mobilization
and war could have on American democracy. Along with his friend
Robert M. Hutchins, president of the University of Chicago, and
other liberals, Hopkins the social worker and Social Gospeler had
strong leanings in that direction—not so much for isolation, perhaps,
as for detachment from Europe. Now, however, he was being power-
fully moved toward a new orientation by his presidential tutor in
world affairs.

While Hopkins carried out his West Coast survey, events in
Europe advanced toward the climax that came in Munich in the early
hours of September 30. In the meeting between the British prime
minister, the French premier, and the German and Italian dictators,
Hitler was given the Sudetenland with its industries and its line of
vital fortresses. Having nothing else to offer at the moment, Roosevelt
and other democratic leaders acquiesced in the agreement, if not with
enthusiasm or even with any conviction; unlike Chamberlain, FDR did
not believe that the capitulation in Munich had produced "peace for
our time." The lasting symbol of the conference and of the appease-

ment policy became, in the world's eyes, the furled umbrella Neville Chamberlain carried wherever he went, in Downing Street or on Hitler's Obersalzberg; it presented itself as a meek counterpart to the Führer's armband with its bristling swastika.

The war scare had blown over, but not the fear of war. Estimates of German air might, not the tally of armed strength on land, constituted the source of the terror that had paralyzed Chamberlain and the French premier, Edouard Daladier, in the face of Hitler's threats: air power, embodied in the bomber, reigned as the new king of battle. The picture that had haunted the western leaders and their peoples was that of London and Paris turned within days to endless heaps of smoking rubble and piles of dismembered corpses. The feeling after Munich of having barely escaped swift destruction found apocalyptic expression in a letter written by Arnold Toynbee to an American friend. "It is probably impossible to convey what the imminent expectation of being intensively bombed feels like in a small and densely populated country like this," said the eminent philosopher of history. "We were expecting 30,000 casualties a night in London, and on the Wednesday morning we believed ourselves, I believe correctly, to be within three hours of the zero hour. It was just like facing the end of the world." "Hitler was not bluffing at Munich," declared the widely popular *Reader's Digest.* "He had irresistible power."

From direct observation (notably, Colonel Charles Lindbergh's hands-on experiences as the guest of Luftwaffe high officers), secret intelligence, economic analysis, personal contacts of various kinds, and other sources, the western powers had built up a detailed image of German air might and the strategy that would guide its use—the image that had paralyzed policy in the days leading up to Munich. Politicians had breathed in this mixture of facts and assumptions so thoroughly that it had become, even more than conventional wisdom, simple common sense. In case of war, it said, the Germans would aim the "knockout blow," the name everywhere given to the expected great air assault. Even so independent a figure as Winston Churchill shared the assumptions. Prominent in the Great War and in the 1920s, now long out of office but still occupying a position that not only gave him access to many official reports and analyses but even allowed him to carry on a kind of intelligence operation of his own, Churchill used Air Ministry figures to support his frequent warnings about the danger posed by German might—well-meant warnings that nevertheless could hardly help adding to the nation's fright.

Were Arnold Toynbee's fears legitimate, and Churchill's warnings justified? Certainly, as intelligence information showed, the Germans had made remarkable progress in the years since Hitler had come to power. Even if his 1935 claim to have achieved air parity with Britain amounted only to propaganda, his country was nevertheless forging a formidable air weapon. Even so, in a 1936 intelligence report the Air Ministry had the opportunity to learn that the Germans had abandoned the development of a four-engine bomber, putting emphasis instead on lighter, twin-engine machines. This change no doubt related directly to the death of General Walter Wever, the leading Luftwaffe apostle of strategic bombing, who left no faithful disciples behind him. Unfortunately, Air Ministry officials missed the cardinal importance of the switch away from a long-range, heavy bomber, and much general discussion turned on numbers of planes, usually exaggerated, not on actual types and what they could do.

An accompanying and unshakable fact was Germany's geographical position, conveniently close to France, to be sure, but tactically distant from England. To pose a genuine threat to the island, Germany would require bases on the English Channel; British policy, of course, had always aimed at preventing such an eventuality in any era or any dimension of warfare. Nevertheless, even knowledgeable high-ranking officers of the Air Staff dreaded the possibility of the knock-out blow; as the recipients of these military leaders' expert advice, politicians bore less responsibility than otherwise might have been the case for joining the ill-informed chorus. In reality, the knockout blow would not come because the Luftwaffe did not—in geography, in doctrine, in equipment, in training—have the ability to deliver it. Leaders and people in the West could have slept far more soundly had they known that the Germans themselves were perfectly aware of the governing facts. Just a week before the Munich conference, a Luftwaffe officer had handed Hermann Göring a special report on the subject; a "decisive war against England," he said, "appears to be ruled out with the means now available."

Leading the way for a French representative who hoped to meet with President Roosevelt concerning aircraft, Ambassador William Bullitt arrived in Washington on October 13, two weeks after the Munich conference. FDR sat up late that night to talk with his old friend, an impulsive and emotional man and a great lover of France and its culture. Bullitt painted the European picture for FDR in full and graphic detail, his performance leading the president to tell reporters the next day that international conditions demanded a fresh look at the state of American defenses. Bullitt also telephoned his friend Jean Monnet: "The President is expecting you. Come discreetly."

Monnet, Bullitt explained to Roosevelt, was a remarkable person who "organized and directed the Inter-Allied Maritime Transport Council; the wheat and shipping pool and all the vast other Inter-Allied organizations during the [World War] when he was only a man of twenty-eight. He then became Under Secretary of the League of Nations and for many years has been engaged in private business." At the same time, the ambassador had assured the French premier that Monnet was clearly the best-qualified person to speak for France in dealings with the American president.

Just six days later Monnet arrived in New York. Since FDR was spending a few days on the Hudson, Monnet made his way to Grand Central Terminal, where he took a train for Hyde Park; his first impressions of FDR's home ("an old patrician mansion, but very informal") took note of the presence of numerous children. After welcoming this visitor—a short, neatly dressed, sallow-complexioned figure who would have been taken anywhere in the universe as a French businessman—the president quickly moved into substantive matters by explaining his view that, far from assuring peace, Munich had opened the way to war. He had begun actions, he told his visitor, aiming at enhancing American military strength, particularly in the air, and the three democracies would have to work closely together to build up superiority over Germany.

The conversation convinced Monnet that "we were talking and always would be talking about the same thing, which is the first and perhaps the only rule if two people are to understand one another." The president concluded it by referring his visitor to Henry Morgenthau in Washington for work on financial arrangements, particularly concerning the tapping of French capital available in the United States, and on the availability of various desired types of planes. The meeting had gone well; a precise speaker and careful (but not always patient) listener, Monnet responded to the president's lack of parochialism and expression of a "wide-ranging" worldview that matched his own. The talk in FDR's little study saw the beginning, the first suggestion, of a new kind of international team.

Just about a month later, on November 14, the president convened a high-level meeting of officials, civil and military, concerned with defense, including Morgenthau; the army chief of staff, General Malin Craig; and Harry Hopkins, still WPA administrator and also, the creator of the president's aircraft industry survey. Doing most of the talking, as frequently happened in such conclaves, FDR explained his view of the U.S. defense picture, focusing on weakness in the air. To counter Axis might, he said, the country should have an air force with a strength of 20,000 planes and an annual production capacity of 24,000. No blandishments could conceivably induce Congress to support the pursuit of such goals, of course, but, said the president, he might win about half his request, which would mean 10,000 aircraft to be produced over a two-year period, 3,750 of them first-line.

These enormous, budget-swallowing figures perturbed the military officers among the president's listeners. Of course the country needed aircraft, but an air force also must have pilots and crews, maintenance teams and supply and other services, all fitted into a rational overall defense establishment. Did the president not understand such points? He did indeed, but "he could not influence Hitler with barracks, runways, and schools for mechanics," and at least one officer in the room read FDR's mind: the planes would be "principally destined not for the U.S. Army Air Corps but for direct purchase by the air forces of Great Britain and France." At the same time, the president did not wish to say publicly that he wanted the taxpayers to fund factories devoted to producing war matériel for foreign countries; on hearing such news, the isolationists would surely hasten to prepare a crucifixion if not an immolation. Since this restraint meant that the president had put himself in the position of seeming to seek an amateurishly conceived program, the ensuing discussion in the room had limited substance, with nobody willing to say so. But it did provide an interesting footnote. Winding up, Roosevelt turned to the brand-new deputy chief of staff of the army, a brigadier general named George C. Marshall, who was attending his first such conference.

The general wanted aircraft, but for the U.S. Army, not for foreign countries, and when the president sought confirmation for his ideas by saying, "Don't you think so, George?" he received a surprisingly frosty reply. "Mr. President," said Marshall, primly unhappy at being first-named by a man he barely knew, "I'm sorry, but I don't agree with that at all."

Roosevelt looked "very startled," and that ended the meeting. This impolitic bluntness, Marshall's associates told him, also had no doubt ended his tour of duty in Washington, and very prematurely. That forecast, with its misunderstanding of FDR's character, would prove notably off the mark.

"The President was under the peculiar difficulty, all the time," one of his close associates later put it, "that if he made any move that looked like getting the country ready for war, he was charged with being a warmonger." On the other hand, he felt that he had to act. "He had a dual policy. One was a policy of peace. The other was a policy of preparing for war." But "each step that he took in favor of one of those policies was construed as an abandonment, or perhaps as insincerity, concerning the other. So it was very difficult for him to move."

6

"THE CAUSE OF SOLIDARITY"

Having met George Marshall for the first time at President Roosevelt's November 14 conference, Harry Hopkins informed the general's office one day in December that he wished to have a talk with the deputy chief of staff. On his West Coast trip to survey aircraft plants the president's investigator had produced an idea that had excited one of his companions, Colonel Arthur Wilson, the General Staff liaison officer with the WPA. (Because his organization depended heavily on army engineers—accomplished civilians would not come on board the WPA for civil service pay—Hopkins had not only developed friendships among them but had overcome some of his prejudice against them as likely conservative opponents of the New Deal.)

Speaking in his customary candid way, Hopkins told the colonel that "the Army and the Navy are sitting pretty to get a lot of money in the next relief bill for the national defense if they can sell the idea to the President." Wilson eagerly reported this news to the War Department, adding that "Mr. Hopkins has the ear of the President as no other man, probably," and so "the Chief of Staff or the Deputy [should] get an appointment with him." Putting an edge on his words, Wilson urged speed: "This question is not a matter of weeks and general staff studies but a matter of fast action and days."

When the army bureaucracy underscored Wilson's concerns about its somnolence by failing to respond within a few days, Hopkins acted directly to arrange a talk with Marshall, which took place just after Christmas. The two men met in the secretary-designate's elegant new quarters, a large, paneled office in the Commerce Department building. For more than an hour they discussed the entire defense scene, with Marshall drawing a picture of American weakness on land and in the air as shocking to his interlocutor as it would have been to any other civilian. (In view of the current size of the U.S. Army, which numbered about the same level of effectives as the army of Portugal, Marshall would later call the United States "a third-rate power.")

Some limited action quickly followed the meeting, as several million dollars of WPA funds quietly moved into the realm of defense, earmarked for creating machine tools for the manufacture of small-arms ammunition. Though hardly a giant step, the switch would give the United States perhaps a year's lead time in an important area of war production. The meeting constituted an enlightening lesson in the continuing education of Harry Hopkins in the world beyond domestic concerns. It also launched a friendship between Hopkins and George Marshall.

Then, in the spring of 1939, serious illness struck Hopkins again— not a recurrence of the cancer, the doctors said, but friends and relatives nevertheless feared that his internal upsets and other symptoms amounted to more than "flu" of one kind or another. Pressed to intervene, FDR turned Hopkins over to his own navy physician, Rear Admiral Ross McIntire, an affable ear-and-nose doctor and presidential fishing companion. This well-meant move by the president could charitably be characterized as no great favor to the patient. When Hopkins began having "trouble with his legs," as one of his sons described it, and "spent more and more time in bed," family and friends became increasingly worried. "You always had the feeling that Harry was delicate," said Franklin Roosevelt, Jr., recalling a visit he and his mother paid Hopkins at his little house in Georgetown, to which he had moved after Barbara's death. "There was no complaining, even though you could see he was a very sick guy. Harry never complained." Eleanor Roosevelt, said her son, "was tremendously fond of Harry and always worried about his health." (Aside from her liking for Hopkins, as FDR Jr. noted, Eleanor had seen Franklin lose his earlier closest confidante and adviser, Louis Howe; Harry would be an equally great loss. "Father would say, 'Now, Harry, get that goddamn thing done. And Harry would have it done two hours later.'" Besides, FDR had a great need of fun, and Hopkins was someone he could "horse around" with.)

Finally the unwilling patient followed Roosevelt's firm suggestion that he go back to the Mayo Clinic; perhaps these renowned doctors could solve the problem. Already, on June 17, Hopkins had told the press that he had abandoned any idea of running for president. His choice for 1940, he said, was Roosevelt, thus facing up to the much-talked-about issue of the third term well over a year before the Democratic convention.

In the early spring of 1939, a "wave of perverse optimism," as Winston Churchill called it, spread across Britain, with ministers ignoring increasing stresses in Czechoslovakia. Neville Chamberlain declared that Europe was "settling down to a period of tranquility," and the home secretary, Sir Samuel Hoare, denounced "jitterbugs" while speaking about the possibility of a five-year peace plan, to be created by three dictators and two prime ministers, that could lead to a "golden age." During these illusory days the U.S. president continued working "prudently but relentlessly," in Jean Monnet's words, toward his objectives. In essence, FDR's strategy, as Monnet saw it, called for him "to advocate in public the cause of solidarity among free peoples, but also that of American self-interest, so that gradually, in practice, solidarity would become total and the common interest emerge." Lacking the support of an obvious and important element of self-interest, Monnet well understood, any policy would rest on sand. At the moment, regardless of what illusions the British government might hold about the world, a major task loomed ahead for the president—trying to create enough support to bring about modification of the Neutrality Act so that the Americans could supply munitions to friendly countries at war.

Sir Samuel Hoare's golden age quickly proved to be stillborn. On March 15, in violation of everything he had said and signed, Adolf Hitler sent German forces across the new Czech border and into Prague; this invasion, together with the secession of Slovakia from the republic, marked the end of the twenty-year existence of the Czech state. At first Chamberlain seemed unperturbed by Hitler's arrogant trampling on the Munich agreement, but within a few days it struck the prime minister that the Führer had gone back on the business deal they had made, defrauding him (and thus the country) like a shady contractor paving a street with inferior materials and thereby cheating the mayor and the good ratepayers of Birmingham. Hitler's word had proved to be worthless and Hitler himself lacking in courtesy.

On March 31, as the European pot continued to seethe, the prime minister appeared in the House of Commons to declare a formal reversal of Britain's course. Looking a very worn seventy, "gaunt and ill," with "the skin above his high cheekbones parchment yellow," Chamberlain announced a new and startling British policy. "In the event of an action which clearly threatened Polish independence and which the

Polish Government accordingly considered it vital to resist with their national forces," the prime minister said, "His Majesty's Government would feel themselves bound at once to lend the Polish Government all support in their power." A British guarantee to Poland: from a position of detachment amounting almost to isolation from the Continent, the government had now yielded up control of its own foreign policy, putting the decision for war and peace for Britain into the hands of a group of colonels many hundreds of miles away from London. The German move into Czechoslovakia had destroyed the government's illusion that by avoiding a direct collision with Nazi Germany, Britain's own life might be spared.

After Munich, Americans, whatever their views, had followed the turbulent events across the Atlantic, not only in their newspapers but also through radio news. Innovation in this rising medium was being shown by Bill Shirer and a group of hastily recruited CBS reporters, who were covering the European scene under the direction of a remarkable, somber-voiced young man, Edward R. Murrow, a leader not only new to broadcasting (as were most of his fellows) but new to the reporter's trade itself. Stung by all he had seen and relayed to listeners in America from his London microphone since the previous summer, Murrow gloomily expected the democracies to continue capitulating to Hitler and thus the turmoil of 1939 to end in another Munich.

Back home, however, most people took a different view. Responding to a *Fortune* magazine poll, three out of four Americans questioned saw war coming in Europe in the near future. *Would* the United States get into it? *Should* the United States get into it? The isolationists spoke with clear and strong voices. Their position rested on their belief in the Atlantic and Pacific oceans as great protective moats, as shields rather than highways, and in the inviolability of the thousands of miles of air above the seas. Hence, "they did not believe it essential to the security of the United States that these oceans and the shores opposite our own be always in the control of ourselves and of friendly, peaceful nations."

In an eloquent plea for Americans to stay out of the European power game, former President Herbert Hoover, who had won almost reverential fame for his humanitarian work in the World War, spoke of the horrors of trench warfare. Americans should not engage in such fighting again except "in this hemisphere alone and in defense of our firesides or our honor." Leery of any effort smacking of a new crusade to make the world safe for democracy, isolationists could point to the the last try, which "resulted in at least 15 dictatorships replacing prewar constitutional governments." "If we enter fighting for democracy abroad," said Charles Lindbergh, "we may end by losing it at home."

At this point, advocates of detachment from Europe and its troubles faced the opposition not of "interventionists" actually wishing for the United States to go to war but of persons wanting the country to intervene sufficiently in international affairs to prevent the outbreak of war. This position found succinct expression in the conclusion by the syndicated columnist Dorothy Thompson that "we are already engaged in a struggle which will certainly result in war or in the defeat of this whole American way of life without war, unless we are willing to use right now the political and economic weapons which are in our hands."

Trying to develop the kind of policy advocated by Thompson, so that the United States might indeed help prevent war, FDR worked continually on the Neutrality Act, aiming carefully at influencing Congress toward revision without making himself the issue and thus politicizing it. His weakened political position since the 1938 elections meant that his arguments about the importance of Britain and France to American security and the danger posed by Nazi Germany were taken by many simply as efforts to distract public attention from problems at home by interfering in European matters. If necessary, it appeared, isolationist senators would even stage a filibuster to keep the Neutrality Act unchanged.

FDR experienced a frustrating spring, talking and cajoling, but one procedural setback followed another. Then came the event that forced the president's hand. On June 11, the Foreign Relations Committee voted twelve to eleven not to send an embargo-repeal bill to the full Senate—to allow this key deterrent action, as FDR considered it, to die in committee. The president could not let this move pass, whatever the odds, and a week later Senate leaders, Democratic and Republican stalwarts all, trooped into the upstairs oval study in the White House for an evening's discussion, complete with the clubby atmosphere provided by a drinks tray.

The meeting proved to be a session in which Roosevelt had to draw on his lifetime's training in masking his feelings, speaking lightly (except for one moment of exasperation) and saving his resentments for later disclosure only to his intimates. Despite all his well-marshaled and chilling arguments, the "master word-painter" made little progress with the Senate lions—one of whom, the shaggy and cantankerous William E. Borah of Idaho, was even known as the "Mountain Lion." Frustratingly, Senator Warren Austin of Vermont told the president that if a problem should arise abroad, it could be dealt with at that time; if the president then wanted revision of the Neutrality Law, he could call Congress back in a special session. With that approach, of course, any opportunity for revision of the law to serve as a deterrent to the dictators would have vanished. If Austin, a Republican but not an opponent of the administration's foreign policy, took a position against change, that made the chances of change appear slim indeed. By most accounts of the meeting, Vice President John Nance Garner, a crusty old Capitol Hill veteran from rural southwest Texas, brought matters to a head by turning to Senator Alben Barkley, the majority leader, and asking colorfully and bluntly, "Old Top, have you got the votes to discharge the [Foreign Relations] committee from further consideration of this bill?" When Barkley admitted that he did not, Garner then took a head count of senatorial sentiment and, turning to Roosevelt, said, "You had just as well be candid about this, Cap'n. You haven't got the votes, so why not start from there?"

The issue would now remain in suspension until the next session of Congress began the following January, because, as the president told the press, the senators had so decided: "the responsibility rests wholly on them." Hence, "about all we can do between now and January is to pray that there won't be another crisis, and pray awfully hard."

Events would not wait for the U.S. Senate to act or even to deliberate. In August, after several months of vague negotiations between the European democracies and the Soviet Union concerning possible joint defensive action against Germany had led nowhere, Hitler moved decisively to produce, with Joseph Stalin, a nonaggression pact that left him free to make war without fearing intervention by the Red Army. "Who could have imagined," wrote a British officer, "that two gangsters, who had been heaping the vilest abuse on each other for many years, would kiss and make friends overnight?"

The news came at 2:50 in the morning of Friday, September 1. The White House telephone operator put through a call to the president from Bill Bullitt in Paris, relaying fateful news from Ambassador Anthony Biddle in Warsaw. German bombs were falling on the Polish capital; Hitler's war had already begun, hardly more than a week after the signing of the German–Soviet treaty. Propping himself up on his pillow and lighting a cigarette, FDR placed calls to Secretary of State Cordell Hull and other cabinet officers; then, having alerted his subordinates, he calmly went back to sleep. At 6:30 he was reawakened by another call from Bullitt, telling him of Premier Daladier's declaration that France would fight. FDR acknowledged the news and then, impressively, he returned to sleep again. But a third call forty-five minutes later, this one from Ambassador Joseph P. Kennedy in London reporting Chamberlain's affirmation of Britain's pledge to Poland, convinced him that he was now awake for the day, and after cheering up his depressed ambassador he rang for his valet.

Despite the reported firm declarations by Daladier and Chamberlain, no Allied military action followed for two days, while the two countries served Hitler with ultimatums demanding the withdrawal of German forces from Poland. Though surprised that this time his enemies seemed to be accepting his challenge and he was actually going to have a major war, the Führer had no intention of calling off his bombers and panzers, and on Sunday the third, Britain and France formally declared war on Germany. This day also saw an important political event in Britain: the return to the Admiralty of Winston Churchill as first lord, the position he had been forced to give up in the Great War after the failure of the Allied attempt to force the Dardanelles and neutralize Turkey.

That evening the president addressed the country—and the world—describing the background of the conflict and stating the U.S. position. "You must master at the outset a simple but unalterable fact in modern foreign relations between nations," he declared. "When peace has been broken anywhere, the peace of all countries everywhere is in danger.

"It is easy for you and for me to shrug our shoulders and to say that conflicts taking place thousands of miles from the continental United States, and, indeed, thousands of miles from the whole American Hemisphere, do not seriously affect the Americas—and that all the United States has to do is to ignore them and go about its own business." But, "passionately though we may desire detachment, we are forced to realize that every word that comes through the air, every ship that sails the sea, every battle that is fought does affect the American future."

Finally, in unspoken contrast to Woodrow Wilson's plea at the outset of the Great War for Americans to be neutral in thought as well as in action, the president said: "This nation will remain a neutral nation, but I cannot ask that every American remain neutral in thought as well. Even a neutral has a right to take account of facts. Even a neutral cannot be asked to close his mind or his conscience."

Harry Hopkins had left Washington for the Mayo Clinic on August 22. While the tremendous events were unfolding in Europe, he could take part in the great world only through a bedside radio, as the doctors worked to identify his complex malabsorption or malnutrition disorder. They had trouble devising effective treatment because they did not know what was causing the trouble. Hopkins himself described his condition as "some kind of malnutrition" that baffled the doctors. "It resembled everything they'd ever heard of, from beri-beri to sprue. They don't know what cured me, they tried so many things." "Cured" perhaps put it too strongly, but all the work of Mayo medical teams and various navy doctors did prove effective enough to enable the patient to escape the death sentence one of the physicians had given him, though he emerged from treatment with a body that only a remarkably strong will could drive into the kind of action that had always marked him.

Though FDR briskly rejected a proffered resignation as secretary of commerce, Hopkins would prove only a phantom cabinet member, for several months rarely leaving his Georgetown house. Any reasonable observer would have concluded that not only Hopkins's ill-conceived career in elective politics but his whole productive life had reached its end. He did, however, receive an encouraging note from a new friend, the poet, folk-song bard, and Lincoln biographer Carl Sandburg, who wrote after an evening visit: "It was good to see you—so beautifully human—and more alive than so many who can run a mile without stopping."

7

"SEND FOR HARRY!"

I f we are to win this war," Premier Daladier told Ambassador Bullitt just a week after Adolf Hitler hurled his forces into Poland, "we shall have to win it on supplies of every kind from the United States." Reporting this conversation to President Roosevelt, Bullitt added that the U.S. military attachés in Paris put the case more strongly: "They are not sure that the British and French can hold out until trans-Atlantic production can be brought into the struggle." It was obvious, the ambassador summed up, that "if the Neutrality Act remains in its present form, France and England will lose."

As the law required, the president had moved quickly to issue the appropriate proclamations embargoing exports of munitions to the belligerents. As they discussed these documents and their implications, Harold Ickes, Solicitor General Robert H. Jackson, and other members of FDR's circle, sounding like liberal isolationists, "engaged in some rather doleful exchanges about the effect of the war on the social program of the President," noting "the general tendency of the reactionary and moneyed interests to move into positions of importance as the situation became warlike." Not pausing for such speculation, the president asked Jackson to complete a study already underway concerning powers he would assume on the proclamation of a national emergency. In all situations, FDR brought one great advantage to the table. As one of his assistants put it, "Roosevelt knew how to be president." He was "not the kind of fellow who had to go and read the books on how to be a president. He just knew." Beyond that, "he liked being president, enjoyed it."

With the coming of war, Roosevelt, fully in accord with Bullitt's view, immediately returned to his fight for revision of the Neutrality Act, his primary aim being to remove the arms embargo, as the restrictions were generally called. (Under the 1937 revision of the law, sales of supplies such as scrap iron, but not actual munitions, were permitted.) With senators and representatives returning to Washington for a special session of Congress, as Senator Austin had casually foreseen in the last White House discussion, the president met with a clutch of bipartisan leaders to spell out his forecast of a war long and wide in scope. This meeting provided an overture to the main event, a presidential address on September 21 to a joint session of Congress. Roosevelt, unusually grave—reporters caught only one smile during the speech—noted that the arms embargo helped Germany while repeal would favor Britain and France, but attempted to reassure his audience by declaring, "Our acts must be guided by one single, hard-headed thought—keeping America out of this war!"

But the senators and representatives reacted in their own fashion, stalling proceedings just as they had done earlier in the year. FDR had no intention of giving up, however: supplying the sinews of war to the Allies formed the heart of his position and policy. Mounting a political and opinion campaign, he moved shrewdly and carefully, making as much use as possible of surrogates like internationalist Republicans. He was, he told a correspondent, "almost literally walking on eggs."

This deft presidential footwork paid off. After more than a month of FDR's campaign, the Senate gave him a resounding 63-to-30-vote victory on repeal of the arms embargo; the vote roughly matched public sentiment, as shown in a Gallup poll figure of about 60 percent in favor of repeal. The House quickly followed suit and the two bills were reconciled into the final act, which was passed on November 3 and ceremonially signed by the president the following day. War commerce would now be conducted on a cash-and-carry basis: countries at war could buy whatever munitions they could pay for, but they also had to take all the responsibility for hauling the goods away— no charge accounts, no delivery service. Under these provisions, their creators hoped and believed, Americans could avoid the financial entanglements that, it was said over and over, had led to their involvement in war in 1917—an event few wanted to defend in 1939. Keeping U.S. vessels out of harm's way through cash-and-carry completed the equation. In London the *Sketch*, though not one of the more serious papers, succinctly made an insightful point: by this amendment, President Roosevelt would be "able to give material help to the Allies as a means of avoiding giving them military help."

Sweeping from north and south into the heart of Poland, in history's first blitzkrieg, Hitler's Wehrmacht won all the battles against its brave but utterly outclassed opponent. The campaign had unofficially ended by September 19, though Warsaw held out until September 27. Warsaw radio, which had broadcast the initial martial notes of Chopin's "Military Polonaise" every thirty seconds throughout the final week, now fell silent. By this time two Soviet army groups had marched into Poland to claim their country's share of the spoils, in accordance with the "Ribbentrop-Molotov" treaty of August 23.

In the West, meanwhile, the British and French armies stood passively, looking eastward into Germany but taking no action. The Luftwaffe, busy in Poland, delivered no attacks on France—by geographical situation a convenient target—while French authorities asked the

British to abstain from any attempts to bomb Germany, in order not to create a situation in which the enemy might retaliate against French war factories. The Royal Air Force nevertheless did appear over western German towns, dropping clusters of propaganda leaflets intended to persuade the Germans to mend their regrettable ways.

With the battle in Poland over and the blitzkrieg having shown itself a devastatingly formidable way of making war (awed reporters had coined the term to convey the pace and force of the campaign), the strange stillness continued in the West. The war began to acquire nicknames: *drôle de guerre, Sitzkrieg,* and from America probably the most popular tag: the Phony War. Some talk was heard about a possible Allied offensive springing east from Belgium, but it was only talk. Visiting a French mess hall, a British corps commander, Lieutenant General Sir Alan Brooke, partook of a lunch featuring "oysters, lobsters, chicken, pâté-de-fois-gras, pheasant, cheese and fruit, coffee, liqueurs," together with champagne. Were the French really up to fighting a serious war?

The repeal of the U.S. arms embargo meant that the British now became as eager as the French to make arrangements for American supplies of all kinds. Just three days after the revised Neutrality Act became law, the British government set up a purchasing commission in the United States, in accordance with Roosevelt's preference, with a Scottish-born Canadian industrialist, Arthur Purvis, as its head. "As much American as British in his way of going about things," Purvis quickly won admiration for his drive and dedication. In November the British and French merged their Washington commissions, with Purvis as chairman, and, fittingly, Jean Monnet, the practical dreamer, became chairman of the Anglo-French Coordinating Committee, based in London, and thus head of all Allied purchasing operations.

The Allies now entered into a large-scale buying program. Did France have the resources to finance her share? "I'll find the money to buy these planes," Daladier said, "even if I have to sell Versailles." The two democracies ordered aircraft from any company that could supply them, with the result of getting all sectors of the U.S. industry humming, increasing the work force, and converting it all to mass production. But the encouraging figures represented orders placed, not actual deliveries; by the spring of 1940 the total number of planes shipped across the Atlantic in fulfillment of these Allied orders had not yet risen out of the hundreds. "So far as France and Britain were concerned," commented a U.S. official, "both they and we had been too late with too little."

On April 8, 1940, British destroyers began laying a minefield off the Norwegian port of Narvik, with the aim of cutting off the shipment of Swedish iron ore via that port southward to Germany. Later on the very same day, German warships appeared in Norwegian waters and began unloading troops at ports the British themselves had intended to occupy. Though outside the main theater, this operation, about which Clare Boothe Luce and her unconcerned French hosts were informed during her luncheon visit to her Maginot fort, marked the demise of the Phony War.

A month later, after miscalculations, mishaps, and enemy superiority had produced nothing better in Norway than stalemate or Allied evacuations, parliamentary frustration with this fiasco and with the British government's general system for conducting the war led to an uprising in the House of Commons. "The ineptitude of the government as a whole, in spite of the brilliance of some of its members," noted Sir Edward Spears, an outstanding MP who was also a general, was "flabbergasting." Indeed, he declared, "the war could not be won in this way. The nation could not afford to wait any longer."

Spears and his allies, a group including as its chief figure Anthony Eden, had the candidate who could set things right firmly in mind: the first lord of the admiralty, Winston Churchill. But as the debate boiled in the House of Commons, two problems concerned Spears. Since, as civilian head of the navy, Churchill had borne a good part of the responsibility for the Norwegian operation, some members of the House might charge him with much of the blame for its outcome. Perhaps worse, Churchill might rush in to take such responsibility, out of loyalty to the prime minister. Even some of Eden's group had always felt that Churchill, though an extraordinary political personality, did not have the trust of the public, which "was convinced that he was erratic and dangerous."

The sixty-five-year-old Churchill had always attracted the attention of the public, ever since Boer War days at the beginning of the twentieth century when his daring escape from an enemy prison made him a national hero, "the latest and the greatest sensation of the day," and launched him into politics. During the Great War he served as first lord of the Admiralty, the post to which he returned in September 1939, and then as minister of munitions; for five years during the 1920s he held office as chancellor of the Exchequer. By 1930 he had become one of the most experienced of all British statesmen, far superior in background to Stanley Baldwin, the last prime minister under whom he had served.

But by 1930, this chronicle of high-level political success had apparently reached its end, with its subject just fifty-five years old. During the 1930s Churchill found no favor with prime ministers, including his former colleague Baldwin, or with much of the public. In controversies over Britain's relationship to India, a central question of the era, he opposed concessions to rising Indian nationalism, and in speaking of the Indian leader Gandhi as a "half-naked fakir" he presented himself in many eyes as an anachronism, a Victorian figure living amid the fusty glories of a bygone empire.

Many of Churchill's political contemporaries, friends and foes alike, thought of him as a colorful and energetic adventurer, one not bound by party loyalties or other conventional restraints. The opinion of an influential Conservative seemed to express the general view: "I believe in Winston's capability if only he were a bit more steady. But you never know what kite he is going to fly next." More bluntly, a future prime minister said of Churchill: "I think he has very unusual intellectual ability, but at the same times he seems to have an entirely unbalanced mind." Churchill himself said, "I like things to happen, and if they don't happen I like to make them happen." He might have developed the point a bit further: he liked to make *dangerous* things happen. Fighting danger, coping with a crisis, served as a tonic, the best medicine for his internal crises—the "black dog," the moods brought on by chronic depression. The resultant behavior made Churchill seem to many an impulsive and erratic romantic in a depressed and matter-of-fact world whose inhabitants wanted jobs and social security rather than swordplay and glory.

Now, on the afternoon of May 7, began one of the most dramatic, pointed, and passionate debates in the history of the House of Commons. A weary Chamberlain offered a speech of self-defense, which only served to evoke from his hearers a barrage of rare vituperation and execration, ending with a veteran member's demand, borrowed from Oliver Cromwell's scornful dismissal of the Long Parliament almost three centuries earlier: "Depart, I say, and have done with you. In the name of God, go!" The next evening, as the debate wound up and the House prepared to vote on the government's conduct in the war, it appeared that if Churchill's hour was ever to come, it might now be at hand.

On the morning of May 10, the whole war changed. Reports began flooding into Allied headquarters of bombings, strafings, and paratroopers dropping from the skies, of troops pouring into the Netherlands and Belgium. This was the morning on which Clare Boothe Luce, asleep in the U.S. ambassador's residence in Brussels, was shaken awake to be told "the Germans are coming again." So began the six weeks of the most remarkable military campaign since the discovery of gunpowder, ending in the complete French capitulation on June 22. By this time Mrs. Luce had returned to the United States, crying out to her peaceable readers: "Do you know what big guns and incendiary bombs and machine-guns are? Do you know what they can do to houses and to roads and to the people on them?" If you knew, it would "make you squirm with horror, rage, disgust." She had come home an evangelist.

In this new and truly great crisis, Neville Chamberlain told a minister that he believed he ought to stay on at the helm of government. No, the minister said; the new urgency demanded a National Government, which meant a new leader. Lord Halifax? For what it was worth, George VI was known to admire this high-church Yorkshireman— "I, of course, suggested Halifax," the king noted in his diary—and Chamberlain himself would find him a congenial choice. Halifax also had the vocal support of the famous (or notorious) Virginia-born Lady Astor. But in a meeting the previous afternoon with the prime minister and Churchill, Halifax had ruled himself out; in wartime, he said, the prime minister must sit in the Commons, the body on whose approval any government depended.

Earlier in the day, Churchill had been given a piece of advice that may well have affected the destiny of Britain. Two members of his personal circle, Lord Beaverbrook and a younger intimate, Brendan

Bracken, both insisted that when the talk turned to the prime ministerial situation, Churchill *must not speak first*; if he should do that,
his friends feared, he would gallantly express his willingness to serve
under Halifax. When the foreseen moment did come, Churchill, following the advice of his friends, stared out of the window onto the
Horse Guards Parade; Halifax, who seemed genuinely not to want the
job, then made his statement.

And so, wrote Churchill, "it was clear that the duty would fall upon
me—had in fact fallen upon me." Responding to the situation like a
true man of destiny, he felt not anxiety but relief: finally the nation
had the leader it needed! The nation also had acquired a leader whose
view of America differed sharply from that of Neville Chamberlain.

When he heard the news, President Roosevelt offered a mordant,
far from lofty comment reflecting both a widespread view of Churchill
and personal concerns in the Roosevelt family. "I suppose Churchill
was the best man England had," FDR said in a cabinet session, "even
if he was drunk half the time."

On the same day, May 10, the White House guest list for dinner
included the name of Harry L. Hopkins. Still secretary of commerce,
though he had been unable to spend much time in his office, Hopkins
had managed to contrive a number of initiatives related to national
defense, such as plans for stockpiling strategic materials and for
recruiting workers for war production. After dinner he accepted President Roosevelt's invitation to spend the night and promptly found
himself installed in a two-room suite that included the bedroom President Lincoln had used as a study. In an unintended and heightened
emulation of the situation in the popular recent play *The Man Who
Came to Dinner*, Hopkins would not only stay for the night but at the
president's insistence would make the White House his home base for

the next several years. In this time of crisis FDR, as a reporter noted, "discovered that it was very convenient to have his old friend close at hand." This observation actually understated the case: the president needed not only the companionship and counsel of a close friend but an extra pair of eyes to keep up with the flow of cables that now poured in from overseas—the flow that on the afternoon of June 10 had led FDR to issue the order: "Send for Harry!"

Hopkins was excellent company—"a charming, charming person," and "very considerate of the people he was dealing with"—and more and more FDR had discussed major issues with his friend and sought his opinions. "I think," said Franklin Roosevelt, Jr., "my father was a person who relied on people he sort of chemically got along with."

After Hopkins had been living in the White House for about two weeks, working at the card table set up in his bedroom as his desk, the president asked one of his house guest's assistants how well he thought Harry was bearing up under all the strain. The assistant declared that he had not seen his boss looking so well in two years. It was just as FDR had thought: as he had learned some years earlier, his friend was a man who thrived on crisis. Though FDR's treatment by direct challenge could not make Hopkins robust, the man who came to dinner nevertheless became strong enough to be on call for unusual assignments and to begin to fill a special role in the president's service.

Hopkins also brought a bit of his outside life into the mansion, arranging to have the *Daily Racing Form* delivered to his suite. This enabled him to take part in the flourishing White House gambling subculture, in which everybody below stairs played the horses. The servants also seemed to enjoy better meals than were served to the great figures upstairs, as was suggested one day when Hopkins suddenly appeared in the servants' dining room. Had he managed to get lost in the maze of service rooms, whatever he might have been doing there? No, he said, he had in effect followed his nose, led through the rooms by the smell of stewed chicken. Could he have some, instead of the lunch that was awaiting him upstairs? The cooks cheerfully obliged, sending him off with a complete meal in doggy bags.

Now that Harry had become a resident of the White House, his appreciation of food, his fondness for minor-league gambling, his love of New York night life, and his general enjoyment of less-than-edifying pleasures began to weigh on the puritan soul of Eleanor Roosevelt. This behavior, she felt, hardly befitted a national leader of social action. What surprised "some of us," she observed, "was the fact that Harry seemed to get so much genuine pleasure out of contact with gay but more or less artificial society." She had, indeed, long had similar feelings about anything that seemed frivolous in her husband's makeup. "I did not like this side of Harry," she said, "as much as the side I first knew." Beyond that, as Harry moved more and more into the president's orbit, sharing both his concerns and his diversions, Eleanor heard the laughter and felt the loss of her ally since 1933. Plainly, she resented it. She was overheard saying that "Franklin had changed Hopkins, and not for the better."

On May 14, only four days after the German attack began, with enemy forces flooding out of the Ardennes and across the Meuse River, Bill Bullitt called the situation "one of the most terrible moments in human history." Paul Reynaud, the French premier who had succeeded Daladier, had "implored" the ambassador to obtain more airplanes from the United States, he reported to FDR, but "I told him I feared there were none to be had." Frantically, Reynaud telegraphed appeals directly to Roosevelt, who assured him that the United States was making the greatest possible effort to supply the Allies with urgently needed material.

On June 14 the premier, utterly desperate, told the president: "France can continue the struggle only if America intervenes to reverse the situation, thus rendering Allied victory certain." If the United States did not pledge to enter the war immediately, "you will see France go down like a drowning man and disappear, after having thrown a last look toward the land of liberty from which it expected salvation." In this scene of rapidly vanishing hours and days, Roosevelt could offer encouragement but could do little of a practical nature to help keep the French ship of state afloat. Two days later Reynaud was gone as premier; his successor, the old and constitutionally pessimistic Marshal Philippe Pétain, moved quickly and efficiently toward the capitulation that came on June 22.

For many Americans, the armistice signed in the forest clearing at Compiègne meant that a whole supposedly permanent world had come to an end. As terrible proof of it, the Eiffel Tower now served as a giant flagpole for a swastika banner.

8

DECIDEDLY UNNEUTRAL ACTS

A little before one o'clock in the morning of May 15, just five days after the Germans launched the great invasion in the West, Joseph P. Kennedy, the fifty-one-year-old Boston adventurer-tycoon who served as President Roosevelt's ambassador to the Court of St. James's, met with the new prime minister at the Admiralty building. Seeming to take for granted the existence of a total community of interests between their two countries, Churchill had summoned Kennedy partly to make it clear that he looked westward, across the Atlantic, for the help Britain needed: the era of standoffishness with America had ended, at least at the top.

The ambassador represented a class of officials not unusual in the Roosevelt Administration: persons who differed with the president on many, often important, issues but who nevertheless retained their positions. Sometimes straightforward political considerations seemed to be the principal factor in these situations, while others appeared to involve the working of the president's complex temperament. Many Washington hands had regarded the choice of an Irish Catholic for the London embassy as a typical bit of Rooseveltian caprice, but Kennedy himself noted that others had applauded the choice because his background would render him "proof against British wiles." Even before his despairing call to FDR in September 1939 announcing that Britain was going to fight, the ambassador had felt that Germany had become too powerful to be challenged; he had not only supported the appeasement policy but had become a confidant of Neville Chamberlain. Most important, he believed that the United States must stay out of a European war, and, since he did not keep his opinions to himself, he had become widely tagged as a defeatist. "There is no doubt that a considerable number of people over here have resented Mr. Kennedy's utterances concerning the war," Ed Murrow told his radio listeners, who could have little trouble in concluding that Murrow included himself among them.

In response to Churchill's statement about the need for help from America, Kennedy asked what, realistically, could the United States do? It was too late for money to make any difference, the U.S. fleet was far away in the Pacific, and, said Kennedy, "we haven't sufficient airplanes for our own use." Churchill replied that he would ask the president for any planes the Americans could spare and also—demonstrating his full awareness of the potential U-boat menace to the shipping lifeline between America and British ports—"the loan of 30 or 40 of [your] old destroyers."

Kennedy left the meeting in a pessimistic mood. The British seemed to expect a short war, which meant a losing war. But they would never give up while he remained in power, Churchill had told him, "even if England were burnt to the ground"; instead, the government would move to Canada, taking the fleet with it, and fight on. But Churchill, Anthony Eden, and a third member of the group present, Sir Archibald Sinclair, "were very low tonight although they are tough and mean to fight." The American ambassador, a professed teetotaler, noted with some concern that on a table next to the prime minister's chair sat a tray "with plenty of liquor on it" and that he was drinking a Scotch highball as they talked; nor was it, Kennedy naïvely felt, "the first one he had drunk that night." The affairs of Great Britain might have been put into the hands of "the most dynamic individual" in the country, but were they in the hands of the best judgment? Beyond that, the ambassador wondered, how sound an investment of scarce American resources would Britain represent?

In speech and performance, Churchill had made his determination clear from the moment he had first appeared in the House of Commons as prime minister, when he presented his program with the terse, beautifully balanced declaration: "I have nothing to offer but blood, toil, tears and sweat." The aim, the new prime minister said, was victory—"victory at all costs, victory in spite of all terror; victory, however long and hard the road may be; for without victory, there is no survival."

On May 20, just ten days after the offensive had begun, General Heinz Guderian led his tanks into Abbeville, a town all the way across northern France on the Somme River with access to the English Channel, thereby cutting the British off from their base at Cherbourg. Puzzlingly, for reasons the Allies could not know but could only be thankful for, the Wehrmacht now halted its panzers in the northwest, giving British troops the opportunity to gather on the beaches of Dunkirk. As the Luftwaffe pounded the area, the men, said one of them, hid "like rabbits among the dunes." Then, in the huge effort labeled Operation Dynamo and lasting till June 4, the men were plucked from the shore and ferried home across the Channel by an array of naval craft—destroyers, sloops, minesweepers, patrol boats—joined, as time went on, by private yachts, tugs, lifeboats from ocean liners, and other small vessels. Of the forty-one destroyers engaged in this one operation, six were sunk and nineteen damaged. The total figure of men rescued reached an astonishing 338,226; the navy had hoped at best to save perhaps 45,000 before the Germans overran the area.

While many of the French charged their ally with wholesale deser-
tion, the British people hailed Dunkirk as a deliverance, a true miracle:
the British Expeditionary Force had escaped from what seemed certain capture, and the island now had defenders. But the soldiers had
not returned with the highest morale. As an official of the War Office
later said, "The Dunkirk episode was far worse than was ever realized
in Fleet Street"; to keep this knowledge under wraps, the government
shrouded the scene in total censorship. Churchill told the House on
the day the Admiralty concluded Operation Dynamo that the people
must realize that "wars are not won by evacuations." (Offstage, he
called Dunkirk "the greatest British military defeat for many centuries.") And, though the soldiers had come home, they now belonged to
a force without weapons; all of their arms, munitions, and equipment
remained on the other side of the Channel. The bill was huge: 7,000
tons of ammunition, 90,000 rifles, 2,300 guns, 400 antitank rifles,
8,000 Bren guns (light machine guns), and 120,000 vehicles. All the
stepped-up output of the war factories had been lost; the urgency of
the need to replace as much of this equipment as possible was tran-
scendent. Despite all that, Ed Murrow told his radio listeners back
in America, Churchill believed that Britain could defend herself and
"outlive the menace of tyranny." The prime minister said simply, "We
shall never surrender!"

"There was," reported Murrow, "a prophetic quality about that
speech."

While wishing Britain and France well, the U.S. government and most
Americans had felt little anxiety about the course of the war, even
after the Allied misadventure in Norway. The Allies had stood off the
Germans for four years in the first war (hadn't they?), though it was
true, many remembered, that the Americans had provided the drive

for the final victorious push. Certainly the eventlessness of the Phony War had posed no threat to any American's complacency. But now reports of the irresistible German sweep across France, capped by the launching of the rescue attempt at Dunkirk, showed how profoundly this new war differed from its predecessor of a quarter-century earlier. People across the United States were shocked into taking a new look at the world. England herself might be small, but everyone had grown up seeing a fourth of the big wall map in red, for the British Empire, the largest ever known. On the other hand, the Nazi leaders were mere upstarts, appearing in the movie theater newsreels as little better than freaks—Hitler with his Charlie Chaplin tramp's mustache, Hermann Göring bulging in his uniform, the sly and shrunken Dr. Goebbels. Their talk of "supermen" had always evoked derisive laughter and soon would even inspire a satiric popular song about "super-duper supermen."

Yet the freakish upstarts threatened now to destroy the established order. "For the first time in many years," said a citizen of Clarksville, Tennessee, "people in this little town are no longer finding arguments for Germany's aggressions." A woman in Massachusetts commented, "Whether we like Allied policies or not, it is necessary for the U.S. to recognize its stake in an Allied victory." And such a victory might not be the issue. With France crumbling and Britain forced off the Continent, a frightful, previously unimagined possibility suddenly became clear: "German victory," two reporters wrote, "sweeping and decisive enough to change the whole face of the world we live in."

Following his early-morning conversation with Joseph Kennedy, Churchill proceeded to send his request directly to Roosevelt, simply bumping up the numbers to "forty or fifty of your older destroyers." (In fact, Paul Reynaud had beaten Churchill by a day with a request for destroyers.) Churchill also asked for several hundred aircraft and various kinds of supplies, and his message included a direct warning:

"The voice and force of the United States may count for nothing if they are withheld too long." On May 21, General Marshall ordered the chief of ordnance to determine what kinds of materials could be considered surplus, and thus legally available for sale, and what were essential to the defense of the United States.

Then, within a few days, the British Army's loss of its weapons and equipment at Dunkirk created a wholly unexpected crisis, which the U.S. Army, on Roosevelt's impetus and under Marshall's direction, met with an unprecedented act of faith. Citing his lack of authority to make such arrangements, the president had declined Churchill's requests for destroyers. But now, drawing on stocks of weapons manufactured for the World War, the Americans moved to rearm the British Army, defying the risk of seeing the weapons end up in German hands. Even before the Dunkirk crisis, Roosevelt had urged the army to interpret "surplus" generously. "The President was not a legalistic-minded person," his younger friend, the newly appointed attorney general Robert H. Jackson, later reflected. He had "a tendency to think in terms of right and wrong, instead of terms of legal and illegal"— though, as the summer of 1940 progressed, FDR would display keen awareness of the relationship of both of these categories to the permissible scope of presidential action. Right now, he was placing his first tangible bet not only on Britain but on the new prime minister. This certainly did not represent traditional neutrality.

The first freighter bearing the American weapons was plowing northeastward out in the Atlantic when the news came that Marshal Pétain had asked the Germans for an armistice. This development presented a fresh kind of emergency, because the combining of the British and French purchasing programs meant that not only the emergency arms but all of the orders the Allies had placed in the United States might now be in jeopardy. Given full authority to handle this unprecedented situation, Arthur Purvis had already been at work to save the orders for Britain; a bitterly disappointed and humiliated French colleague told him that Britain must take over all the French contracts or none of them: "You cannot pick our bones after we have fallen." And the demand for speed was urgent; at any moment a message from France might strip the representatives of their authority. After the final papers were signed in his apartment at three o'clock in the morning of June 17, Purvis, who had no instructions from London beyond the injunction to do whatever was necessary, reflected that with his lone signature he had now committed his parsimonious— and dollar-shy—superiors in Whitehall to spending some $600 million (the equivalent of many billions some decades later). Within five hours, when the normal business day began, the Treasury Department would freeze all French assets in the United States.

The urgent appeal to President Roosevelt for American destroyers remained a central issue for Winston Churchill. But as desperate events unfolded across the Atlantic, the president had to face some grim possibilities. If a British defeatist administration should find itself in armistice negotiations with Hitler, he asked the ambassador, Lord Lothian, the Royal Navy might become a supreme bargaining counter, might it not?

The ambassador referred the question, both delicate and important, to his chief in London. Too much optimism or too much pessimism—either might produce an unwanted reaction in Washington. Expressing disappointment about another turn-down on the destroyers, Churchill said bluntly in a cable to the president, "If members of the present administration were finished and others came in to parley amid the ruins, you must not be blind to the fact that the sole remaining bargaining counter with Germany would be the fleet," and he proceeded to add even more bluntly: "if this country was left by the United States to its fate no one would have the right to blame those then responsible if they made the best terms they could for the surviving inhabitants." Then came the counterbalancing soothing remark: "However, there is happily no need at present to dwell upon such ideas."

A little over a month later, Churchill cabled Lothian a more detailed picture of the possible grim future: "Never cease to impress on President and others that, if this country were successfully invaded and largely occupied after heavy fighting, some Quisling Government would be formed to make peace on the basis of our becoming a German protectorate. In this case the British Fleet would be the solid contribution with which this Peace Government would buy terms," all of which would mean that "feeling in England against United States would be similar to French bitterness against us now."

But despite his doggedness, and his pointing to the increased demands on the Royal Navy that would now be made by Mussolini's entrance into the war on June 10—the "Italian outrage"—Churchill still won no destroyers. Indeed, his chances of getting American war vessels of any kind soon worsened, because of a flare-up of at least partially ethnic politics. On June 28 the Senate amended an appropriations bill to forbid the disposal of any army or navy matériel unless the service chiefs certified the items in question as "not essential to the United States." This sudden development represented the work of Senator David I. Walsh of Massachusetts, not only an isolationist but also a Boston Irishman who never shed any tears at the sight of England in trouble. Which aspect of his outlook weighed more heavily in his present calculations was perhaps difficult to know, but either way the important fact was that Walsh chaired the Senate Naval Affairs Committee.

As a preeminent national leader, Franklin Roosevelt necessarily lived along many parallel lines at the same time, with few opportunities to deal with problems simply one by one. While trying to cope with questions of international life and death, he also had to perform his varied duties as head of one of the great political parties of a very large country and to be aware of the possible relationships between the two tracks. Now, in the summer of a presidential election year, he needed to take certain specific steps if he intended to remain in the White House. The possibility of a third term for Roosevelt served as one more item to inflame rabid anti–New Dealers, who gave vent to loud outrage at the prospect, while FDR took delight in a caricature showing him as a jaunty Sphinx with uptilted cigarette holder, carefully keeping his plans to himself.

Probably, until well along in the spring of 1940, Roosevelt was an unusual kind of Sphinx who did not know the answer to his own questions; in any case, he shrewdly held on to the influence he had over events by keeping secret his intentions, though in January, to his intimate Henry Morgenthau, he had expressed what was likely his predominant feeling: "I do not want to run unless between now and the convention things get very, very much worse in Europe." And in June the fall of France produced just that situation.

Harry Hopkins had seen the third-term picture clearly a year before, and now, with his fleeting presidential aspirations far behind him, he found himself dispatched to the Democratic convention in Chicago with a new assignment, one calling for him to perform as a purely political operative: he would coordinate the process that would lead to his boss's nomination for a third term. He carried out the task with drive, efficiency, and blunt realism, and soon after his return he resigned as secretary of commerce, expecting after a period of further rest and recuperation from his illness to become director of a Roosevelt innovation, the library being built at Hyde Park as the depository of the president's papers. But this idea for a new career would have an even shorter life than some of Hopkins's other plans and expectations.

In early July, Winston Churchill received a report that brought a measure of balance to British estimates of German air strength. An analysis of information produced and correlated by code-breakers and intelligence officers strongly suggested that the Luftwaffe possessed only about 1,250 first-line bombers, half the total the Air Ministry had previously thought, and only a fraction of the reserves with which it had been credited. It was the kind of information that could have braced Chamberlain, Daladier, and other western leaders had they possessed it two years earlier. The RAF would still have to fight off the enemy, but a more manageable enemy, and the danger of invasion, though not disappearing, did not loom quite as large as before. The prime minister even began to give some thought to ways Britain could ultimately take the offensive in the air.

Even so, on July 31, after a break in his continuing pleas for the loan or sale of U.S. destroyers, Winston Churchill returned to his quest with a memorable declaration: "Mr. President, with great respect I must tell you that in the long history of the world, this is a thing to do now." With Britain losing a destroyer a day to enemy action, he said, "We could not keep up the present rate of casualties for long."

Aside from the legal constraints by which he felt bound, Roosevelt had continued to fear the possibility that American ships or other war matériel would end up in German hands. The French fleet, which had not been sailed to British ports (as Churchill had requested) before the conclusion of the armistice at Compiègne, had remained a looming threat, though following the capitulation the Germans had refrained from seizing it. Then, on July 3, Churchill and the Royal

Navy had given the world a strong and convincing demonstration of the nation's resolve. A British squadron attacked a powerful French fleet at its North African base near Oran, damaging a battle cruiser and destroying two battleships; a few days later an air attack at Dakar disabled another battleship. These bold strikes, beating the Germans to any contemplated takeover, could not be considered the actions of a country, whether facing invasion or not, that believed itself on the edge of defeat.

Looking at the map in this summer of 1940, contemplating the world in geopolitical terms, the president had could see the nightmarish prospect that would be presented if Britain went down—the whole of Eurasia dominated by Hitler and his associate, if not active ally, Joseph Stalin, supported by the Italian navy and the remnants of the French navy, with the British fleet as a probable great new asset. Against this truly mighty coalition, possibly reinforced by Japan, would stand the United States as the only nontotalitarian great power in the world.

Talking with Robert Jackson one afternoon at the height of the Battle of France, the president had made an empathetic leap across the Atlantic. Churchill, he said, had to decide how much of the RAF's strength to throw into the battle. If he committed all of it, and the Allies nevertheless lost the fight, then Britain would be left defenseless against air attack. But if he held it back for home defense, then the French would accuse him of abandoning them, and his own people would blame him for not using his full strength while he still had the help of the French. "We'd better be thinking about this," Roosevelt said. "It is not much different [from] the questions we may have to face if things continue as they are going now."

But those old destroyers, analogous in FDR's mind to the British fighter squadrons that had been demanded in France: how could they be declared surplus, not essential for American defense? The chief of naval operations, Admiral Harold R. Stark, who under the new Walsh amendment would have to make such a declaration, could hardly do that, since he had recently pointed out in a congressional hearing that the navy was currently hastening to recondition one hundred of these vintage four-pipers for American defense purposes.

Rising public sentiment, as well as pressures from members of his own cabinet, could only reinforce Roosevelt's own desire to find an answer to the dilemma, but with a presidential campaign in progress, with isolationist sentiment still strong—particularly on Capitol Hill—and with Anglo-American interwar tensions far from forgotten, what answer might he find? What might the plan be, and how could it be sold?

The answer, coming from an unexpected source and seeming almost like a coincidence, began to take shape in a cabinet meeting on August 2. In mid-June, for reasons both symbolic and practical, the president had moved to create a kind of coalition cabinet (although, of course, the concept of cabinet responsibility does not exist under the American system of government) by appointing two of the most prominent Republicans, the veteran statesman Henry L. Stimson and Frank Knox, publisher of the *Chicago Daily News* and 1936 vice-presidential candidate, to the positions, respectively, of secretary of war and secretary of the navy. In the August 2 cabinet meeting the president led off with Churchill's letter of two days earlier. Then Knox, new to this context, reported that just the previous evening, in a talk with Lord Lothian, he had asked the ambassador whether the British had ever thought about selling some of their Atlantic and Caribbean possessions; no, they had not, Lothian replied. Knox's question had not come out of the void; as it happened, he had for some time maintained in his newspaper that the United States should acquire Caribbean bases to protect the Panama Canal.

Secretary Hull saw procedural problems in any arrangement of this kind and "obviously was not happy at the initiation of such a negotiation by the impetuous Knox," while Roosevelt, Jackson felt, considered the notion "something of a hobby of Knox's to which he did not expect British agreement." But the very next morning brought a cable from Churchill to Lothian agreeing to the idea, with the bases being leased, not sold. "It is understood," said the prime minister, "that this will enable us to secure destroyers and flying-boats at once." The following day Lothian made the formal offer of the bases to Hull, who actually favored the idea but nevertheless met the ambassador with various legalistic concerns and insisted on the involvement of all the American republics, a subject of obsessive concern to him.

At this point the president still believed that the transaction required congressional approval. But now Churchill proposed that the arrangement be treated essentially as two transactions—a gift of destroyers from the United States to Great Britain and a gift of bases from Great Britain to the United States. If it was simply a "swap," as Hull called it, it would look like a bad business deal for Britain, since there was no comparison in intrinsic value between the bases and the venerable destroyers, and, in addition, Churchill wanted to make the grand gesture of giving these territories to the United States. FDR explained to the prime minister that he lacked the power to give away U.S. property. "But what Winston can't get," Roosevelt told Jackson, "is that even if I had the legal power, it would not be politically possible just now to make a gift of these destroyers." One had to acknowledge, as a columnist noted, that "seeming to make a 'Yankee trade' out of everything" plays an important role in American political psychology.

At one point in the ongoing conversations, Churchill, viewing the swap as a demeaning idea, declared to Jackson, "Empires just don't bargain." Jackson produced a quick return thrust: "Republics do." As the bizarre transatlantic bickering proceeded between two leaders seeking to achieve the same purpose, the Germans, on August 13 (*Adlertag*— Eagle Day), launched a great air assault aimed at winning control of the skies over England. Whether or not Hitler actually contemplated an invasion of the island, such an operation could not take place until the Luftwaffe had achieved air supremacy, which it intended to do by using its superior numbers to break the RAF. To safeguard the country in a situation of possible invasion, the Royal Navy had to control the "narrow seas," as Churchill called the Channel and adjacent waters. The arrival of fifty destroyers from America, whatever their vintage, would enable the Admiralty to bring in an equivalent number of modern ships from duties in the Mediterranean and elsewhere, replacing them on these patrols with the old four-stackers.

By the middle of August the president had begun to believe that the whole deal might not, after all, require congressional approval with all its evasions and delays. Failing to receive a promise from the Republican presidential nominee, Wendell Willkie, to enlist the support of congressional Republicans—though Willkie himself, no isolationist, supported the idea—FDR began to move toward making the deal by executive order. As long as the negotiations concerned only the ships, "the President never entertained the idea of proceeding without the specific approval of Congress," Jackson declared, but the inclusion of bases in the negotiations altered everything. FDR, ever mindful of the approaching election, still did not quickly change his mind.

After the president revealed that the administration was negotiating with Britain to acquire naval and air bases in the western hemisphere, he won support from the arch-isolationist Senator Burton K. Wheeler, who in an impressive display of senatorial institutional memory argued that since such a deal clearly would strengthen U.S. defenses, the Americans could treat the new bases as a partial payment on Britain's old World War debt, one of the many causes of postwar friction between the two countries. He was glad to see, he said, that "the President is not considering trading American destroyers for these naval bases and thereby weakening our own defenses." FDR could hardly find such support helpful, and he cautioned reporters not to speculate that the discussions involved a trade of destroyers. Nevertheless, what the newspapers called "usually well-informed legislators" were insisting that such a deal was not only in the works but well along.

On August 18 Bill Bullitt, newly returned from France where, as the ambassador of the leading neutral power, he had presided over the peaceful transfer of Paris as an open city from the French authorities to the German occupiers, took the stage. In a characteristically impassioned address he urged Americans to write and telegraph Congress demanding the adoption of selective service and also declaring their support for the sale of the destroyers to Britain. "How many Americans," he asked, "are playing the dictators' game without knowing it?" Though Senate isolationists quickly charged the ambassador with trying to lead the United States into war, the public seemed to share his point of view. A Gallup poll released the same day showed that, in either of two alternate wordings of the question about destroyers for Britain, respondents gave strong support to the idea: 62 to 38 and 61 to 39. Walter Lippmann searched his bookshelves and dug up an apposite thought from James Madison: "With the British power and navy combined with our own, we have nothing to fear from the rest of the world."

Earlier a group of eastern legal mandarins, prominently including Dean Acheson, had presented the opinion that the president already had ample power to sell the destroyers to Britain with no quid pro quo required; Attorney General Jackson, who agreed with this opinion, nevertheless saw the exchange of the ships for valuable bases as better because unassailable. For some time the president, however, hung onto one feature that had held a prominent place in his thinking from the outset—that the prime minister declare that the Royal Navy "would never be turned over to the Germans or sunk, even if England surrendered or was defeated." But FDR came to see that the intention, not the statement of it, was what mattered, and that Churchill could hardly be expected to publicly include a dire possibility in the terms of any arrangement; the prime minister played his part by embodying such a pledge in a cleverly worded statement suggesting that the German fleet, not the British, was the one likely to be sunk.

Legal advisers then produced the idea of splitting the bases into two groups, one of which Churchill would magnanimously present to the United States; in return for the other group, as a Foreign Office/State Department draft agreement put it, "the United States Government wish for their part to make some contribution towards the security of the United Kingdom and the defensive strength of the British Navy in the Atlantic." Therefore the U.S. government would immediately transfer to His Majesty's Government "50 destroyers, 20 motor torpedo boats, a certain number of aircraft and rifles."

So the deal was made. Fortunately for all the parties, both Churchill and Roosevelt favored leasing rather than outright sale. The prime minister in effect was granting the United States an option to build naval and air bases on British territory, which would remain British. The attorney general felt that the president had full power to negotiate a leasing arrangement without the involvement of Congress; on the other hand, enlarging the nation through annexing the territories, and thereby creating new groups of citizens, Jackson saw as an entirely different matter. FDR not only saw the same point but saw it in all its implications. He told Jackson that the United States must not assume any responsibilities for the civilian population of the islands and must not in any way become involved in race relations there. The British had managed such matters admirably, he believed, with no legal discrimination. The president felt that the last thing either the islanders or Congress needed was for the Americans to export their racial policies to the Caribbean.

Churchill later called the transfer of American warships to Britain "a decidedly unneutral act by the United States." According to all precedent, it would "have justified the German Government in declaring war upon them." He saw no fear of that, he said, and "the President judged that there was no danger." Certainly not. The deal represented a big and courageous step for Roosevelt to take in the midst of a presidential campaign, but it was just what it was; FDR had no intention of turning it into a step toward a war he did not want.

So an Anglo-American alliance had been born. But the qualitative and quantitative questions had no answers: What kind of alliance? And how much of one?

9

THE POLITICAL CALCULATING MACHINE

O n the twenty-third of November, arriving back in the United States after a trip home to London, Lord Lothian emerged from the Pan-American Atlantic Clipper at LaGuardia Airport's seaplane base to astonish a cluster of waiting reporters by declaring, without fanfare or even a phrase of introduction: "Well, boys, Britain's broke; it's your money we want."

No one could have imagined a less elegant or subtle statement by a diplomat—and concerning the ticklish matter of finances, at that. Had Lothian simply blurted out his observation without thinking? Apparently not. Moving over to newsreel microphones, the ambasador not only did not recant but instead reaffirmed his point that Britain was reaching the end of her financial resources and must have U.S. aid for "planes, munitions and ships for the tough year ahead." Almost all of the gold and securities owned by Britons had now gone to pay for imports; the Americans would now have to fill the need. Arriving in Washington that same evening, Lothian, a genial man who liked reporters and dodged no questions, told interviewers that Britain could continue paying cash for American war material for only another six months, possibly a year.

The ambassador's remarks not only caused considerable consternation in London, they resounded through the high-level corridors of Washington. Secretary Morgenthau felt profound displeasure, which he forcefully expressed to Lothian. By making such a bald public statement, Morgenthau said, Lothian had given isolationists ample ammunition to attack the filling of British orders for arms, since, if Britain was officially broke, she could hardly pay the cash required by the cash-and-carry law.

Morgenthau and his experts concluded that, after all their purchases since the war began, the British currently had just $2 billion in assets of all types available to back purchases in the United States. Thus, although like other observers the secretary wondered what had moved Lothian to make his declaration, without even the courtesy of a warning, he essentially agreed with the ambassador's point. That did not hold true for President Roosevelt, who told Lothian that before asking for U.S. financial help the British must liquidate their investments in the western hemisphere; differing with Morgenthau, the president believed that this move could produce as much as $9 billion. Only with the cupboard bare beyond question, it seemed at the moment, would the president feel able to take the question to Capitol Hill. In no case would any action occur before the convening of the new Congress in January 1941.

A little more than two weeks later, on December 11, Lord Lothian canceled a speaking appearance because of illness, and before that night was out he had died. Those who dealt with him had not realized that he had been suffering from the ravages of uremic poisoning and related kidney failure—untreated because he was a Christian Scientist. According to his faith, his disorder had reality only in the illusory material world, not in the real world—that of the spirit—yet, as irony would have it, his last great preoccupation had concerned heavily material questions. Since, among its many symptoms, uremia frequently produces a loss of mental clarity, perhaps all the speculation about Lord Lothian's motives in speaking out at LaGuardia had simply been beside the point.

The British Treasury had earlier dispatched an imposing senior official, Sir Frederick Phillips, to discuss money with the president and the secretary of the treasury. In essence, Phillips had the mission of quietly making the kind of point that Lord Lothian would raise publicly a few months later: at some point in 1941, Britain would have used up her assets convertible into dollars and hence would need very large credits. FDR made no promises, but Phillips appeared to see the essential point: the Americans had no choice but to get the goods to Britain one way or another, and the British had no choice but to accept whatever the Americans decided to do. But time was moving fast.

As for the fears of the isolationists that American aid to Britain would constitute an inevitable slide into full participation in the war, most British leaders would have agreed, differing only in that they would have recast the thought as an expression of hope rather than of fear. Despite any public government protestations to the contrary, salvation through American belligerence constituted the hope and aim of Churchill's policy. He had expressed it quite succinctly to his son, Randolph, one morning, as he was shaving. He had decided how he would win the war, he said: "I shall drag the United States in." According to Randolph, his father delivered the line "with great intensity."

Those who knew Churchill, including the Germans, would not have been surprised at this plan. Even well before the war, in a 1936 conversation with Joachim von Ribbentrop, then Hitler's ambassador to Britain, Churchill had uttered a warning against Nazi adventurism and warmongering: "Do not underestimate England. She is very clever. If you plunge us all into another Great War, she will bring the whole world against you like last time."

Not quite all British leaders shared the prime minister's view, however. Many, perhaps most, of these dissidents knew little about the United States and disliked what they did know; unlike Lord Lothian, these were the types whose habitual condescension produced a reciprocal dislike on the part of Americans, and of other foreigners as well; "the special sting of this 'arrogance,'" commented Lord Eustace Percy, "has always been its aloofness." In addition to active dislike, some of these people, many of them industrialists of one kind or another, deeply resented the increasing dependence of Britain on the United States as signaled by the appeals for aid, and some openly wondered whether the game was truly worth the candle—whether by resisting the Germans the British were simply exhausting themselves while the Americans, in the friendliest way, pushed the British Empire into bankruptcy.

The news of Lord Lothian's death reached President Roosevelt on his post-election cruise aboard the U.S.S. *Tuscaloosa* in the Caribbean. Now about to move into his third term, he had left behind in Washington groups of advisers with the mission of finding solutions to the central financial question, which the ambassador had crystallized for everybody. Officially, the president would be taking a look at some of the island spots received by the United States in fulfillment of the destroyers–bases deal, but he made no claim for the trip as a working mission. He and the other members of his small party, including Harry Hopkins and the sociable Dr. McIntire, would spend most of the time fishing—which FDR favored because, with his means of recreation limited, it was one he could enjoy—loafing, and engaging in the relaxing horseplay he loved. As a companion, said Robert Jackson,

Roosevelt was "irresistible and inimitable. He liked people, almost any people," and "a more considerate man or one less inclined to stand on the position that a presidential word was a command" had never occupied the White House.

Behind his mask of carefree fisherman bantering with his cronies, FDR would allow his mind to grapple with the financial problem. "I didn't know for quite a while what he was thinking about," Hopkins said later. "But then I began to get the idea that he was refueling, the way he so often does when he seems to be resting and carefree. So I didn't ask him any questions."

On December 9, as the *Tuscaloosa* lay off Antigua, the president received a full measure of food for thought. During the morning a seaplane splashed down nearby and a pouch of mail for the White House was transferred aboard the cruiser. The collection of correspondence proved to contain a formidable *pièce de résistance*—a long letter to the president from Winston Churchill. As it happened, German bombs had smashed into the House of Commons just the previous night, and so on the day Roosevelt was pondering Churchill's letter the prime minister was sadly inspecting the ruin of the chamber that had been in many ways the great love of his life.

The writer of this special letter had not worked alone; he had the help of two important British representatives to the United States who were in England in November—Lothian, who urged Churchill to give Roosevelt the full picture of Britain's needs, and Arthur Purvis, who provided details to fill in the picture. During the same period, Phillips had made another trip to Washington, this time to meet with Morgenthau to present a full appeal for a gift or a loan—whatever transaction could be arranged—but Lothian believed that Churchill must directly and fully seize Roosevelt's personal attention. In the midst of all the stresses and financial privations, Lothian made one of his greatest contributions to his country's cause by persuading the prime minister to adopt, in the letter and in other dealings with Washington, a style of trust rather than one of bargaining and haggling. (The prime minister had been, for instance, on the point of making a complaint about the poor condition of the mothballed destroyers that had come from America.) The letter took shape through the last half of November and, after three weeks of literary labors, its principal author sent it off to the president.

Assuming a stance much like the approach a corporation president might use in reporting to the board of directors, Churchill told Roosevelt that, since the year 1940 was ending, "I feel that you will expect me to lay before you the prospects for 1941." Lothian had argued for a full statement because, unlike some of Churchill's other associates, he believed that the president sincerely was working to help Britain and should be given as much useful evidence of the need as possible. Writing as though Britain and the United States had actually entered into an alliance, Churchill declared it to be Britain's duty "in the common interest, as also for our own survival, to hold the front and grapple with the Nazi power until the preparations of the United States are complete."

The bulk of the letter contained a picture in depth of the entire strategic situation, with particular emphasis on shipping. "The decision for 1941," said Churchill, "lies upon the seas." He wanted U.S. convoys, and more destroyers, and extended naval patrols. But, perhaps curiously, in view of the impetus from Lothian and the contributions of Purvis, Churchill paid less attention to the question of money, the issue on which all turned. Finally he said, "The moment approaches when we shall no longer be able to pay cash for shipping and other supplies." This statement, of course, simply represented an acknowledgment of the abundantly established point. "I believe you will agree that it would be wrong in principle and mutually disadvantageous in effect if at the height of this struggle Great Britain were to be divested of all saleable assets, so that after the victory was won with our blood, civilization saved, and the time gained for the United States to be full armed against all eventualities, we should stand stripped to the bone." The president would surely feel that it would not be to the "moral or economic interests of either of our countries" for the United States to squeeze Britain dry.

Roosevelt read and reread the letter, Hopkins noted, and the two discussed it as they sat on the deck of the *Tuscaloosa*. Clearly its contents had deeply impressed the president, though the prime minister had not actually produced new facts or unfamiliar ideas. But the eloquent presentation and summary of the situation had perhaps stirred up new whirrings and clickings in FDR's "political calculating machine," as the historian Samuel Eliot Morison characterized the presidential mind when it was addressing a public issue.

The letter also made a profound impression on Harry Hopkins. What must the author of such a letter be like? How much of him would be "mere grandiloquence" and how much "hard fact"? Hopkins decided that he must find out.

In a discussion of the campaign season of 1940, Professor Morison described the president's political calculating machine as "an intricate instrument in which Gallup polls, the strength of the armed forces and the probability of England's survival; the personalities of governors, senators and congressmen, and of Mussolini, Hitler, Churchill, Chiang, and Tojo; the Irish, German, Italian, and Jewish votes in the presidential election; the 'Help the Allies' people and the 'America Firsters,' were combined with fine points of political maneuvering." With due whirring and clicking, this unique contrivance had produced the unprecedented destroyers-bases deal with Britain—and not simply as an individual act but as part of a subtle, new kind of aid to a friendly country at war. Now, with the election solidly won and FDR off on holiday aboard the *Tuscaloosa*, had the machine made use of the time to crank out a new plan or synthesis to deal with the current question?

The president returned to Washington on Sunday, December 16. The next afternoon, delighted that their greatest source of news had come home, reporters crowded into the office and up to the presidential desk with its famous clutter of knickknacks. Roosevelt looked well, relaxed and tanned. As though he had summoned the reporters for no purpose at all, he said to them, "I don't think there is any particular news," but the remark could have fooled nobody; the tone was light and bantering, and the cigarette holder fiercely uptilted.

That morning, telling Henry Morgenthau, "I have been thinking very hard on this trip about what we should do for England," FDR had sounded out the secretary about the idea his thinking had produced, then he asked, "What do you think of it?"

"I think it is the best idea yet," the secretary responded.

"What would you think if I made a statement like this at my press conference this afternoon?"

"Fine," Morgenthau said. "The sooner the better, because the people are waiting for you to show them the way."

Now, facing the reporters, the president declared: "In the present world situation of course there is absolutely no doubt in the mind of a very overwhelming number of Americans that the best immediate defense of the United States is the success of Great Britain in defending itself"—not wishful thinking on the president's part; the opinion polls consistently reported it, though they also reported fears that the British might not succeed in their self-defense. And so, "quite aside from our historic and current interest in the survival of democracy as a whole in the world, it is equally important from a selfish point of view of American defense that we should do everything to help the British Empire to defend itself."

In the last few days, Roosevelt said, he had "read a great deal of nonsense by people who can only think in what we may call traditional terms" about finances. What people should remember was that "in all history no major war has ever been won or lost through a lack of money." What American defense now required was greater production facilities; here British orders were "a tremendous asset," because they created "additional facilities." Carefully emphasizing his focus on American self-interest, FDR discussed the best way to achieve the desired increase in productive power—not by repealing legislation and lending Britain money to be spent in the United States nor by manufacturing war matériel and then giving it to the British. These "banal" ideas did not fit the situation. Somewhat wordily, the president then presented the essence of his thought: the United States should manufacture the materials and then divide them between the two countries "as the military events of the future would determine." Those materials going to Britain would do so either under lease or as purchases "subject to mortgage." If indeed "the best defense of Great Britain is the best defense of the United States," it followed that these materials would make a greater contribution to America if they "were used in Great Britain than if they were kept in storage here."

Moving from the general background—innovative as it was—into the kind of specific illustration he always favored, the president told the reporters: "What I am trying to do is to eliminate the dollar sign, and that is something brand new in the thoughts of practically everybody in this room, I think—get rid of the silly, foolish old dollar sign." Well, FDR had certainly offered his audience a novel way of looking at the national currency, which may have seemed less foolish to some people than to others, but he quickly moved on to an analogy; the idea had been playing in his mind since a conversation with Harold Ickes several months earlier. "Suppose my neighbor's home catches fire, and I have got a length of garden hose four or five hundred feet away; but, by Heaven, if he can take my garden hose and connect it up with his hydrant, I may help him put out his fire." In such a situation, you don't make your neighbor buy the hose; you simply lend it to him and get it back when the fire is out. If it should be damaged, the neighbor would of course replace it. A gentleman always has the obligation to repay in kind: "I think you all get it."

Apparently the press did indeed get it. Though reporters raised a few legalistic questions about ownership, nobody asked how, after winning a war with Germany, the British could replace ships, aircraft, and other kinds of garden hose that had been destroyed or damaged in the fighting. "There were probably very few," said Robert Sherwood, "who had any expectation that we would ever get the hose back," but he and others saw FDR's determination, at the outset of the new relationship, to prevent another generation of the name-calling and haggling over war debts that had soured the 1920s and 1930s and had molded many still-existing attitudes. The Dutchess County squire and his needy neighbor would deal like gentlemen, and together they would surely get water on the fire.

10

"REPOSING SPECIAL FAITH AND CONFIDENCE"

F ending off inquiries from both Americans and Britons about details of his plan, the country squire celebrated his traditional family Christmas, while allowing suspense about his intentions to build in the press and among the public. The British, who had the most at stake, felt sharp frustration at the presidential silence, with some particularly perturbed at a presidential action just before Christmas. Roosevelt had telephoned Admiral Stark requesting him to dispatch the *Tuscaloosa* to Cape Town to bring back British gold, and he told Secretary Morgenthau that he wanted it insured. If the Treasury did not already have a suitable policy, Morgenthau said, he would insist that the British arrange to pay for the coverage. Graceless though it seemed, this kind of gold transaction had been suggested by Sir Frederick Phillips to pay for current purchases. "Americans are being *very* tiresome about financial matters," grumbled Sir Alexander Cadogan, permanent undersecretary (and thus chief civil servant) at the Foreign Office. "Maybe Pres. wants to be able to show Congress that he has got all he can out of us." Associates in London and at the British Embassy in Washington stayed vigilant and busy restraining their frustrated prime minister from sending off protests and complaints. Dominating everything stood the question: whatever Roosevelt might mean with his idea, even if all went well, what would happen with the money during the weeks or months before his mysterious program emerged from the chambers of Capitol Hill?

Then, on Sunday evening, December 29, FDR played host to a gathering in the oval diplomatic reception room on the ground floor of the White House. The guest list included not only the expected cabinet members and other political figures but the uncrowned king of Hollywood, Clark Gable, and his consort, the "screwball comedy" star Carole Lombard, all sitting on flimsy gilt chairs jammed together as the temperature rose in the crowded room. The party also included an unseen audience of millions, tuning in on their radios, curious like the rest of the world to hear what the president would say in this well-publicized address, his fifteenth fireside chat—and, to be sure, his first speech since his victory in the election.

He was not going to talk about war, the president declared at the outset of his address; instead, he would talk about how to keep out of war. Americans needed to realize that, just as in March 1933, the country faced mortal danger—this time the greatest in its history. Because the election had safely been won, FDR felt free now to name names: the Nazis must be defeated. "It is a matter of most vital concern to us," he declared, "that European and Asiatic warmakers should not gain control of the oceans which lead to this hemisphere." The Nazis aimed at using "the resources of Europe to dominate the rest of the world." The central factor and motivator: "If Great Britain goes down, all of us in the Americas would be living at the point of a gun—a gun loaded with explosive bullets, economic as well as military." The United States must therefore do everything it could to "support the nations defending themselves against attack by the Axis." Acknowledging that this policy would entail risks, Roosevelt declared that these risks were smaller than those the country would run by allowing Great Britain to be defeated. This course represented the best chance "to keep war away from our country and our people."

The president gave no name to the picture he drew, which at this point seemed more policy than actual program. As he summed it up, "as planes and ships and guns and shells are produced, your government, with its defense experts, can then determine how best to use them to defend this hemisphere. The decision as to how much shall be sent abroad and how much shall remain at home must be made on the basis of our overall military necessity." The president concluded with a ringing definition of his practical aim, perfect for his purposes: "We must be the great arsenal of democracy."

This memorable capsule identity, probably gleaned by Hopkins from a newspaper editorial, no doubt contributed to what quickly became clear: the speech had been a remarkable success. Telegrams, reported Steve Early, the press secretary, were running one hundred to one in support of the president's views. A Gallup poll showed 61 percent of the public favorable with only 24 percent opposed. Even better were the reports on the public's actual familiarity with the speech: 59 percent of those polled had heard it and another 16 percent had read it in their newspapers; the combined 75 percent set a record for FDR. He had given this great, attentive public a clear goal: to defeat Hitler with American help but without American soldiers going into battle.

Now would come the move into the trenches: the preparation of a bill and the negotiating on Capitol Hill that would enable the bill's provisions to emerge, substantially unchanged, as a law. Not everyone on the Hill believed that the president meant what he said. Aid Britain without entering the war? Not likely.

The president ordered Henry Morgenthau's Treasury staff to get to work on the bill he wanted. The secretary had just the man for the task—Oscar Cox, an imaginative and hard-working lawyer from Maine who by January 2 had produced a basic draft.

In the 1930s, in the interest of harmony with Eire, the British government had negotiated away their right to base destroyers at three ports on the Irish coast. Now, with the continuing submarine menace and with invasion always at least a possibility, Ireland had taken on immediate strategic significance. It would be desirable, many in the government felt, to receive rights to use at least one of the ports; perhaps, some thought, the United States could be helpful in such discussions, or U.S. Navy vessels could be based in an Irish port. On December 13, Churchill had cabled Roosevelt about questions relating to food supplies for Eire. The prime minister told the president that the British needed the tonnage for their own supply, and besides, he added bluntly, British seamen took it amiss that they had to run the risks involved in these operations while Eamon de Valera, the president of Eire, was "quite content to sit happy and see us strangled."

Ireland and Irish questions had constituted a vexing factor in relations between the United States and Britain throughout the century since the famine of the 1840s had begun creating "Irish America," as some of the English called the transatlantic consequences of the great disaster. At the moment, Churchill wanted to know what attitude Roosevelt would take if the British should decide to concentrate their tonnage on supplying themselves. The president saw a possible approach in the thought that a leading Irish-American might provide the answer; such a person, Joseph P. Kennedy, perhaps, or General William J. Donovan, could go to Dublin to negotiate concerning the various issues.

In conversation with Hopkins, FDR produced a variation of his favored approach to any problem. "You know," he said, "a lot of this could be settled if Churchill and I could just sit down together for a while."

"What's stopping you?" Hopkins asked.

Well, the president said, with no British ambassador in Washington and, with the departure of Kennedy from England, no American ambassador in London, such a meeting simply could not be arranged.

No one could suppose that the participants in such a meeting would have to confine themselves to talk of foodstuffs for Ireland, and Hopkins seized his chance. "How about me going over, Mr. President?"

FDR rejected the idea immediately: Hopkins had too much work to do in Washington, particularly in regard to the State of the Union message, the Third Inaugural speech, and the dealings with Congress over the bill for aid to Britain—shortly to become known as lend-lease. But he would be of no use in that battle, Hopkins declared; Congress would pay no attention to him.

Certainly FDR had many reasons for seeking a direct, personal contact with Churchill. As president of the United States, he needed to know how genuine was Churchill's defiance and resolution, and that of his government. The Royal Navy's July 3 attack on the French fleet at Oran had impressed many Americans, notably including the president, but it was also true that the British government had appeased Hitler in 1938 and early 1939; there had been talk of negotiations after the fall of France, and in just the past few months a kind of German peace offensive had involved some diplomatic discussions. If the Americans now made great efforts to send aid, might it not be wasted or fall into German hands? As two reporters noted, with reference to the peace blitz, the president "wished to discover the extent of the softening, in what quarters the forces of appeasement had shown recovery, and how Churchill was meeting them."

There was also the question of Churchill's drinking. Was the prime minister a drunk, with all that such a condition would imply? This question genuinely concerned the president; for one thing, he had seen the ravages of alcoholism in Eleanor's family, with her father and her brother.

Beyond these points, the Americans and the British had actions and policies of urgent importance to discuss at the highest level. If the president himself could not go to England—and, in view merely of all the logistical problems such a trip would involve, Hopkins's "what's stopping you?" had probably been deliberately naïve—then what better than a personal representative to carry out the mission . . . not an ambassador, a political appointee, but a *personal* representative, an extension of himself, serving just as Eleanor Roosevelt had often served, to sit at that table with Winston Churchill? Though Hopkins had no diplomatic experience of any kind, FDR, characteristically, would see that lack as anything but a handicap; his friend had many times over proved himself a quick learner in many contexts. "Harry had a very clear mind," said FDR Jr., and a "simple way of expressing himself so he didn't leave any questions or doubts"; if questions did arise, however, "my father would ask him a question. Harry would answer very explicitly," and he "had a marvelous way of setting forth his conclusions, his thinking." Besides, a columnist noted, Hopkins had a "capacity to get inside another man's mind." Steve Early summed him up as a good reporter, a genuine tribute from the veteran newsman. So, alert, lucid, engaging, and untainted by the State Department, Hopkins seemed just the man FDR would want for the assignment.

Nevertheless, the president said no, and in the following days he stuck to that unwelcome answer. He would josh Hopkins with cracks like "I hear life in those air-raid shelters is pretty congested, Harry," but discussion went no further than that. With plenty of work to do, Hopkins had to sublimate his intense curiosity about the personality and nature of Winston Churchill. He, in fact, had his doubts about the prime minister, but it appeared that they would simply have to remain unanswered questions.

During the morning of Friday, January 3, Hopkins, stretched out in his bedroom-office in his frayed dressing gown, took a phone call from Steve Early.

"You're on the spot, Harry," the press secretary said.

Suspecting some sort of practical joke, a common occurrence in the Roosevelt White House, Hopkins responded cautiously: "What do you mean?"

The president's press conference had just ended, Early said, and he was calling because Roosevelt had told reporters that he was sending Harry Hopkins to England as his personal representative, there being no U.S. ambassador in London. Incredulous, Hopkins made Early repeat the news and then asked him to come up to the Lincoln room to provide a firsthand account.

"Think of it!" Hopkins, truly moved, said to Early. "Just think about it for a minute. I was a social worker. My father was a harness maker and my mother was a schoolteacher. And I'm going over to talk to Winston Churchill and the men who run the British government. If that isn't democracy, I don't know what is."

Just to make absolutely sure of the whole thing, Hopkins then arose and dressed, and went downstairs and over to the West Wing. "Did you say that, Boss?" he asked. Smiling, the president confirmed the news. Then he would go right away, Hopkins said. "I'm not going to hang around here. I know what you'll want me to do, go over to the State Department for instructions and get the views of a lot of people." That hardly seemed likely, but in any case FDR agreed that a long talk between the two of them would serve as his representative's briefing. In answer to persistent questions from the reporters concerning Hopkins's role and title and the purpose of his mission, the president had responded, wholly in character, "He's just going over to say 'How do you do?' to a lot of my friends" and would be in London "for two or three weeks so that he can talk to Churchill like an Iowa farmer." (Perhaps the Iowa-born Hopkins had once shown Roosevelt some of his verse, with lines like "An Iowa farmer always looks in the dark.")

Serious about making his escape before the State Department could waylay him and burden him with advice, Hopkins telephoned Juan Trippe, president of Pan-American Airways, who told him a Clipper would be leaving for Lisbon the following Monday. He would be on it, Hopkins assured Trippe. During the weekend FDR found time for the promised long talk with his special representative, who also squeezed in a courtesy call with Secretary Hull and wisely accepted suggestions that he see Jean Monnet, whom he had not met. Remarkably, when Monnet's country surrendered and fell out of the war, he had offered his services to the British, who had very sensibly accepted with no fuss about nationality, and had dispatched this uniquely pragmatic and internationally minded Frenchman to Washington, where he was now established on the British Purchasing Commission, working with Arthur Purvis. Monnet gave Hopkins one piece of explicit advice: Go to the top—don't spend your time with any ministers except the prime minister. "Churchill *is* the War Cabinet. Everything will be simpler if you can establish a close link between Roosevelt and him." Monnet later expressed the surprise he had felt that contacts were being arranged for Hopkins with various ministers and civil servants—thus giving "Roosevelt's alter ego . . . what amounted to a ministerial mission," suitable for a secretary of state, "whereas the real gap in the Alliance was the lack of direct and constant communication between the two men at the top." Believing that Hopkins had to initiate the needed transatlantic dialogue forthwith, Monnet made the point with Felix Frankfurter, who, though a Supreme Court justice, uninhibitedly kept fingers in various political pies and, as a friend, had been sought by Hopkins as a potential ally in his effort to win the assignment. Frankfurter then brought Hopkins and Monnet together at his house. During the conversation Hopkins, who had his own hero, came out with "I suppose Churchill is convinced he's the greatest man in the world!"

Frankfurter pounced on him: "Harry, if you're going to London with that chip on your shoulder, like a damned little small-town chauvinist, you may as well cancel your passage right now." But Hopkins did not recant, and when he left Washington his shoulder still bore at least a piece of that particular chip. He also carried a formal commission from the president: "Reposing special faith and confidence in you, I am asking you to proceed at your early convenience to Great Britain, there to act as my personal representative."

Averell Harriman took the European war with total seriousness. A severe ulcer that had put him in the hospital the previous April resulted, he believed, from his frustration over the lack of effective action by the Allies, going back to their acquiescence in the German occupation of the Rhineland in 1936. Denouncing the doctors in a note to his stepson, Harry Payne Whitney, Harriman reported that they gave him only "half a glass of milk mixed with cream every two hours," adding that "the big event in my life is going to be having a baked potato the day after tomorrow." On the very day he recorded these austerities, the Germans moved into Denmark and launched the Norway campaign, and before he had recuperated sufficiently to return to his Wall Street office, the Wehrmacht had routed the Allied armies in the Low Countries and France.

In late May, when President Roosevelt had accompanied his call for greatly increased production of war materials by establishing the National Defense Advisory Commission, Harriman moved into action, pressing his services on a commission member, Edward R. Stettinius, Jr., of U.S. Steel, who had taken on the responsibility for industrial materials. Speeding east from the Union Pacific headquarters in

Omaha, Harriman swung by New York and quickly got himself set up in Washington as coordinator of the transportation of raw materials; by the end of the week he had also addressed himself to the condition of the railroads themselves, many of which sorely needed an infusion of energy to lift them out of the Depression doldrums.

Within a few weeks Harriman was concerning himself more with the raw materials themselves than with their transportation. Still later, when the ineffectual advisory commission (a Rooseveltian first step) gave way to the Office of Production Management, Harriman took charge of the industrial materials division. To get the job, he had to persuade the OPM director, William S. Knudsen of General Motors, to see him as more than merely a mallet-wielding, sun-worshipping play-boy. One of Harriman's Wall Street partners could have offered helpful information here: "Goddammit, the rest of us go down to the office and hit it from nine to five, and slave away to put together these [deals], and Averell comes in between polo and something else, and damned if the bastard doesn't pull off the biggest deal the company has ever had."

In the exercise of his new duties, Harriman's drive for efficiency ran head-on into the antimonopoly stubbornness (or devotion to principle) and irascibility of Harold Ickes. When Harriman, working to increase the supply of aluminum for aircraft production, wanted to allocate electric power to Alcoa instead of the newer and smaller Reynolds Metals, "because they took so long to do things," he ran into an Ickes veto; Reynolds had been created for the purpose of bringing competition to the field, and Ickes saw to it that the company got the power. Harriman said with some hyperbole that the decision cost the United States 70,000 planes; his stint at OPM did not prove to be a happy chapter in his life.

Harriman spent Christmas at Sun Valley, enjoying the challenging ski runs his resort boasted but also keeping a close eye on developments in Washington. If the United States was indeed to become the Arsenal of Democracy, as the president had just proclaimed, then business needed to truly mobilize to play its part in the great effort, and he had to have a full part in that effort—something beyond the bureaucratic. On hearing the news of Hopkins's mission to England, he immediately telephoned his friend, literally begging to join him. "I've met Churchill several times," he pointed out, "and I know London intimately." He even offered—no doubt more seriously than not—to carry the bags. But Hopkins turned him down. He had to take the trip alone, he said, though he would want to see his friend when he got back. Hopkins spoke vaguely with Harriman, rather as Roosevelt had spoken with him, but that closing hint held promise.

Driven by Juan Trippe himself, and accompanied by his three children and his daughter-in-law, Hopkins appeared at the LaGuardia Pan-Am terminal at eight o'clock on Monday morning, January 6. Having begun only two months before the war started, transatlantic passenger flights had the glamour of novelty; they were also time-consuming. The Clippers took the trip in three legs, made necessary by the limited range of the aircraft: New York to Bermuda—five hours; Bermuda to the Azores—fifteen hours; Azores to Lisbon—five hours. Those times, together with the hours needed for refueling and the frequent complications caused by hostile weather, meant that a flight could take days. Hopkins approached travel by air reluctantly, but at least the big flying boat would offer comfortable seats, real tables for dining, with china and cutlery, and actual bunks for sleeping.

The waiting reporters had little success in drawing Hopkins out about his mission, or about anything else. He parried a series of questions with the simple statement that he did not wish to add anything to what the president had said." How long would he be gone? "I will be back when I have finished. It won't be too long." He apologized to the newsmen for not being able to say more, though he did produce one solid piece of information: he would not be succeeding Joe Kennedy as ambassador in London. "There is no chance," he said, "of my taking a diplomatic post."

Looking hard for some hidden significance in the mission, reporters brought up the World War activities of Colonel E. M. House, President Woodrow Wilson's alter ego and influential traveling representative who visited European capitals in various attempts to promote peace talks. Rumors in Washington had speculated that Roosevelt might be using Hopkins in a similar way. When asked directly about a possible parallel with House, Hopkins "flushed for a moment," according to one reporter; another thought he "appeared ruffled." He shook his head.

Despite the role he had recently been playing as an all-purpose presidential deputy, some of the news analysts presumed that, as a social worker and leading New Dealer, Hopkins would confer with British labor leaders so that he could report to the president on "social trends in England as a result of the war." They also conceded that, to be sure, he might well talk with British leaders about "the President's plan for lending arms."

The only Clipper passenger going all the way to Lisbon, Hopkins joined five travelers for Bermuda and one for the Azores. As the neutral window on Europe and escape hatch from the Continent, the Portuguese capital had become a colorful center not only of transportation but of intrigue and espionage. Hopkins would not linger there, however; as soon as a flight could be arranged, he would be off on the last leg of his journey, to the south coast of England.

Carrying a newspaper and two paperbacks given him by friends— *The Blood of the Conquerors*, a western story, and *Honorable Picnic*, a notable French novel (translated) about Japan—Hopkins stepped onto the Yankee Clipper, which at 9:23 a.m. began churning out into the little bay called Bowery.

11

"A SMILING GENTLEMAN"

I n November 1922, for the first time in the century, Winston
Churchill had lost an election. The collapse of Lloyd George's
postwar coalition, Churchill's remoteness from the current concerns of his Dundee constituents, and an appendectomy (then still a
serious operation calling for an extended rest) combined to take away
his seat in the House of Commons. In the following year the Liberal
association in West Leicester (near Birmingham) chose him as their
candidate, but the campaign proved raw and sometimes violent. Speaking in London, he was almost hit by a brick and a young man smashed
a window of his car. Hecklers accompanied him everywhere, with the
Great War's Dardanelles disaster, which the public had determined to
be Churchill's chief sin, constantly thrown in his face. Unfortunately,
the local newspapers offered little help.

A young acquaintance, twenty-two-year-old Brendan Bracken,
entered the fray as an almost compulsively eager volunteer, working
the district and enjoying some success with the press, including talking the influential *Guardian* into providing better coverage. But the
national balance of forces as well as local sentiment did not favor the
Liberals, who were rapidly being superseded in the House of Commons by the Labour Party, with the result that Churchill suffered a

bad defeat. He had, however, acquired a permanent and transcendently loyal friend.

Bracken seemed to have arrived on the scene almost without background; intimations were heard of a difficult childhood in Ireland and then, it seemed, he had gone to Australia to live with an uncle. Returning from the antipodes and seeking a bit, at least, of a public school education, he had worked his way into Sedbergh in Yorkshire by his persuasiveness, enhanced by his successful pretense to be three years younger than he was.

After the setback at West Leicester, Churchill lost at the polls one more time, in Westminster, before, in 1924, winning the seat for Epping (now as a Conservative, if not yet quite declared). Bracken, staying close and helping his older friend, also put his brashness and drive to effective use in his own career, both in South African gold-mining enterprises and in publishing, becoming the proprietor of the *Financial News*. By the time he was twenty-nine Bracken had won a seat in Parliament, from a London constituency.

Tall but homely, with what Americans would call Coke-bottle glasses, Bracken was the sort of man dismally described as "unattractive to women," and some acquaintances thought him not only brash but "clumsy and uncouth." One of his physical attributes caused considerable comment and speculation—a great tangle of red hair, a quality he shared with Churchill in hue though he had a far greater quantity of it. So close did the two become—as a young man Bracken would let himself into Churchill's house in Sussex Gardens after the family had gone to bed and tuck himself up on the couch for the night—that rumor declared him to be Winston's natural son. Clementine Churchill became concerned enough to ask her husband if the story had any truth to it, a question to which he returned the audaciously careless answer: "I've taken the trouble to look the matter up, but the dates don't coincide." Bracken also, said Freda Dudley

Ward, a prominent London figure and more-or-less official mistress of the Prince of Wales during the 1920s, had "a romantic and ardent if somewhat selfish nature like Churchill's."

Though some called him brash, those who liked Bracken thought of him as "ebullient," and he could very effectively "dispel prime-ministerial gloom and induce good temper." Indeed, said one of Churchill's principal secretaries, when dealing with Churchill, Bracken "was invariably in high spirits, bursting with optimism and discounting bad news or depressing forecasts." These qualities took on particular value when, in 1940, Bracken became the new prime minister's parliamentary private secretary, a position of scope and influence and one that established him as a resident of 10 Downing Street, living in the house of his hero.

When Churchill was told that President Roosevelt was sending him a guest named Harry Hopkins, the prime minister said simply, "Who?"

Some who knew of Hopkins expressed surprise at the news; the Virginia-born Lady Astor thought of the visitor as a "nice Sunday-school teacher" who might get the wrong impression of England through associating with the hard-drinking prime minister. Indeed, Hopkins's background as a social worker and reformer continued to label him in many circles. The eminent Washington columnist Raymond Clapper presumed in print that the special representative's assignment called for him to study the new kind of democratic state the war was presumed to be creating in Britain. "Necessarily there are many intangibles and matters of judgment in assessing personalities and trends," Clapper said, "and Mr. Roosevelt's understanding of them undoubtedly will be sharpened thru the observation of one so closely attuned to his own mind as Mr. Hopkins"—an insightful point, even if the columnist had aimed it at the wrong specific target. In any case, no one in England seemed to fear Hopkins as a new Colonel House arriving with an unwelcome presidential peace plan in his bag.

One person, at least, had a shrewd idea if not of Hopkins's precise mission, at least of its likely importance. Several years earlier Brendan Bracken had met Hopkins on the Long Island croquet-playing circuit, and at the end of the day his new American acquaintance had given him a ride into New York. Hopkins, Bracken wrote his Long Island host, Herbert Bayard Swope, "struck me as being the embodiment of all that is intelligent, honest and aggressive" and was "a first-rate talker."

More recently Bracken had sent his congratulations when FDR named Hopkins secretary of commerce. "When I read the news of your appointment," said Bracken in a wide-ranging letter, "I felt that at long last intelligence and initiative must mark the relations between your Department and men of business in the United States"—a sentiment that could have been expressed by another notable businessman, Averell Harriman, who had seen early that Hopkins was a doer, not merely a do-goodish dreamer as some critics liked to claim. To increase prosperity, Bracken went on, the administration now needed to soft-pedal social reform in order to win the cooperation of "middle-aged and old people." This necessity might "be maddening to zealous reformers, but you will forgive a foreigner," Bracken said justly, "for pointing out that the United States is one of the most intermittently conservative nations upon earth." In this circumstance, Bracken believed, Hopkins might well repeat the kind of success Lloyd George had achieved early in the century in a comparable office, president of the Board of Trade, as a radical "who surrendered none of his principles, but also aired none of his dogmas." Hopkins said in his reply: "I certainly wish that you were just around the corner so that we could sit down for a real session together."

Now such a moment had arrived, in circumstances unforeseeable two years earlier. The American guest, Bracken told Churchill, was the closest person to Roosevelt, and his visit could therefore possess incomparable significance.

For all the differences between Bracken and Hopkins, it was a case of one fixer recognizing and understanding the importance of another. Brendan Bracken himself, not some Foreign Office functionary, would be on hand to greet Hopkins when he arrived on England's shores.

After waiting in Lisbon for a day, during which he met the Portuguese dictator, Antonio Salazar, Hopkins flew to Poole Bay, near Bournemouth on the south coast of England, arriving at about five o'clock on Thursday, January 9; the entire journey had taken almost three and a half days, only one day less than modern ocean liners made the passage in peacetime. As the passengers came off the plane, the waiting Bracken saw no Harry Hopkins among them; he went aboard to find his exhausted acquaintance slumped in his seat, not even up to releasing his safety belt. Hopkins had to rest on land for a while before he could tell his host that he was ready for the train trip up to London.

As for the train itself, it showed how seriously Churchill had taken Bracken's view of the visitor's importance. Following the prime minister's instructions, said the general manager of the Southern Railway, "arrangements were made for the most modern Pullman cars to be formed in the train. The conductors wore white gloves; a good meal, with liquid refreshment, was available, together with papers, periodicals, etc. Mr. Harry Hopkins was obviously impressed."

Though he noted the bomb damage to the ports, Hopkins also saw the countryside looking as serene as he remembered it from his earlier trips. Turning to Bracken, he suddenly asked a typical kind of question: "Are you going to let Hitler take these fields away from you?" Bracken, not given to short statements or answers, nevertheless said simply, "No." The question represented the special representative's first try at a test of British resolution.

As the time moved past seven o'clock, Hopkins had his first brush with the continuing blitz. The Luftwaffe, taking advantage of the winter darkness, arrived with incendiaries and seemed almost to be chasing the train; bombs fell on the line behind it as it rolled into Waterloo Station. When the car carrying their distinguished visitor left the station, the railway general manager noted "the intense relief on the faces of the train crews."

Although a formidable schedule had been created for Hopkins, beginning with dinner at No. 10 Downing Street that very evening, he obviously needed to rest; the meeting was put off until the next day. Herschel Johnson, chargé d'affaires at the American embassy and thus de facto ambassador, shepherded Hopkins to Claridge's, the grand red-brick hotel in Mayfair. The two had a quiet dinner in Johnson's room, punctuated by the noise from the antiaircraft batteries in Hyde Park nearby, and were joined briefly by the U.S. military attaché, the articulate Brigadier General Raymond A. Lee.

The dispatch of Hopkins to London had struck this officer as astonishing: the man suffered from extremely poor health, as Lee knew from an interview with Hopkins the preceding June, and in the general's view he had little to offer in the present situation. "Here is a man," Lee said, "who eight or nine years ago was only an obscure social worker, who managed to prevail upon the President and the New Dealers" to allow him to hire three million workers and spend hundreds of millions of dollars. He was not a success with the WPA, Lee believed, "and finally turned it over to my old friend Pink Harrington, of the Engineers, whose real mission was to liquidate all the extravagance which had been common under Hopkins' administration." Hopkins had moved on to become secretary of commerce, "where he was of no consequence at all."

Fortunately for everybody, Hopkins did not have access to the general's diary, with its antipolitician and specifically anti–New Deal prejudices and misstatements. As the general gave the distinguished visitor a far from cheerful summary of Britain's military situation, he noted, with some objectivity, that Hopkins was "quiet, unassuming, and very much to the point."

The meeting between Hopkins and Johnson held importance for both men. Johnson would serve as Hopkins's link with the State Department and thus the president, and for the chargé it provided the opportunity to size up the president's representative and hence the president himself, his aims and intentions. A veteran of the blitz, and at times almost a casualty of it, Johnson was looking for help, and what struck him, he later said, was the "intensity of Harry Hopkins' determination to gain firsthand knowledge of Britain's needs and of finding a way to fill them." Most Americans on missions to London busied themselves trying to determine whether the British really needed what they were asking for, Johnson said, but "Harry wanted to find out if they were asking for *enough* to see them through." Hopkins had come to London not to carp and criticize but to encourage and cooperate. It was, Johnson seemed to feel, about time.

At 10:30 Friday morning, after a briefing from the U.S. naval attaché, Rear Admiral Robert L. Ghormley, Hopkins with marvelous resilience entered on his memorable day with a call at the Foreign Office, where he met the new chief, the debonair Anthony Eden. Not one to mince words as a reporter, Hopkins in his notes for Roosevelt characterized the foreign secretary, Churchill's chief political ally, as "suave, impeccable, unimportant." Further, "the words were quite right but carried no conviction for I am sure the man has no deeply rooted moral stamina." Throughout his career Eden, with his looks and style, had to an unusual degree elicited varying reactions from those with whom he dealt, but if Hopkins had not come to Britain to criticize, he certainly had not come to inflate or flatter anyone either. Even so, his judgment of Eden was surprisingly venomous: "I fancy Churchill gives him high office because he neither thinks, acts—much less [says] anything of importance."

Before the conclusion of this limited-courtesy call, Eden graciously took Hopkins to Sir Alexander Cadogan's office to meet the permanent undersecretary. Neither man seemed aware of the importance of the other. Cadogan noted his offhand impression of the American visitor: "Seems simple and nice"; Hopkins, perhaps not yet aware of the central role played by the permanent head of a ministry—and by this particular permanent head—made no mention of the encounter in his notes.

At 11:30, Hopkins, accompanied by Johnson, moved on to meet with Lord Halifax, who had just given up the post of foreign secretary to become, at the prime minister's behest, ambassador to the United States. Although Halifax had stood in the same relation to Neville Chamberlain as Eden to Churchill, Hopkins much preferred him to Eden, characterizing him as "a different and somewhat tougher breed." He "has no side—has been about—I presume is a hopeless Tory—but that isn't too important now if we can but get on with our business of licking Hitler." Hopkins noted that Halifax was leaving for America the following Tuesday "aboard a British cruiser." Actually, dramatizing for various purposes the importance of Halifax's mission, Churchill was sending him across the Atlantic on Britain's newest battleship, the *King George V*.

After an interlude back at Claridge's to freshen up, Hopkins was driven to Downing Street for the encounter he had wished for since he and FDR had discussed Churchill's letter on board the *Tuscaloosa*. "No. 10 looked a bit down at the heels," Hopkins noted in his account for FDR, which had a journalistic tone throughout; he learned that the street had been bombed heavily, with considerable damage being done to No. 11, the residence of the chancellor of the Exchequer next door, and that the prime minister was no longer "permitted" to sleep in No. 10.

Bracken, whom Hopkins readily identified as Churchill's "man Friday," met the visitor at the door of No. 10 and showed him about "the old and delightful house that has been home of prime ministers of the Empire for two hundred years. Most of the windows are out—workmen over the place repairing the damage." After the tour Bracken led Hopkins to a small dining room in the basement, poured him a sherry, then left him there to await the anticipated encounter with the man who, since the previous summer and the Battle of Britain, had grown into the legend that both fascinated and perturbed the American.

"A rotund—smiling—red faced, gentleman appeared—extended a fat but none the less convincing hand and wished me welcome to England," Hopkins reported. "A short black coat—striped trousers—a clear eye and a mushy voice was the impression of England's leader as he showed me with obvious pride the photograph of his beautiful daughter-in-law and grandchild." The daughter-in-law was Pamela, née Digby, who shortly after the beginning of the war had married Churchill's only and greatly cherished son, Randolph.

"The lunch was simple but good—served by a very plain woman who seemed to be an old family servant," Hopkins continued, including in his account details that seemed as much for his own future use as for the president's edification. "Soup—cold beef—(I didn't take enough jelly to suit the P.M. and he gave me some more)—green salad—cheese and coffee—a light wine and port. He took snuff from a little silver box—he liked it." Hopkins enjoined Missy LeHand, Roosevelt's secretary, to save the letter for him, as well as to read it (it seemed all-purpose, diary as well as report); FDR of course delighted in the specific, so all the details in the picture his personal representative was painting may have given him an interesting extra insight or two.

Turning to the big picture, Churchill and Hopkins ranged over a variety of subjects, beginning with a matter close to the visitor's own heart—the possibility of a meeting between the president and the prime minister. "There is no question but that he wants to meet the President," Hopkins noted, whenever and wherever such a meeting might prove feasible; Roosevelt had suggested April, and Churchill even spoke of staying as long as two weeks, expressing his eagerness to talk face to face instead of communicating at long range. He could "go on a cruiser and by accident meet the President at the appointed place."

To dispose of another possible problem, Hopkins told the prime minister straight-out about "a feeling in America that he, Churchill, did not like America, Americans or Roosevelt." Responding to the charge with a vigorous denial, the prime minister bitterly blamed Joe Kennedy, who had gone home to offer FDR his resignation, for the spreading of the story, and he ordered a secretary to produce the congratulatory telegram in which he had expressed "warm delight" at FDR's reelection; in fact, Churchill had expressed himself to the president more strongly than that: "I did not think it right for me as a foreigner to express any opinion upon American politics while the election was on but now I feel that you will not mind my saying that I prayed for your success and that I am truly thankful for it."

With that out of the way, Hopkins could go on to talk about his mission. Churchill "seemed pleased," he noted with some understatement, and the prime minister certainly took the point: he "several times assured me that he would make every detail of information and opinion available to me and hoped that I would not leave England until I was fully satisfied of the exact state of England's need and the urgent necessity of the exact material assistance Britain requires to win the war."

Churchill then swung into an overall strategic survey, expressing "with obvious pride his own part in the war to date—he didn't *know* that England could withstand the onslaught after France fell—but he had felt sure that it could." (Not completely sure, however. One weekend the previous summer, his daughter-in-law later recalled, he had looked around the lunch table, saying to the family, "'If the Germans come, each of you can take a dead German with you.' This is not mock heroics," Pamela declared. "He was in dead earnest, and I was terrified. 'I don't know how to fire a gun,' I told him. 'You can go into the kitchen and get a carving knife,' he said.")

Now, in 1941, Churchill did not fear invasion, and if the enemy should attempt it "we shall drive them out." He could not find a good face to put on the situation in Greece, which he declared, simply, "lost," but he expected much better results against the Italians in North Africa and he thought cooperation in Northwest Africa might be possible with the Vichy French government if the Germans should try to move in. He reposed great faith in air power: "In general, he looks forward with our help to mastery in the air and then Germany with all her armies will be finished." Churchill then bound up the point, saying that the war "will never see great forces massed against one another." For the prime minister this statement, with its almost unlimited trust in air power, represented a wish and a hope, and also his intention, as long as he had anything to say about it, to see that the path to victory would indeed not lead across bloody continental battlefields. A quarter-century earlier, in the Great War, his advocacy of the operation to force the Dardanelles had shown his drive to find a way out of the slaughter the "great forces" were inflicting on each other in the deadlock of the Western Front. Beyond that, Churchill's summary and conclusion would fit Roosevelt's approach and allay American fears in two dovetailed ways: U.S. production, together with British efforts, would produce the matériel that would win the victory, and it would come without the need for mass armies—no more millions of dough-boys in the fields of France, making the world safe for democracy. Altogether, Churchill had shown that Britain was holding her own, that he was firmly in charge, and that he had a plan for victory. Britain therefore represented a good bet for America to make—that was the prime minister's case, which he presented with his usual persuasiveness. He did not talk about his desire, and that of the cabinet, for the United States to enter fully into the war, as an active belligerent.

"Thus I met Harry Hopkins, that extraordinary man," Churchill wrote later. "His was a soul that flamed out of a frail and failing body," the prime minister said, in recognition of the intensity that had also touched Herschel Johnson. "I soon comprehended his personal dynamism and the outstanding importance of his mission." The nature of the mission obviously gave Hopkins no power to make commitments of any kind, but during his talk with Churchill, as the prime minister recalled it, his new American friend delivered himself of a remarkable statement:

"The President is determined that we shall win the war together. Make no mistake about it.

"He has sent me here to tell you that at all costs and by all means he will carry you through, no matter what happens to him—there is nothing that he will not do so far as he has human power."

Now what did Hopkins say and what did Churchill hear? Hopkins makes no mention in his notes of having delivered such a fervent if brief speech, and certainly Roosevelt had not sent his special envoy to England to make an undying pledge of any kind. Churchill surely would have liked to have heard such words, and Hopkins to have been empowered to deliver them. Perhaps, in his new surroundings, after a night of the Blitz and under Churchill's unfamiliar and remarkable spell, he became a bit carried away, though the wording as Churchill recorded it rang only faintly of Hopkins or of the president.

But was not Hopkins almost perfectly attuned to Roosevelt's thinking, his aims and purposes? To one side of it, a very important side, indeed, but "to describe Roosevelt," said an old friend, "you would have to describe three or four men for he had at least three or four different personalities." Frances Perkins called him "the most complicated human being I ever knew."

"Never let your left hand know what your right hand is doing," FDR once said to Henry Morgenthau, one of his oldest friends.

"Which am I?" asked Morgenthau.

"My right hand," replied Roosevelt, "but I keep my left hand under the table."

That indeed seemed to Morgenthau "the real way he works." No one could expect even the most sensitive alter ego to reflect the whole mind of such a prismatic personality—but part of it, yes. Hopkins knew what he believed; Roosevelt must believe it, too.

Hopkins's working day had not ended with the three-hour session with the prime minister; now came separate press conferences at the U.S. embassy with British and American correspondents. The reporters had arrived by three o'clock, the scheduled time, but no Hopkins was to be seen. General Lee, who was on hand, observed that Hopkins "no doubt was being subjected to all of Churchill's brilliancy, boldness and blandishments." Since Hopkins could hardly walk out on Churchill, as Johnson explained to the waiting reporters, the meeting got under way only after an hour's delay.

After Hopkins told the reporters that, not knowing how to conduct such an interview, he would leave the questioning up to them, one man, after an interval of silence, asked, "And what have you done today, Mr. Hopkins?"

Sitting behind the desk that had been used by the departed Joe

Kennedy, Hopkins paused for a moment, then said, "I got up this morning about eight o'clock and took a look out of the window for the weather. Then I went into the bathroom and turned on my bath and when the tub was full I got into it. Then the telephone began to ring . . ." As he continued in this vein, with details of his breakfast and his clothing, including a discussion with the valet about detachable collars, the reporters at first sat silently but then began to chuckle as they realized the visitor was gently putting them on by literally answering the question. "What interested me chiefly," said Lee, who seemed able to look past his prejudices and respond to Hopkins as a person, "was that by answering this question in that manner he had established, without very much delay, a common meeting ground and a mutual interest," with the result that the reporters "felt that they had a fairly good acquaintanceship with him and other questions came more easily." That held true even though Hopkins was not at liberty to say much of substance.

The session with the American reporters proved a bit rougher. Seeming nervous and looking frail, one reporter thought, Hopkins sat "tapping the arms of his chair and looking as though he might burst with secrets." Clearly impatient at "the necessity of behaving like a clam," Hopkins told the reporters that he could say nothing about his mission, except that it concerned matters of mutual importance and urgency and it would take him from two to four weeks to complete. One reporter, obviously a bit impatient himself, considered the conference "equally embarrassing for the journalists and for the President's envoy." The envoy was, of course, faithfully following orders, and he did earn a favorable mention for having spent the preceding night in his own room, not in the hotel shelter. Lee paid tribute to Hopkins for his manner, not greeting reporters "with the suave, toothy, and inane grin which was characteristic not only of [Joe] Kennedy, but of all the bright young politicians, who seem to think that a vacuous grin is all that is needed to get by." Hopkins simply answered questions as fully as he could.

A working dinner at Claridge's topped off Hopkins's demanding first full day. He had arrived in England determined to see Ed Murrow as soon as possible, and when the broadcaster received the summons to Claridge's he presumed that Roosevelt's representative was granting him an interview. On arriving, however, he discovered that the flow of information would be going in the other direction. Hopkins, a regular listener to Murrow's celebrated "This is London" broadcasts, with all their background and sometimes foreground noise of planes and bombs and antiaircraft fire, knew "how wide an acquaintance Murrow had and how implicitly trusted he was, so that, as the censors at BBC explained it, 'they told him everything.'" The two men spent about five hours together, by Murrow's estimate, with Hopkins asking questions about British political figures and the state of the national morale. Hopkins also suggested that Murrow "go home and talk to a few people." Murrow stiffened at that: "I'm a reporter, without political ambition," and added, perhaps curiously, that he certainly did not "propose to go home and do political propaganda." He did not appear to realize that his radio reports, at once dramatic and introspective, constituted propaganda of the most vivid and effective kind, far beyond the dreams of professionals in the trade.

Hopkins's appointment list for the next two days, January 11 and 12, said simply: "With the Prime Minister." What that meant was that he now had an engagement for one of the most quintessentially English and often most useful of all occasions—the country weekend.

12

"THE PERFECTION OF HUMAN SOCIETY"

For the past twenty years British prime ministers had enjoyed the use of Chequers, a more-or-less Tudor mansion in Buckinghamshire, as an official country residence. Early in the war, however, German reconnaissance planes had overflown the area, and in the summer bombs had fallen nearby. Telling Churchill that the long, broad gravel drive, pointing like a great arrow to the house, made it an easy target to spot "when the moon was high," his chiefs of staff and security people urged him to find a safer country location. (No one presumed to suggest that the prime minister remain in town on bright weekends.)

Hence, one Tuesday in early November, Churchill had summoned Ronald Tree, a member of Parliament and a friend though not an intimate, to ask, "Would it be possible for you to offer me accommodation at Ditchley for certain week-ends?" Tree, the son of American parents who had chosen to live in England, had remarkable connections: his grandfather was the original Marshall Field, his stepfather was the dashing Admiral Sir David Beatty of Great War renown, his great-uncle was the American ambassador to Italy, his wife's aunt was Lady Astor. In Ditchley Park, which stood in Oxfordshire not far from

Blenheim, he and his wife had created a jewel of a country seat—eminently suitable as weekend headquarters for a prime minister, particularly since, unlike Chequers, it was masked, appropriately enough, by a fine stand of trees. Tree himself loved the place: it had "a welcoming quality that I have never known in any other house."

He "told Churchill, of course, that we would be delighted to have him," Tree said, though he swallowed hard when informed that the prime minister would like to pay his first visit the very next weekend. Since Tree was fully occupied as parliamentary private secretary to the minister of information, the burden of preparing for the sudden prime-ministerial invasion would fall on the lady of the manor, Nancy Tree, who showed herself fully equal to the challenge. All proved in order on Friday afternoon, when Churchill's caravan arrived with officials and secretaries and an "antiquated armoured car" which the prime minister refused even to enter and which was consequently banished to the garage. Engineers had installed a new telephone system, complete with scrambling equipment, and a company of Oxford and Bucks Light Infantry—actually a collection of raw recruits, though armed with machine guns to fight off air attacks—took up positions around the house. After the weekend Tree recorded "no complaints about the food and drink"; indeed, Churchill found his stay so satisfactory he declared his intention to return the following Friday, "high moon or no high moon."

Thus began a pattern, Churchill descending on Ditchley with an entourage—not a large group, but including Clementine and perhaps another family member or two, a cabinet member (Anthony Eden was a particular favorite), a general or an admiral, friends, civil servants, and secretaries, and always Brendan Bracken. Another regular, although he would not spend the night but would drive back to Oxford in his antique Rolls, was "the Prof," F. A. Lindemann, Churchill's influential adviser on all matters scientific. Though the company always consisted largely of colleagues of the prime minister, they were associates to whom he was close personally and with whom he could relax and enjoy a weekend even though he brought his responsibilities and his schedule with him from London.

As for Churchill's personal staff, noted a member of the Cabinet Secretariat, "so far as we were concerned he drew no sharp distinction between his private life and his official duties," because he "never stopped work, wherever he was, and wanted some of us to be continuously on hand" as, characteristically, he delivered himself of messages scourging bureaucrats and, often ignoring lines of political and military authority, hung over the shoulders of distant commanders, concerning himself even with the activities of individual divisions. Churchill himself followed his idiosyncratic daily schedule, which called for him to spend the morning in bed, though awake and dictating letters and memos; nap generously during the afternoon; then stay up till the wee hours, fueled by what were obviously weak if uninterrupted (as Joe Kennedy had noted) whisky-and-sodas. As compensation for responding to his demands, those who worked for Churchill "were taken freely into the family circle," in London or in the country. And "nothing was drab or dull: it was all shot through with colour and contrast."

Some eighty years earlier the eminent American historian and diplomat John Lothrop Motley had employed a memorable phrase in talking with a young friend about the good points of life in England. "The London dinner and the English country house," said Motley, represented "the perfection of human society." The younger man, Henry Adams, who as the son of the American minister had attended a number of such dinners, felt that his older friend could hardly be serious, at least with respect to the food; he did not know of "a good cook or a good table in London." As for the country house, Adams decided after some reflection that Motley was probably thinking of places in which "the tone was easy, the talk was good, and the standard of scholarship was high"—not Germanic scholarship, to be sure: "Nothing that seemed to smell of the shop or of the lecture-room was wanted." All of that might be very well for some literary types, Adams grudgingly conceded, but it was also true that "one might stay in no end of country houses without forgetting that one was a total stranger and could never be anything else."

At lunchtime on Saturday, January 11, escorted from London by Churchill's naval aide, Commander Tommy Thompson, Harry Hopkins arrived at Ditchley for his first encounter with the latter-day version of perfect human society: the harness maker's son was weekending with "Winston Churchill and the men who run the British government." But into this challenging company Hopkins brought with him one great personal asset; as a reporter described him, "he can get along in almost any company, from the inhabitants of the tenement sections of Chicago to the Long Island society set." He also had another asset: his lengthy lunch and talk with Churchill had seen the beginning of a friendship between the two men.

This weekend's group consisted of Clementine Churchill; Venetia Montagu (widow of a cabinet minister); Bracken; Jock Colville, assistant private secretary to the prime minister; and Churchill himself. When Hopkins arrived, the host and hostess had both gone off on urgent duties—Nancy Tree, who operated canteens, had been called to Portsmouth to help the victims of the previous night's heavy bombing. Though no host or hostess was present, "Mr. Hopkins arrived," noted Colville, "and his quiet charm and dignity held the table"—no mean feat for anybody with Churchill as one of the company.

Speaking of the lend-lease bill, which had been introduced in the Senate and the House just the day before, Hopkins told these very interested listeners that it would certainly arouse controversy but he fully expected it to pass. He also brought up a curious point about the continuing cross borne by the British government, the Duke of Windsor, who had recently taken a publicized cruise with Axel Wenner-Gren, a Swedish industrialist whom the United States government considered "a dangerous pro-Nazi." If American officials received him, Hopkins said, it was only "to let him talk." Hopkins pleased his listeners by observing that the decline of the Windsors' support in the United States, where they had been darlings of press and public, had resulted from the winning impression made by the king and queen on their visit to America in the summer of 1939.

After his successful launching at lunch, Hopkins was taken by Bracken for a tour of Blenheim, the ducal seat of the Marlboroughs and Churchill's birthplace—and the largest privately owned palace in Europe. Returning for tea, they found the social group augmented by Oliver Lyttelton, president of the Board of Trade; the charming Marquesa de Casa Maury, previously famous as Freda Dudley Ward; and Professor Lindemann. Bracken passed on the encouraging news from Hopkins that President Roosevelt was determined that Britain should have the material she needed to win the war, and Hopkins's mission was to determine what the country needed.

After dinner, a meal that reflected little wartime austerity, served dramatically in an elegant dining room lit only by candles, Hopkins spoke of the profound effect of Churchill's speeches on all Americans across the country. Modestly, though clearly pleased, the prime minister responded that he had hardly known what he was saying; he simply felt that "it would be better for us to be destroyed than to see the triumph of such an impostor." People last summer wanted to hear him say that whatever happened to the army, Britain would still fight

FDR received his famous Scottie, Fala, as a present in 1940, shortly before this picnic photograph was taken on Sunset Hill in Dutchess County, New York. Four years later the terrier would play the central part in one of the funniest passages in all of political oratory: the president's campaign appearance at a Teamsters Union convention would forever be remembered as the "Fala speech."

Support of the New Deal earned Averell Harriman (center) the derision of many fellow financiers, who classed him as one of President Roosevelt's "tame millionaires." (The use of ramps, together with the help of an aide, enabled FDR to appear to be walking.)

As he lounged in various postures, Harry Hopkins sometimes struck observers as enigmatic, but quickly his directness, often expressed profanely, took over. His candor, often caustic, did not alienate reporters but instead appealed to them. As the leading symbol of the New Deal, next to the president himself, Hopkins always made good copy.

On March 11, 1941, President Roosevelt signed the Lend-Lease Act, thus capping a two-month debate in the Senate and the House of Representatives. By this time Harry Hopkins had completed his remarkable mission to Winston Churchill as FDR's special representative, and just the day before the signing Averell Harriman had departed for London to begin the practical work demanded by the new partnership.

Chequers, a 16th-century country house in Buckinghamshire about 50 miles northwest of London, has served since the 1920s as the weekend retreat for British prime ministers. Hopkins and Harriman both spent time here with Churchill; Hopkins, whose mission took place during the winter, found the place so drafty that he often kept his overcoat and hat on indoors.

The beauty of Clementine Churchill (shown here at Admiralty House in London, in 1940) had literally rendered Winston speechless when the two first met at a ball in 1904. Since then the verbal situation had changed greatly, with each freely giving advice and counsel to the other. In the days following her husband's becoming prime minister, Clementine earnestly cautioned him against sarcasm and rudeness.

When Churchill's daughter-in-law, Pamela, gave him a grandson (October 1940), the prime minister was determined that the boy be named after him. Here are baby Winston and his glamorous mother at about the time she would meet the handsome and wealthy presidential envoy, Averell Harriman. Motherhood would prove no hindrance to the relationship she developed with him.

Though his polo-playing and other pursuits had caused some to class him as a playboy, Harriman in fact was a driving worker who from his desk in Grosvenor Square directed the activities of Americans in London on a variety of assignments, long-term and short-term. He expected the same kind of dedication from his subordinates.

When Hopkins arrived in Moscow in late July 1941 as the president's emissary, he came with the highest credentials. FDR had told Joseph Stalin: "I ask you to treat Mr. Hopkins with the identical confidence you would feel if you were talking directly to me." Hopkins's optimistic conclusions from his meetings proved to be sound.

Shortly after the Japanese attacks on American and British territories and installations in the Pacific, Churchill set off for Washington to begin crafting a full-scale alliance with the United States. On December 22, having just arrived, the prime minister—probably not feeling as somber as he looked—was greeted by FDR on the south portico of the White House.

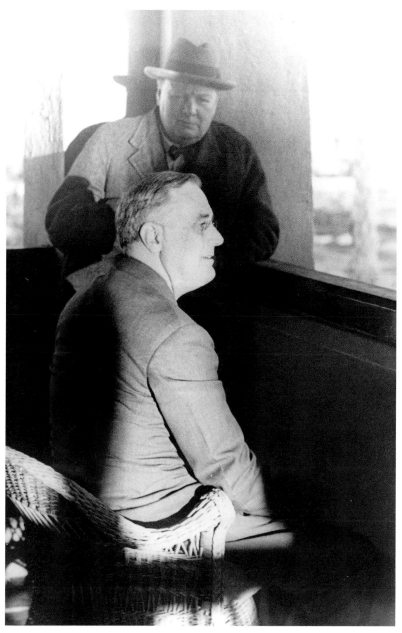

After the conclusion of their conference at Casablanca in January 1943 (at which the Allies issued their demand for "unconditional surrender"), Churchill insisted that the president join him in a two-day excursion to Marrakech, "the Paris of the Sahara." From the tower of a villa the two statesmen watched the sunset on the snows of the Atlas Mountains.

At one of the most important of the wartime conferences, at Tehran (November–December 1943), Roosevelt was supported by his now veteran team, Harry Hopkins and Averell Harriman. At FDR's behest, Harriman had recently—and reluctantly—given up his post in London to become ambassador to the Soviet Union.

The last Big Three conference in which Roosevelt participated took place at Yalta, in the Soviet Crimea, in February 1945. When Harriman, now with more than a year's experience in Moscow, arrived in the Crimea, he was already concerned about the president's physical condition. Churchill had remarked that ten years' search would have turned up no worse place for a conference than Yalta.

on. And he had done so. Now the text of the president's lend-lease bill, which he had seen that morning, had given him the feeling that a new world had come into being. He was looking to a United States of Europe—a favorite theme—which must be built by the British, not by either the Germans (hardly surprising) or the Russians. With the Germans, tyranny and brute force would predominate; with the Russians, communism and squalor.

British war aims? What to say to this American emissary, this one-time social worker? "We seek no treasure, we seek no territorial gains, we seek only the right of man to be free; we seek his right to worship his God, to lead his life in his own way, secure from persecution. As the humble labourer returns from his work when the day is done, and sees the smoke curling up from his cottage home in the serene evening sky, we wish him to know that no rat-a-tat-tat of the secret police upon his door will disturb his leisure or interrupt his rest. We seek government with the consent of the people, man's freedom to say what he will, and when he thinks himself injured, to find himself equal in the eyes of the law. But war aims other than these we have none."

What would the president think about all this? Churchill wanted to know. In "a remarkable contrast to the ceaseless flow of eloquence to which we had listened," said Colville, Hopkins, replying slowly and thoughtfully and "exaggerating his American drawl," spoke of there being two kinds of men, those who talked and those who acted, and that the president, like the prime minister, belonged to the latter group. He had heard Roosevelt express similar ideas to Churchill's, he said, but, more to the point, "Mr. Prime Minister, I don't think the president will give a damn for all that." (Some also heard him say, "I don't give a damn for your cottagers.") Lyttelton reacted with shock: Had everything just gone wrong? But after pausing, Hopkins said, "You see, we're only interested in beating that son of a bitch in Berlin."

Laughter swept the room. Churchill hastily expressed hearty

agreement; he had merely wanted to let Hopkins—and, of course, the president—know that he was looking to the future. But he and his associates were rapidly coming to see that their visitor did not fit any stereotype they may have held; not austere in any way, he chain-smoked, liked to drink, and enjoyed other normal pleasures, and now he had displayed a distinct touch in pricking the prime minister, sharply but not offensively. He had a certain offbeat raffishness, with a mordant humor and a lively wit; his clothes hung loosely on his frame. Such a type appealed to Churchill—"a sophisticated outsider with a touch of loucheness"—and the prime minister's own background of course included two unconventional Americans of primary importance, his adventuress mother and his grandfather, an imaginative and often risk-running New York financier and entrepreneur; indeed, he shared more traits with these ancestral Yankees than with his Marlborough relatives.

With a single comment Hopkins had advanced his friendship with Churchill a long step forward, moving quickly out of the total-stranger role to which Henry Adams had believed country-house visitors to be consigned, but of course Ditchley with Churchill could hardly be called a conventional country-house scene. As Jock Colville noted, Churchill took to Hopkins at once, and their friendship progressed from that point. Though inevitably a friendship of the special type having limitations imposed by the respective responsibilities of the principals as powerful figures who, however common their cause may be, nevertheless serve different national masters and divergent interests, it rested on genuine mutual liking. Quite apart from questions of influence, a Churchill biographer would note, "Hopkins quickly acquired a personal position in the Churchill court."

In redoing and modernizing Ditchley after acquiring it in 1933, the Trees had given special thought to the library. Inheriting the space as two small rooms, they had knocked down the wall between to create a big room, about fifty feet by twenty, with two marble fireplaces and towering bookcases reaching to the cornices. Armchairs and a large sofa were assembled from various corners of the house and re-covered in red leather, and the Trees added a white Hepplewhite desk, large enough for four persons to write at it without jostling each other. "It was in this room that we usually assembled before and after dinner," Tree said, and so it became the stage on which Churchill gave Hopkins and the others of the company a special performance on Sunday evening.

"Churchill was not a great conversationalist," said Lord Normanbrook, of the Cabinet Secretariat. "He was not much interested to hear what others had to say," but "as a soloist, in pursuing and embroidering his own theme, he was supreme." At about midnight, armed with his usual cigar, the prime minister took up his position in front of one of the two fireplaces and entered on an appreciation and analysis of the war as it had unfolded thus far. Earlier the group had engaged in general talk, mostly about America, with a bow to Hopkins concerning the U.S. government's efforts to cope with unemployment by providing jobs instead of simply leaning on the dole. Churchill wanted to know what the Americans would do when they had accumulated all the world's gold and then everybody else decided that it had no use except for filling teeth. Hopkins amused his listeners by replying that the Americans could use their unemployed to guard the gold.

While everybody was watching the current film *Night Train to Munich*, starring Rex Harrison, news came that German dive-bombers had appeared in the Mediterranean and had sunk the cruiser *Southampton* and damaged other vessels. Churchill later talked with Hopkins about this sinister incursion—previously, the only Axis air activity in the Mediterranean had been by the Italians; the prime minister took this development in stride, keeping his guest up until four o'clock with this reminder that anywhere the prime minister went became a war command post. But first came the centerpiece of the evening, Churchill's monologue, given especially for Hopkins's benefit.

Beginning with a look to the future, the prime minister assessed relative populations as a factor in the war, observing that while Germany had 60 million people that could be relied on (satellites not figuring here), the British Empire and the United States (which he credited with 120 million, about 10 million below the actual current figure) together far outclassed the enemy, as was also the case with reference to courage and resolution. He did not believe that Japan would enter into war against the combined Anglo-Americans, and, while he expected the Germans to take over Unoccupied France, he saw a benefit here: the French would react to this move by opposing the Germans in North Africa.

With that optimistic look at the overall prospect, Churchill went back to pick up the history of the war from the point at which the Phony War had turned into the real thing: the Norway campaign, the ill-advised rush of Allied armies into Belgium, the struggle for air supremacy, the war in the North African desert, and the possibility of invasion of Britain. He hailed the attack on the French fleet at Mers-el-Kebir, Oran (over which Churchill himself had shed tears), as the deed that had shown the world that Britain meant what it said—it was determined to fight on—and declared his confidence in the country's ability to resist a German attempt at invasion.

"I think," Colville noted, "Hopkins must have been impressed."

The performance, presumably a blend of ideas and expressions the prime minister had already had in mind and those that came impromptu, lasted two hours. Churchill's conversation was "less rhetorical than his written prose," said Normanbrooke, but even in ordinary meetings one would hear memorable sentences or phrases. Tonight Hopkins was indeed impressed, not surprised by the prime minister's eloquence but profoundly struck by the depth of his knowledge of the entire situation and the detail that enriched that knowledge. "Here was one who certainly knew his stuff," as Sherwood put it in expressing Hopkins's feeling, "who could recite fact and figure and chapter and verse, and in superb English prose." Definitely, Hopkins was dazzled. Though it had been authoritatively stated two thousand years ago that no man can serve two masters, Hopkins, for all his unquestioned loyalty to Roosevelt, might have wavered. He had told Colville that Roosevelt had sent him to find out "whether the reports sent to the President by Ambassador Kennedy are as incorrect as he thinks they are." He had definitely found the answer to that question.

Coming to understand Churchill represented a necessary process to be undergone not simply by important American visitors but by the associates and staff members of 10 Downing Street and related offices. Young Jock Colville (twenty-five in 1940), who had served Neville Chamberlain as a private secretary and regretted his chief's departure from power, saw the country running a terrible risk with Churchill, involving "the danger of rash and spectacular exploits" and the possibility of being "maneuvered into the most dangerous position it has ever been in." He had listened with approval as a friend castigated the Conservative leaders who had "weakly surrendered to a half-breed American whose main support was that of inefficient but talkative people" of the same ilk—Lady Astor and Ronald Tree. Within just a few days, however, Colville found himself conceding that, for all its faults, the new administration had drive.

The situation had also produced a new Winston Churchill. Colonel Ian Jacob, military assistant secretary of the War Cabinet, noted how, as first lord of the Admiralty, Churchill involved himself in the activities of other departments: the "outbursts of interfering inquisition that he had unloosed at meetings had not proved easy to tolerate." Now, with Churchill having become prime minister, "we foresaw a stormy future, and we wondered how this difficult and seemingly erratic character would get on as the leader of the team in a situation of such grave urgency."

Jacob's question contained its own answer. Churchill with his energy and flow of ideas had indeed never limited himself to his own departmental turf, either in the Great War under Prime Minister Herbert Asquith or in this new war under Neville Chamberlain, and he had regularly ruffled the feathers of many of his more conventional colleagues. He had at times been unrelenting in his drive to see his ideas put into effect, but now his situation was transformed—no longer a number-three or number-two man, he had become number one, with the whole war as his purview and therefore with authority over all departments. No longer did he have to wheedle and hector; he could issue orders. "We soon saw," Jacob said, "that the methods which produced friction and heat among his equals and superiors were exactly those that produced action when employed by a Prime Minister toward his subordinates." Nor did Churchill any longer have to advertise himself or to dream of what might be: on May 10, 1940, he had reached the top of the pole. He could therefore organize everything— his daily routine, the conduct of cabinet business, and the management of the war—exactly as he wished.

Hopkins returned to London from Ditchley on Monday, and the next day he dispatched two messages to FDR, the first a brief cable to bring the president up to date.

PERSONAL AND CONFIDENTIAL FOR THE PRESI-
DENT AND THE SECRETARY OF STATE FROM MR.
HOPKINS:
    Weekend with Churchill. Leaving for tour of naval bases with
him today. Saw King yesterday. Well and confident. He sends warm

regards to you. Your message received well here. Am urging Govern-
ment here not to create or accentuate differences between us pending
passage of Bill. What is your best judgment as to when Bill will
pass? Hope there will be no major amendments. Can we be informed
relative to the Bill from time to time? Going here pretty rough. Am
seeing everything from bombs to President's cousins. Letter by mes-
senger. All well.

Hopkins enlisted General Lee, who was returning to Washington, as his messenger to deliver his letter to the president. Writing rapidly, on the small pages of hotel stationery he had used for his first set of notes, he worked almost up to the minute he had to leave the hotel to set off with the prime minister for the tour of naval bases. "The people here are amazing from Churchill down," Hopkins told FDR, "and if courage alone can win—the result will be inevitable. But they need our help desperately and I am sure you will permit nothing to stand in the way." As a good reporter, he could not resist adding that "some of the ministers and underlings are a bit trying but no more than some I have seen."

He then moved to his main point: "<u>Churchill</u> is the gov't in every sense of the word—he controls the grand strategy and often the details—labor trusts him—the army, navy, air force are behind him to a man. The politicians and upper crust pretend to like him. I cannot emphasize too strongly that he is the one and only person over here with whom you need to have a full meeting of minds.

"Churchill wants to see you—the sooner the better—but I have told him of your problem until the bill is passed. I am convinced this meeting between you and Churchill is essential—and soon—for the battering continues and Hitler does not wait for Congress."

Dismissing the idea that Churchill disliked Roosevelt and America—"it just doesn't make sense"—Hopkins declared: "This island needs our help now Mr. President with everything we can give them."

More personally, Hopkins observed: "There is no time to be out of London so I am staying here—the bombs aren't nice and seem to be quite impersonal. I have been offered a so called bomb proof apartment by Churchill—a tin hat and gas mask have been delivered—the best I can say for the hat is that it looks worse than my own and doesn't fit—the gas mask I can't get on—so I am alright." There was much to tell, Hopkins said, but it would have to wait—"for I must be off to Charing Cross."

This letter, though coming early in Hopkins's stay in England, represented the cornerstone of his mission. "Churchill is the gov't in every sense of the word"—that was the lesson the president's representative had learned in only half a week; it was just as Jean Monnet had said back in Washington. Even if Hopkins was unwittingly exaggerating—the political story inevitably had more to it than that—he had answered the president's first question: Is Churchill a good bet for us? And Britain? "This island needs our help now, with everything we can give them."

As for his being "out of London," Hopkins had rejected any talk of a house in the country, away from the bombs—he hadn't come to the city just to run away from excitement and danger. Delightedly, he would make do in town with the tin hat and the unusable gas mask.

13

"WHITHER THOU GOEST"

Harry Hopkins's schedule for Tuesday morning, January 14, called for meeting Winston Churchill at King's Cross station, a departure point for northbound trains, and not Charing Cross as he had told FDR in his letter. Fortunately, with the aid of the embassy staff, he got to the right place and onto the prime minister's special train, bound for Scotland. Hopkins's information-gathering process out in the field would begin in the rawest and dreariest part of the British Isles, the Orkneys, site of the Home Fleet's famous base, Scapa Flow. (In flashes of unconscious Great War–era nostalgia, Churchill would speak of the fleet as the Grand Fleet, and the office wall behind the first lord's desk in the Admiralty building still held his special map case from the old days, including a hand-printed listing of steaming distances between British and German ports.)

In the correspondence President Roosevelt had begun with Churchill at the beginning of the war, the then–first lord had chosen to sign himself "Naval Person," and after becoming prime minister had modified the alias to "Former Naval Person." But, having decided to dramatize the appointment of Lord Halifax as ambassador to the United States by sending him to America in the new battleship *King*

George V, appropriately escorted by a flotilla of destroyers, Churchill, still very much a naval person, wanted to see the vessel off on its mission and to visit the fleet, which he had not seen since changing jobs in May. He would also make use of the train journey and the shared experience to get to know Hopkins better. On Monday he had cabled Roosevelt: "I am most grateful to you for sending so remarkable an envoy, who enjoys so high a measure of your intimacy and confidence."

Once Churchill had learned the general nature of Hopkins's mission, he began to woo and thus to use his visitor; but this visitor had come to England, as Herschel Johnson saw, precisely to be used. As he took Churchill's measure for himself—a task that moved along briskly—he wanted and needed to see the country's real requirements; he did not have to concern himself with determining the financial framework within which these needs should be met or with what degree of belligerency the United States ought to adopt. He had come to England as the president's reporter.

The choice of Halifax for the Washington embassy represented a gamble for Churchill, perhaps more of one than he realized. The new ambassador, having some years earlier put in a demanding stint as viceroy of India, had not wanted this or any other posting that would take him out of England again (a sentiment held even more strongly by Lady Halifax), and in the ranks of those formulating and carrying out the appeasement policy he had stood just behind Neville Chamberlain himself. In May 1940, as the front in the west was collapsing and British troops fell back on Dunkirk, Halifax had argued in cabinet for going along with the French and sounding out the Germans on peace terms. Churchill unflinchingly opposed the foreign secretary (although surprisingly conceding that the moment for such an inquiry might come later, after Britain had shown that she could not be defeated), but found his position threatened for a day or two before he succeeded in snuffing out the idea.

The prime minister confirmed his position by the Royal Navy's attack on the French fleet shortly after France's surrender, showing not only the Americans but likewise the residual appeasers in his own cabinet that the Britain he headed was in the war to stay; having declared Hitler to be the Antichrist, he could hardly look to peace negotiations and a resumption of diplomatic relations with the Führer and his regime.

There was also the not-insignificant fact that Halifax had no knowledge of Americans and little regard for them; as he would soon write in a private note, "they strike me as very crude and semi-educated." Such condescension, not in the least unique, represented exactly the persistent transatlantic problem identified by the former diplomat Lord Eustace Percy. This attitude seems to have rested most heavily on the fact that an American was viewed not as a foreigner, with his own national culture and habits, but as an even more deplorable creature, an Englishman manqué. Yet when sounded out by London, Washington had seemed to welcome the idea of Halifax as ambassador, whereas it had shown little enthusiasm for Lloyd George, Churchill's earlier, and unrealistic, proposal. And Hopkins had responded favorably to Halifax on meeting him, "hopeless Tory" or not.

On an entirely different level, moving Halifax to Washington would open the door for Anthony Eden's return to the Foreign Office, where Churchill wanted him. Halifax, whose continuation in high office attested to the remarkable durability of British politicians regardless of the results of the policies they espoused, accepted the appointment with at least outward grace; Churchill salved it by keeping the ambassador as a member of the War Cabinet, a function to be exercised whenever he was in Britain.

On the final leg of the northward journey, Churchill and his party, including Clemmie as well as Hopkins, woke up to a blizzard but continued on to Thurso, on Pentland Firth, whence they proceeded by minesweeper to Scapa Flow. As the ship turned into the anchorage and sunlight suddenly pierced the clouds, General "Pug" Ismay, Churchill's closest military aide, decided that Hopkins must not miss the sight of the "might, majesty, dominion and power of the British Empire" as symbolized by these great vessels; if ill fortune befell these ships, the American visitor should know, "the whole future of the world might be changed, not only for Britain but ultimately for the United States as well." But Ismay found Hopkins shivering in the wardroom, too cold to work up much excitement about the Home Fleet. In a while, thoroughly chilled in the dank air and biting wind, Hopkins, looking for a sheltered spot on deck, sat down on a large object but moved without demur when a petty officer informed him that he had taken refuge on a depth charge.

After a farewell lunch with Lord and Lady Halifax aboard the *King George V*, Churchill began his inspections both of the vessels at anchor and of shore installations; Hopkins spent much of the next two days in bed. On the day the party left the naval base, in transferring from one vessel to another Hopkins almost fell into the icy water when the step of a ladder gave way; two quick-acting seamen saved him from that dangerous misfortune, while Churchill helpfully called, "I shouldn't stay there too long, Harry. When two ships are close together in a rough sea, you are liable to get hurt."

This was the first of various kinds of inspections and visits in which the prime minister would show his American friend a great deal, if not literally everything, and would also show off to the public this representative of the president of the United States who had come to

Britain to help in the great cause. In Glasgow, Churchill took Hopkins on a whirlwind tour of the city's civil-defense facilities, including an inspection of anti–air raid personnel formed up in ranks like a large military force. Finally exhausted, Hopkins tried to lose himself in the crowd but Churchill, calling "Harry, Harry," invariably dug him out, though by now on this wintry Scottish tour the prime minister himself was showing the effects of a heavy cold.

In an unscheduled speech to some two hundred people who seemed to expect an address, Churchill presented his listeners with a blunt assessment of Britain's situation. "Before us lie many months of having to endure bombardment of our cities and industrial areas without the power to make equal reply," he said, not sweetening his message except to observe that the coming dangers might not be quite as great as those through which the country had just passed—but, still, "dangers which if we neglect anything might be fatal, mortal. Before us lie sufferings and tribulations."

Turning to his companion on the platform, Churchill said that Hopkins had come "in order to put himself in the closest relation with things here," and, with a nod to Roosevelt, "he will soon return to report to his famous chief the impressions he has gathered in our islands. We don't require, in 1941, large armies from overseas. What we do require are weapons, ships and aeroplanes." How would Britain pay for them? "I watch with deep emotion the stirring processes by which the democracy of the great American Republic"—an ingenious bit of political-party fence-straddling—"is establishing its laws and formulating its decisions in order to make sure that the British Commonwealth of Nations is able to maintain, as it is maintaining at the present time, the front line of civilisation and of progress."

At a dinner given by Tom Johnston, the regional commissioner for Scotland, Hopkins was asked for a few words. After pausing, he rose and said quietly, "I suppose you wish to know what I am going to say to President Roosevelt on my return. Well, I'm going to quote you one verse from the Book of Books in the truth of which Mr. Johnston and my own Scottish mother were brought up: 'Whither thou goest, I will go, and where thou lodgest, I will lodge; thy people shall be my people, and thy God my God.'" Another pause. Then: "Even to the end." So Nancy Astor had not been completely off the mark in her view of Hopkins—the soul of the Social Gospeler shone through the exterior of the presidential envoy. Tears flowed from Churchill's eyes.

News of Hopkins's brief remarks, spreading across the country, seemed to give a tangible boost to the national morale. Though perhaps a bit transported by his admiration for his hosts, Hopkins spoke in good faith. He thought he knew the president's mind. But Franklin Roosevelt was an eastern Episcopalian, not a midwestern Social Gospeler; he was president and not an adviser, and he was playing a careful game in the real world.

The republic's stirring processes had formally begun to move in Washington on January 10 with the introduction of the lend-lease bill—"an act further to promote the defense of the United States, and for other purposes"—in the House and the Senate. The House parliamentarian, applying what seemed a numerical pun, tagged the bill H. R. 1776—a neat switch on history. The parliamentarian had more than a game in mind, however; he hoped to provide a bit of patriotic cover for the majority leader, John W. McCormack, who represented heavily Irish South Boston, where his sponsorship of a program to aid the English spalpeens would hardly strengthen him with constituents.

An official characterized the clamor across the country following the introduction of the lend-lease bill as "the final stage in a running national debate that had been going on in the United States with increasing vigor since the fall of France." Even after the stirring and tragic events of the previous summer, the debate had moved slowly, noted the official, Edward R. Stettinius, Jr., and the pace with which the United States had proffered aid to the countries battling the Axis had thus proved correspondingly slow. That was because, Stettinius believed, the situation demanded a great consensus: "a mere majority is not a sufficient foundation when drastic and far-reaching action is necessary to protect the nation in time of peril."

During the preceding summer two organizations had entered the debate—first, the Committee to Defend America by Aiding the Allies, which took formal shape on May 17, a week after the great German attack in the west. Chaired by the famous Kansas editor William Allen White, a Republican, it advocated supplying Britain and France with arms and war materials but did not argue for U.S. entry into the war. There soon followed a counter-organization, the America First Committee, a rallying point for isolationists or antiwar activists, founded at Yale with leadership by such young men as Gerald Ford, Potter Stewart, and Kingman Brewster; General Robert E. Wood of Sears, Roebuck agreed to serve as chairman. Both groups built up nationwide organizations, held mass meetings—with Colonel Lindbergh as the star attraction for America First—and waged extensive advertising campaigns. Though America First attracted a number of fringe types, the range of its adherents included many of the old liberal isolationists as well conservatives. "The 'Great Debate' was impressively orderly and nonviolent," commented a historian; "emotions mounted as concerned Americans earnestly jousted verbally on what were literally life-and-death issues. Passions grew, and so did intolerance of conflicting foreign policy views. Increasingly, many on each side saw their adversaries in the debate as not merely wrong, but evil and perhaps subversive as well." With each side wrapping itself in the flag, the debate became to some extent a contest of labels, "warmongers" versus "appeasers," and some of the debaters flourished bare knuckles indeed. And now, the introduction of the lend-lease bill, with the committee hearings that would follow, would bring focus to the debate, giving senators and congressmen the chance to summon onto the national podium the voices they favored.

Striking divisions of opinion marked the two camps. Among former presidential candidates, Al Smith, James M. Cox (with whom FDR had run as vice-presidential nominee in 1920), John W. Davis, and the just-defeated Wendell Willkie supported the bill; Alf Landon and the veteran Socialist campaigner Norman Thomas opposed it; the only living former president, Herbert Hoover, not only attacked it but served as the godfather of the opposition. He favored aiding "other countries to defend their independence," the ex-president said, but Congress must consider "the suggestion of enormous surrender of its responsibilities." This theme found aggressive expression in a statement by the racket-busting Manhattan district attorney, Thomas E. Dewey: "The President's so-called Defense Bill would bring an end to free government in the United States"; among its dangerous provisions, it would give the president the power "to give away the whole Navy; to give away every gun in the Army; to give away every American airplane." (Since the president indeed wished to push everything possible across the Atlantic for use in the actual fight, Dewey's perception had a basis in fact, though FDR had not given anything away and would hardly dispose of his beloved navy to anybody.) The legislation had "the possibility of making the President of the United States the greatest war lord of all time," said the *Cleveland Plain Dealer*, but the newspaper believed that he would use this tremendous power wisely, "to the end that the blessings of freedom and democracy will be preserved, not only in this hemisphere, but in Europe."

A varied parade of witnesses, mostly distinguished, began passing through the committee rooms of Capitol Hill—cabinet members, ambassadors, university presidents, preachers, labor leaders, businessmen. Were the American people "about to commit suicide," as Robert M. Hutchins had said in a radio discussion, or did Americans' "only hope as a free people" lie in the defeat of the Axis powers, as President James B. Conant of Harvard declared in his testimony? The witnesses presented a lively and important spectacle, the hearings attracting the attention not only of political commentators but of the *Washington Post*'s society editor, who wanted to let her readers know which influential capital ladies were in attendance.

More than the success of a frontal assault on lend-lease, many of the bill's proponents feared the damage that could be done by flank attacks through amendments hampering its working or even in effect nullifying it. Yet supporters had to acknowledge that the president sought unprecedented powers. "No bill like it had ever been introduced," noted Roosevelt's Dutchess County neighbor, the isolationist congressman Hamilton Fish, who took it on himself to invite witnesses to testify on "the President's dictator bill."

While Congress engaged in its own dealings with the lend-lease concept, the administration continued its efforts to bridge the gap with Britain, financially and materially; an immediate shortfall of something like $225 million loomed. Arthur Purvis, back from London with a memorandum of needs and costs (some of which had appeared in Churchill's letter to the president), played an important role in the discussions with Morgenthau. Commenting that Roosevelt's "sense of trading and intuition" were "absolutely amazing," Morgenthau also noted that when Purvis asked FDR what he proposed to do in the interim period—before the anticipated passage of the lend-lease bill—"the President hedged on this thing beautifully. He gave Purvis no satisfactory answer." But the secretary did not enjoy the same privilege of evasion: he had the assignment of working out with

Purvis and Sir Frederick Phillips some kind of arrangement for the short run. The group succeeded, through various improvisations, in producing a workable plan, but it could only be temporary, because it increased Britain's financial liabilities; only the adoption of lend-lease could attack that problem.

What Roosevelt really wanted, Morgenthau had decided at the outset, was a blanket authorization to produce war material without any stipulation about which country it was for; the president would make the decision in each case according to current need. That would be excellent, Morgenthau thought, but would Congress grant the president such authority? He doubted it. Nevertheless, FDR had given Treasury the assignment of producing the bill, and, said Morgenthau, "he definitely wants it in the blank check form." The department's lawyers actually found a relevant precedent in older legislation and briskly produced the text of the bill that, after vetting by various elders, went to Capitol Hill.

When Churchill had announced the appointment of Lord Halifax as ambassador to the United States, he had expressed the "fervent hope that he may prosper in a mission as momentous as any that the Monarch has entrusted to an Englishman in the lifetime of the oldest of us here." In the manner of Halifax's departure from Britain and his arrival in America, noted an observer, "at last the Democracies had paid due tribute to symbolism." The choice of the *King George V* had attracted wide attention and then, when steaming carefully through thick fog accompanying a blizzard the battleship arrived off Annapolis, no one knew just what was to happen next.

At this point the president intervened. Perhaps making up, at least in part, for a frustration of a quarter-century earlier, when the secretary of the navy had not allowed him to sail out to greet Allied visitors, FDR ignored the storm and, in fur cap and fur-lined coat, had himself driven over icy roads to Annapolis, where he boarded the presidential yacht *Potomac* and sailed out to rendezvous with the *King George V*; the president took as much of a look as the weather allowed at the new battleship, and the *Potomac* acquired two new passengers as Lord and Lady Halifax were transferred aboard. When the yacht arrived back at Annapolis, onlookers could see the president dining with the new ambassador seated on his left and Lady Halifax on his right. The symbolism seemed to speak for itself.

Returning to London on Saturday, January 18, for a brief stop, Churchill and Hopkins moved on to the visitor's second country-house weekend, this one at Chequers. Hopkins was "really a charming and interesting man," one of Churchill's private secretaries wrote to his family. "Winston has taken to him tremendously." The two men put in a telephone call to Roosevelt, and getting into the spirit of the occasion the prime minister took the phone, saying, "Mr. President, it's me, Winston, speaking." Hopkins, however, did not take to Chequers, whose temperature indoors so chilled him that he kept his overcoat on and spent most of his working time in the bathroom—with coat on there as well—because it offered a faint trace of what was said to be central heating (though some believed that the bit of warmth came only from a hot-water pipe that ran through the room). The American awoke "on a cold, dreary morning—and the formal garden of this lovely old place seems very unhappy under the onslaughts of wind and snow and cold. I have just finished my breakfast in bed—of kidney and bacon and prunes—the papers have been read telling of Halifax's arrival and the President's personal welcome. This will please the P.M. no end."

Back in London on Monday, Hopkins found little rest if less

physical exertion than his week's excursion with Churchill had demanded. He spent the next few days in almost constant meetings with cabinet ministers and other high officials and military figures, and Friday morning would see him at Victoria Station for the beginning of another Churchill guided tour, this one taking him to south coast ports.

Hopkins's arrival in Britain appeared to hold great significance for a wide variety of people; letters seeking aid or asking for appointments poured into the U.S. embassy. One letter met him on his arrival— from a sixteen-year-old schoolboy named Harry Hopkins, who, as the visitor's namesake, gave him a formal welcome to the country. Since his mother was French and all her closest relatives were in occupied France, "under the heel of the Germans," the boy said, one could see what the "sympathy and understanding and help" Hopkins brought from America meant to him. A young woman, who had been married only a month when her husband was taken prisoner in the fighting at Calais in 1940, just wanted Hopkins somehow to get "just one letter" to him so that he would know that she was all right.

Lady Astor extended an "urgent invitation" for Hopkins to come down to the famous Cliveden, where she would have people for him to meet.

Newsreel companies were trying for a film interview with Hopkins, and the Associated Press had discovered no photo of the president's representative in their files. Where might they catch him?

Most requests received the same answer: the demands of Hopkins's primary activity, shadowing the prime minister, left him little time for any informal or nonscheduled activities. Embassy representatives had to decline, on Hopkins's behalf, lunch, dinner, or other sorts of invitations from the first lord of the Admiralty and the secretary of state for India, for the chairman of the Labour Party, for the Chinese ambassador, for the former lord chancellor, for the president of Czechoslovakia and Prince Bernhard of the Netherlands, and a number of other dignitaries of various kinds. Hopkins's presence in Britain clearly possessed an enormous symbolic force.

Among the notable events of the crowded week following Hopkins's Chequers weekend, one had particular importance. On Wednesday evening Lord Beaverbrook gave a dinner for the distinguished visitor at Claridge's. Not only one of the country's three or four commanding press barons but also minister of aircraft production, a role Churchill had created for him in the emergency of the past summer, Beaverbrook belonged to the same elite transatlantic group as Hopkins—fixers, men with varying status and titles who devoted much of their effort to making things work for the heads of government. "The Beaver," as he was known, represented an unusual case in this specialized trade; a man of enormous power and energy, he at times proved of unmatched value, while at other times he would seem, capriciously, to be undermining the prime minister rather than supporting him. He and Hopkins had met at lunch with Herschel Johnson on Monday of the preceding week, just before Hopkins dashed off to King's Cross, and, perhaps because of their similarities, had failed to respond to each other as friendly brothers in the same fraternity.

For Wednesday evening, Beaverbrook had invited an array of publishers, editors, and reporters to meet and talk with the president's representative, who had seemed almost mysterious to the press, having since his arrival said very little in public. As journalists, the members of the group felt a natural curiosity about the man and the obviously unusual mission; after dinner, amiably and informally, the host presented the guest of honor to the crowd. Speaking in his usual almost diffident way, Hopkins delivered a message expressing American solidarity with Britain—not surprising to those who knew him but good news to many of those present, including representatives of provincial newspapers as well as the metropolitan press.

Then Beaverbrook pulled off a neat coup; at his urging, Hopkins moved around the table, progressively sitting and talking with persons from the various papers. He had apparently found time for a bit of cramming or had been well briefed; the editors and reporters expressed gratification at his knowledge of their individual papers, and one Shakespearean in the group said that they all went home happily stimulated by this "little touch of Harry in the night." The success of the dinner also warmed relations between Beaverbrook and Hopkins.

Also warmed by the evening, or at least by reports of it, FBI director J. Edgar Hoover reported to President Roosevelt that "it appeared from facial expressions that all the guests were quite happy as the result of the dinner and discussions." Sitting in the coffee room, representatives of the FBI heard comments about "the very charming manner of Mr. Hopkins, his keen insight into current problems and the very remarkable fact that he combined a very charming but almost shy personality with a very vigorous and dynamic mentality. In no instance was any unfavorable comment made ..." FDR seemed amused that, during its study of "various phases of intelligence operations" in Britain, the Bureau was keeping tabs on his special envoy.

14

"THE ALL-SEEING EYE"

On the following Friday morning, Churchill resumed his role of high-level tour guide, taking Hopkins off to Dover, where the visitor could be duly impressed by the heavy gun batteries and could look across twenty hazy miles of Channel to the low hills of Occupied France. "Mr. Churchill himself conducted Mr. Hopkins over some of the most hush-hush parts of our defences in the Dover area," said a reporter, who observed of Hopkins that "in tribute to his keen but unobtrusive methods of investigation, he is known among the high-ups of the Defence Services as 'The All-Seeing Eye.'"

That evening, weekending at Chequers again, Hopkins said that in Dover, when the prime minister passed by, he had heard a workman tell another: "There goes the bloody British Empire." Jock Colville felt that nothing for a long time had given Churchill as much pleasure as that remark. At dinner the prime minister also vouchsafed the view that German invasion could no longer be successful. He now woke up in the mornings like his old self, he said, feeling as if he "had a bottle of champagne inside him and glad that another day had come."

For Sunday, Colville had arranged an outing for Hopkins to a friend's country house, West Wycombe Park, a striking eighteenth-century "stately home" of blended Palladian and neoclassical styles. Afterward the visitor was taken to meet Fred Cripps, the worldly and engaging brother of the austere Labour politician Sir Stafford Cripps, whom Churchill had dispatched to Moscow as ambassador. Clementine Churchill, who seemed displeased at not having been a member of the party, suspected that Hopkins had been lured by the well-known charms of Cripps's wife, Violet; the lady in fact proved so attractive, Colville noted, that Hopkins stayed for lunch.

Hopkins also met another attractive woman during his country-house rounds—Pamela, the daughter-in-law whose picture Churchill had proudly pointed out to him. Just twenty years old, this redhead with a fine complexion that seemed almost translucent struck Hopkins as "delicious-looking"; a longtime friend of Randolph Churchill's, the novelist Evelyn Waugh, liked Pam's "kittenish eyes" and "very friendly disposition." Waugh also noted that "in the nature of things" Pam had "great superiority" of information. She and Randolph, Winston's only son, had been married just since October 1939. Even though Pam had efficiently produced the much-desired son and heir, the relationship could hardly be considered a successful marriage—not because Randolph was in the army and preparing, along with Waugh, to ship out to the Middle East in a Commando unit, but because he ranked as one of the most notorious and obnoxious drunks in the United Kingdom, in an era in which alcoholic behavior was little understood and ineffectually treated.

Baby Winston, not quite two months old in late January 1941, had an impressive array of godparents, among them Lord Beaverbrook and Brendan Bracken. The Beaver, whose close but in-and-out relationship with Winston Churchill went back to the Great War era, had taken on Randolph and Pamela as a sort of protégé couple, frequently having them to stay at Cherkley, his country house in Surrey. A native of Ontario who had built up his wealth in the securities markets,

Beaverbrook (then William Maxwell Aitken) had left Canada under something of a cloud having to do with questionable stock transfers. Arriving in London, the center of the empire, this unabashed adventurer got himself into Parliament and began creating an empire of his own on Fleet Street; one of his newspapers, the *Daily Express*, built up the greatest circulation of any newspaper in the world—more than three million. Always promoting in print his views of the moment, Beaverbrook seemed to prove a critic's point that in Britain, freedom of the press guaranteed the proprietor the right to express his own prejudices as long as the advertisers did not object. Seeming to love the game more than the substance, Beaverbrook delighted in making things happen, in tinkering and goading. His energy and puckish appeal made him a considerable charmer when he chose; like Harry Hopkins, he came from the ranks of the unconventional types that held a special appeal for Churchill.

In one way or another, Beaverbrook would subsidize needy friends; such debtors could repay him simply by giving him information. More than anything else, in fact, Beaverbrook seemed driven by curiosity. His young friend Pamela Churchill likewise loved information; during social evenings at Cherkley, amidst the political doers and social elite of the country, she could learn much—indeed, she had developed what might be called listening skills, the ability to draw people out. She also liked being at 10 Downing Street or Chequers, in the center of things, in close connection with her fond father-in-law. It was perhaps not surprising that, even though she was just out of her teens and had little genuine education, Hopkins could say that she had more information than anyone else in England. He also liked her.

In talk on Sunday evening at Chequers, Hopkins repeated his thought about Roosevelt's concern with the next few months rather than the distant future. In regard to public opinion, Hopkins said, the president faced four groups: Nazis and Communists, who called for a negotiated peace but really wanted a German victory; a group, with which Hopkins identified Joe Kennedy, that wanted to help Britain but not to run any risk of war; a majority that supported the president in sending maximum aid regardless of the risk; and a group of 10 to 15 percent of the people, including Stimson, Knox, and the leaders of the army and navy, who favored entering the war immediately.

The president, said Hopkins, believed that if Britain should lose, America would then suffer defeat herself. He would lead public opinion, not follow it, and his boldness constituted a striking factor in the overall situation. The president did not want war but would not shrink from it. (These were interesting points for Hopkins to make, since many in his third and fourth groups accused FDR of dilatoriness and excessive caution, and, on the other hand, Hopkins himself seemed to have decided on his own to say in various ways, at Downing Street and in Glasgow, that Roosevelt was ready to go to war.)

During the weekend Hopkins had shown the prime minister and General Sir John Dill, chief of the Imperial General Staff, details of the U.S. armament program. It was "gigantic," but Churchill warned Hopkins, on the basis of the British experience, not to expect the full results for about eighteen months. The American also had the opportunity to learn one of the advantages a monarchy enjoyed when politicians needed to reward a supporter: "It is better," said Churchill, "to give a man a peerage than to give him a contract"—hence the value of the House of Lords. But, Colville commented, Hopkins "did not seem to notice."

On Monday, Hopkins rode up to London with Professor Lindemann, who presented him with a book of statistics outlining Britain's assets and her needs. Colville wistfully noted that during the weekend, Hopkins had smoked most of his Chesterfields.

With so many persons to see and so much to do and to take in, Hopkins drew considerable benefit from the extension of his stay in Britain. The president had chosen a new ambassador—John Gilbert Winant, former governor of New Hampshire—and Secretary Hull had suggested that Hopkins stay in London until Winant arrived in early February; overall, Hopkins's mission was growing from the original two weeks to about six.

The new arrangement gave Hopkins an outing with the prime minister on January 31 to Portsmouth, where the two made a "hustling tour" of the dockyard. "Spontaneous cheering greeted [Churchill] wherever he went," noted a newspaper correspondent, "and he gave the 'thumbs-up' sign to dockyard workers who assured him by repeated shouts that they were not down-hearted." The effects of the bombing reminded one of Churchill's secretaries of the damage he had seen in France in the last war. As he had in Glasgow, the prime minister did not sugarcoat his message: the country faced "long and hard" ordeals, but "we shall come through." As on earlier stops, Hopkins was struck by the air almost of reverence with which the workers and the people of the area responded to Churchill.

At Chequers that evening Hopkins produced, from somewhere, a box of American phonograph records, which put everyone in a mellow and sentimental mood, Churchill walking about the drafty and dimly lit Great Hall and occasionally doing a little dance step. "He gets on like a house afire with Hopkins," said the secretary in a letter; indeed, "it is quite extraordinary how Hopkins [has] endeared himself to everyone here he has met." The music Hopkins provided gave the group a perhaps welcome change from a standard late-evening spectacle in the Great Hall—the prime minister pacing slowly up and down in silence, while the phonograph played the same three or four

French marches over and over. No one ever presumed to ask him what occupied his thoughts during these sessions.

Hopkins also spent part of an evening with a celebrated fellow American, Wendell Willkie, the recently defeated Republican presidential candidate, who arrived in England bearing an unusual message from Roosevelt to Churchill: a verse from Henry Wadsworth Longfellow's poem "The Building of the Ship," which the president had written out in longhand. (FDR, curiously, had taken the time to do it during the day of his precedent-setting third inauguration.) A strong supporter of lend-lease, to the disgust of many of his previous supporters, Willkie, Roosevelt noted, "is truly helping to keep politics out over here." As the titular head of one of the two great American political parties, Willkie received a thoroughly high-level reception in England, including a night at Chequers. Hopkins, diplomatically, kept to his own pursuits, meeting Willkie only the one time.

"I think this verse applies to your people as it does to us," Roosevelt wrote in his letter to Churchill, who some days later folded a dramatic, rise-and-fall rendition of the verse into a radio address:

> *Sail on, O Ship of State!*
> *Sail on, O Union, strong and great!*
> *Humanity with all its fears,*
> *With all the hopes of future years,*
> *Is hanging breathless on thy fate.*

"I shall have it framed as a souvenir of these tremendous days," Churchill wrote back, "and as a mark of our friendly relations, which have been built up telegraphically but also telepathically under all the stresses." These lines, wrote Churchill, "were an inspiration." That, and no more, was precisely what the president had intended.

On his first Monday in London, Hopkins had made a quick duty call at Buckingham Palace and departed without fulfilling his formal purpose, delivery of a letter from President Roosevelt to George VI; the embassy corrected this oversight the next day. On January 30, Hopkins returned to the palace to lunch with the king and queen in a session that lasted almost two hours; the detailed account in his diary made it plain that he thoroughly enjoyed himself.

The three lunched in a dining room next to the king's office, with much of the early talk devoted to the royal visit to America in the spring of 1939—a great public-relations coup for Britain, with FDR as the smiling executive producer. The schedule had featured everything from a White House state dinner to a beer-and-hot-dog picnic at Hyde Park, with the king's simple friendliness and the queen's charm and glamour winning over the large crowds that flocked to see the royal visitors. (FDR had been quite taken with the king, who had "an almost American sense of humor" and was "completely natural and put all the 'royalness' aside when in private"; the queen "could *never* quite forget she was a queen," though "a fine person.") Hopkins's eight-year-old daughter, Diana, seeing the queen in jewels and tiara, cried to her father, "I've just seen the Fairy Queen." The queen told Hopkins "quite casually," however, that since the visit she had written three letters to Mrs. Roosevelt with no response, but she would try again. The president had thoroughly enjoyed meeting them, Hopkins assured the king, and he urged his host to keep in touch with Roosevelt.

On asking Hopkins about his expedition to Scapa Flow, King George heard the surprising news that the demonstration firing of a rocket had produced an unexpected result: instead of heading off toward a presumed enemy, the projectile had come streaking toward the American visitor, landing only about five feet away from him. The king commented drily that Churchill had failed to tell him about this incident. "The reason for that," Hopkins rushed to say, "was that the Prime Minister didn't think it was funny and I did!"

The king impressed Hopkins with his detailed knowledge of his military and naval commanders and his evident close attention to all important dispatches, including, Hopkins noted with admiration, one that Hopkins himself "had sent Sunday night through the Foreign Office." Then the king closely questioned his caller about his opinions of British ministers, while adding his own candid comments. "He left me," Hopkins noted, "with the impression that he did not have a very high opinion of many of them, particularly Beaverbrook, who clearly he does not trust, although he recognizes his good qualities." (Few of those close to Churchill had much use for the adventurer-tycoon; Clementine Churchill distrusted and detested him.) "He thinks very highly of the Commander-In-Chief of the military forces"—no such position existed; Hopkins presumably meant Sir John Dill, a schoolmasterly commander who, unfortunately, had an almost total inability to work well with Churchill.

Like everybody else, Hopkins said, the king had "great confidence in Churchill. He discussed quite freely with me the great difficulties this country would have if anything should happen to Churchill, and felt there was no one even remotely as competent as him in managing the affairs of Britain." (This represented a total turnabout by the king, a Halifax man back in May 1940.) The king proceeded to make unflattering comments about various Labour Party leaders, even the generally admired Ernest Bevin ("talks too much and is not a particularly solid man who can be depended on").

Sirens had sounded just as the three sat down to lunch, and as coffee and port were served a bell rang. "'That means we have to go to the air raid shelter,' the king said, so we immediately walked down two or three flights of stairs, through a dark hallway, led by a guard, through several doors and finally landed in a small lighted room with a table and chairs." The royal couple slept in adjacent rooms, so that in case of alarm at night they were already there. The king and queen did not seem to like taking shelter, but apparently, Hopkins decided, they had reluctantly given way after much argument.

Concerning the question of possible British use of the Irish ports, King George declared the prime minister of Eire, Eamon de Valera, "a fanatic who, while not necessarily pro-German, is so bitterly anti-British that his actions amount to the same thing." (The king hardly overstated the case: de Valera's government had gone so far as to forbid newspapers in Eire from acknowledging that any Irishmen were fighting in the British forces.) His Majesty strongly doubted whether President Roosevelt could have any success in trying to get access to the ports. As Churchill later wrote, the denial of the ports "exerted its baneful influence" on British naval operations and security.

Hopkins emphasized the president's determination to defeat Hitler and his deep conviction that Britain and America "had a mutuality of interest in this respect." The British, Hopkins said, could depend upon receiving aid from the United States, at which "they were both very deeply moved." The king hoped and believed that Roosevelt and Churchill could meet in the near future; he "greatly appreciated the President's speeches," he said, and he knew from his visit "what was deeply embedded in the president's mind. He told me to tell the President how much beloved he was by the people of Britain." Earlier, Hopkins had noted: "If ever two people realized that Britain is fighting for its life it is these two."

That same evening, Hopkins met a number of other persons who found themselves in a position to realize the same basic fact about Britain's fight: with an MP, Ellen Wilkinson, he visited several air raid shelters to chat with Londoners, this outing representing one of his rare chances to move outside elite circles.

Quite apart from high-level diplomatic socializing, Hopkins engaged in detailed work having to do with the material side of his mission for the president, distilling his researches about Britain's situation and needs into a lead report and a series of follow-up documents. After mentioning people he had conferred with and places he had seen, Hopkins declared: "I believe that insofar as it is possible to get a picture of the situation here in a short time, I have got a reasonably clear perception not only of the physical defenses of Britain but of the opinions of the men who are directing the forces of this nation. Your 'former Naval person' is not only the Prime Minister, he is the directing force behind the strategy and the conduct of the war in all its essentials. He has an amazing hold on the British people of all classes and groups."

Hopkins spoke of the danger of invasion, which he believed "most of the Cabinet and all of the military leaders" expected by May 1. "The spirit of this people and their determination to resist invasion is beyond praise," Hopkins said; "the Germans will have to do more than kill a few hundred thousand people here before they can defeat Britain. I therefore cannot urge too strongly that any action you may take to meet the immediate needs here must be based on the assumption that invasion will come before May 1st. If Germany fails to win this invasion then I believe her sun is set."

Probably few Cabinet members actually believed at the time that the Germans would mount an invasion; Churchill definitely did not expect it and had not for several months. Various pieces of intelligence had made it plain that, however seriously Hitler may have entertained the idea, he had abandoned it; on October 31 the War Cabinet Defence Committee had concluded that the danger had become "relatively remote." But the prime minister's fondness for Hopkins had not led him to share this information with his guest; national considerations as Churchill saw them trumped any personal feelings. He preferred to keep President Roosevelt concerned about the imminent possibility of German landings. Even so, at Chequers Churchill had freely expressed his view that an invasion would not be successful, and he would shortly demonstrate the point by pushing through, before May 1, the dispatch of a convoy carrying tanks—307 of them—out of England to the British army in Egypt. More than any other politician of the day, he knew from experience—the Dardanelles disaster in 1915—the formidable difficulties involved in amphibious invasion, even before the air became an important element. At the same time, he told the president on January 28, the Germans were "persevering in their preparations to invade this country." But he was not being quite truthful; intelligence decrypts had indicated otherwise.

Nevertheless, those responsible for the fate of Britain could not allow themselves to forget that the Germans had produced spectacular surprises in 1940 and might have more tricks in their bag for the current year. From the German point of view, their officials told the Japanese foreign minister in March, the question was not how to win the war but how to conclude the war that was already won. One way or the other, they suggested, the end would come soon.

"I am convinced," Hopkins concluded his substantive points, relying in this respect on both what Churchill had and had not told him, "that if we act boldly and promptly on a few major fronts we can get enough material to Britain within the next few weeks to give her the additional strength she needs to turn back Hitler."

In subsequent cables, proceeding with great assurance as if lend-lease had already become law, Hopkins produced a cumulative report that represented a notable achievement in collating highly diverse materials. Some of the information supplied by the British had an admirable explicitness: in the general category of bottlenecks was

"LIST OF ITEMS URGENTLY REQUIRED FROM U.S.A." This particular list dealt with aircraft and related items; for instance, the RAF had received 315 Tomahawk (Curtis P-40) fighter planes, but 100 lacked propellers. With reference to the bottlenecks, the cover letter noted that Hopkins had "very kindly offered to give this matter his personal attention."

Hugh Dalton, minister for economic warfare, sent Hopkins, at his request, a memorandum on leaks in the British blockade of the Continent—for example, copper coming from Latin America to Russia or Japan and going on from there to Germany. Here, it appeared, the United States was talking a strong game but not acting, and Dalton hoped that Hopkins could stiffen Washington to take "the necessary decision of principle." This message was followed by a memorandum so thorough as to constitute almost a textbook on blockade.

Hopkins reported on Britain's need for heavy bombers to attack German factories. "It is absolutely urgent," he wrote, "that the maximum number of B-17 BSC's or D's in addition to the twenty already agreed upon be released without delay." To "prevent fatal loss of time," the aircraft should be sent complete with armaments and spare parts; men who knew how to fly and maintain the planes should deliver them. If air corps pilots ferried the planes, they would gain valuable experience and at the same time allow RAF pilots to remain with their fighting units. Beyond that, since the weather and the effects of enemy attacks combined to hamper the training of pilots in Britain, Hopkins suggested that at least five American flying schools be turned over to the authorities for this purpose.

Other messages concerned rifles and ammunition, the need for more merchant shipping tonnage (Britain's net loss thus far in the war: two million tons) and for more old destroyers ("I have seen destroyers being repaired at several yards and have had repeated evidence of the almost desperate speed with which they are trying to get these ships back with the fleet") and more PBY patrol planes for spotting submarines, and other matters of supply.

Though hardly privy to Hopkins's secret messages, a political correspondent for Lord Beaverbrook's *Daily Express* had enough inside information to declare that Hopkins had "made one of the most comprehensive surveys of Britain at war ever attempted, and there is no doubt that his report to the President will be a document of historic importance." Hopkins's report "should give President Roosevelt a vivid picture of our defensive and offensive plans and preparations, the state of public morale—which Mr. Hopkins finds extraordinarily high—and our needs in various kinds of war supplies." Thus, said the reporter, Hopkins was concluding his "quiet look round" in Britain.

Hopkins tended to have adventures and misadventures with his clothing. Early in his stay in London he had acquired a number of items of the highest quality—a sweater, several shirts, socks, and underwear from Sulka and Austin Reed. Now, on Saturday, February 8, after he had checked out of Claridge's, the staff discovered that the visitor had left behind four shirts (collar attached) and other bits of laundry, which, the embassy soon informed him, could not be forwarded to him by diplomatic pouch but would go by parcel post. If the hotel staff could have prevented the problem, they would surely have done it—they were devoted to this unusual visitor. One of the valets had kept a regular eye on Hopkins so that he could check collar and tie before the guest left for an appointment. Another valet, appalled at Hopkins's crumpled gray felt hat with its upturned and undulating brim, kidnapped it one morning in a gallant but ineffective effort to block it into respectability. A waiter who brought Hopkins his morning coffee, toast, and fruit termed him "very genial—considerate—if I may say so, lovable—quite different from other ambassadors we've had here."

That Saturday morning, weekending as usual at Chequers, Churchill was working on a radio speech to be delivered the following evening, and when Hopkins arrived to pay a farewell call he found himself pressed into service, thereby becoming surely the first person ever to serve both an American president and a British prime minister as a speechwriter. The day stretched late into the evening, with Hopkins finally saying goodbye and heading off on a special train for Bournemouth, near the Poole flying-boat base, for scheduled departure the next morning.

Unfavorable weather forced postponement of the flight for a day, however, and Hopkins and his companions—Bracken, Commander Thompson, and a security officer, Lieutenant Anthony McComas—listened to the Sunday night address in the hotel lounge. Beamed to America and aimed at American opinion, this was the speech in which Churchill delivered the Longfellow verse sent by Roosevelt. He went on to say: "What is the answer that I shall give in our name to this great man, the thrice-chosen head of a nation of 130,000,000? Here is the answer which I will give to President Roosevelt:

> *Put your confidence in us. Give us your faith and your blessing, and under Providence all will be well. We shall not fail or falter. We shall not weaken or tire. Neither the sudden shock of battle nor the long-drawn trials of vigilance and exhaustion will wear us down.*
>
> *Give us the tools and we will finish the job.*

The speech made its particular contribution to the lend-lease debate with that memorable last sentence. The prime minister added the assurance: "We do not need the gallant armies which are forming throughout the American Union. We do not need them this year, nor next year; nor any year that I can foresee." Certainly, Churchill, as he had earlier said, did not relish or expect the collision of mass armies; certainly Roosevelt hoped that the "tools" could indeed do the job. But whether Churchill, even with the faith he and some of his associates had developed in strategic air power—as in the B-17s for which Hopkins was pressing Washington—foresaw no role at all for American armies is quite a different question.

"It has been a great pleasure to me to make friends with Hopkins, who has been a great comfort and encouragement to everyone he has met," Churchill cabled Roosevelt.

"He is an outstanding liberal of the very best type," the *Manchester Guardian* said of Hopkins, quoting an unnamed person who knew him well. "He has, I understand, been taken into the confidence of the British Government as no foreigner has ever been, not even a French Prime Minister when our alliance with the French was at its height." (In its reference to "height," the *Guardian* was presumably thinking back to the Great War.)

Speaking of the visitor's attempts to avoid publicity, the *Evening Standard* declared that he had earned two nicknames for himself: "Poker Face" and "Oyster."

"Mr. Hopkins is an American whose charm is entirely devoid of self-consciousness," noted a *Daily Telegraph* commentator. "Though he does not worry about dress, he was occasionally bewildered during his London stay." One evening, it seemed, Hopkins appeared to dine with the prime minister wearing a dinner jacket. To his surprise, he found Churchill "in something closely resembling pyjamas." Returning the next evening, "determined to conform with custom," Hopkins arrived "in a somewhat battered lounge suit. It was only to find his host in a dinner jacket." After that, the reporter observed, Hopkins "gave up trying to guess what rules governed the customs of the strange people he had come to visit." (Of course, Churchill, a dedicated wardrobe hobbyist, could hardly be taken as an exemplar of British style.) "Only recently out of hospital," said the *Telegraph*, "Mr. Hopkins must have found his contact with Mr. Churchill at once bracing and trying," what with a trip in a northern blizzard and nightly talks going on till three o'clock.

What Hopkins himself thought found brief but sincere expression in a formal little note he left for Churchill:

> *My Dear Mr. Prime Minister:*
> *I shall never forget these days with you—your supreme confidence and will to victory—Britain I have ever liked—I like it the more. As I leave for America tonight I wish you great and good luck—confusion to your enemies and victory for Britain.*
>
>

Ever so cordially,
Harry Hopkins

Never forget these days? Of course he wouldn't—the boy from Iowa had just had the adventure of a lifetime. Perhaps these amazing days had provided a measure of recompense for all the pain and privations his frail body had suffered; they had certainly provided a kind and level of excitement he would never have experienced as the director of a library up in Dutchess County.

15

"A NEW MAGNA CHARTA"

With a thirty- to forty-mile-an-hour wind whipping the waters of Bowery Bay into whitecaps, the landing was not proving a happy one. Though the Yankee Clipper had arrived at 8:04 a.m., about forty-five minutes ahead of its revised schedule, maneuvering the big flying boat on the surface presented the Pan-Am skipper, Captain A. L. McCullough, with a stiff challenge. After failing several times in his attempts to taxi his ship in to the landing float, the captain had to call for help. The airport authorities sent out a motor launch and crewmen fastened a line to the prow of the clipper, creating a sea anchor that allowed McCullough to end his hour-long effort to bring the ship in.

At the terminal a distinguished group awaited one of the disembarking travelers. Confronted by a battery of newsreel cameras as he emerged from the Clipper, the last passenger wore the shapeless gray hat that had resisted the ministrations of the valet at Claridge's and had given his British friends much amusement; London hatters had offered him replacements, and seeking this one as a souvenir of the memorable visit, Brendan Bracken had made a lavish bid of £100 for it. The passenger saw, close by, an old friend, who had walked down almost to the end of the float. "Hello, there, Fiorello," Harry Hopkins called to the mayor of New York. The welcoming group also included David K. Niles, who had been assistant secretary of commerce under Hopkins; Hopkins's son David and his wife, who had been in the bon voyage party on January 6; and Hopkins's good friend Averell Harriman—but none of the onlookers could have eyesight penetrating enough to catch the passing of an invisible torch.

Primed by an analysis that had appeared in the *News Chronicle* some days earlier, reporters at LaGuardia knew what was being said in London: "When Mr. Hopkins reports to the President there are few secrets of the War Cabinet that he will not be able to repeat. He has, so to speak, lived in the Prime Minister's pocket ever since his arrival on January 9, and has attended conferences in Downing Street from which all but a few of the Service chiefs are always excluded."

What, then, had the president's emissary concluded from his unprecedented access to the inner workings of the British government and from his observations in his travels about the country? Seeming for a moment reluctant to talk, Hopkins then declared, "One thing I can say is this: I don't think Hitler can lick these people. I think he's up against as tough a crowd as there is, and I think they have the military stuff, with the help we can give them, to win. It won't be a stalemated war." He added, in response to another question, that "the British people are determined to win. They don't need our men, but they badly need some real help from us." The British had a "wonderful" spirit, he said, with no "doubts about winning."

More personally, Hopkins said in answer to questions that he had experienced many bombings but he did not "want to overemphasize the air raids. There were sometimes six or eight alarms a night, but I didn't go through any more than anybody else." What about Winston Churchill? "I think Mr. Churchill is a great man and a great leader," he responded. "He is leading all the people—labor, the armed forces, everyone." In answer to a question about a possible invasion, Hopkins said, "I think most of the people there are expecting an invasion soon." Pressed for specific information about preparations to meet the danger, including Britain's needs for destroyers or any other specific war matériel, Hopkins said drily, "Well now, we could get into a detailed discussion of the situation," thus concluding the discussion.

Smilingly apologetic to the reporters for having spoiled their Sunday by the early hour of his arrival while, a reporter noted, seeming impatient to get on with his duties, Hopkins left the terminal for a meeting at the Hotel Roosevelt, in midtown, with John Winant, who had not gone to London as early as Secretary Hull had expected and would therefore receive his briefing from Hopkins in New York. He wanted to tell the new ambassador, Hopkins said opaquely, "those things I thought would help him."

Winant, a three-time governor of New Hampshire, had served since 1939 as director of the International Labor Organization, an affiliate of the League of Nations; he also had been FDR's first chairman of the Social Security Board. Sometimes described as "Lincolnesque," Winant, a shy man with awkward gestures, often twisting and turning as if he had caught an arm in the lining of his coat sleeve, struck some as an odd choice for ambassador to the Court of St. James's, and he appears to have been picked only after Bill Bullitt declined the honor. When Henry Morgenthau suggested to the president that Winant might not have the kind of financial position that would enable him to take the job, FDR displayed no interest in the point, contenting himself with saying, "If he has any money troubles, they are his wife's." The secretary let it drop.

In any case, Winant's involvement with labor issues fitted him to play an extended version of the role that newspaper reporters had imagined for Hopkins in England as an observer of the war-driven social revolution believed to be in progress; linked on the one hand with the Conservative Churchill, Roosevelt through Winant could establish continuing contact with Labour Party leaders, who had favored the appointment. Winant had immediately celebrated his selection by declaring in a nationwide broadcast that victory in the war must be followed by the building of "a democratic world of tomorrow," based on social justice and economic security. Welcomed by the *Times* of London, the new ambassador, said a former colleague in Geneva, represented "an example of the best product of American democracy."

The meeting with Winant gave the weary Hopkins a chance to rest, and, taking advantage of the light Sunday afternoon traffic in midtown Manhattan, he stayed at the Roosevelt until 3:10, leaving for Penn Station just in time to catch the 3:30 train to Washington. On disembarking from the parlor car at Washington's Union Station, Hopkins had another round with reporters, telling them that the British were "desperately in need of help." He looked fit and was in good spirits, the newsmen noted, and he assured them that with American assistance Britain would win the war. Eyeing Hopkins's swollen black briefcase, the reporters jealously presumed that it held secrets for the president's eyes alone. Personally, the trip had changed Hopkins in one respect; always a reluctant flier, he spoke enthusiastically about his trip home—even though the Clipper had been delayed in the Caribbean by weather. "It's just like riding in a baby carriage," he said. "Not a bit rough."

The trip had also brought about something of a change in an entirely different realm. Aghast at Hopkins's absentminded handling of confidential materials, security authorities had pointed out his need to improve, but to make sure of things Lieutenant McComas had accompanied him on his homeward journey—a needed move because his luggage contained secret technical papers as well as political documents. Story-hunting New York reporters, fishing for a connection between the Irish Guards lieutenant and Hopkins, learned only that the officer had recently been serving with the Imperial General Staff and had been detached for a brief mission to Washington, after which, he said, he would return to "our little war over there."

Stepping into a limousine sent by the president, Hopkins was driven back to the big house that had been his home for the past eight months; he arrived in time to join a birthday dinner for Elinor Morgenthau, the secretary's wife. After the socializing, FDR and his emissary talked till two o'clock in the morning, and with the president having cleared his schedule as much as possible, more talk followed the next day.

An American correspondent in London had offered a shrewd guess about what the special representative would say to the president when he returned home. Hopkins had come to London, said the correspondent, "prepared to make a realistic diagnosis. He asked for all the facts, bad as well as good, and he got them," and "some of them will not make pleasant reading"—or listening—"for the President." In particular, Hopkins would "certainly blast the easy and wishful idea that the British people are so brave and strong that the Germans cannot lick them. He seems to have been impressed by the British fortitude but not by the idea that this fortitude would necessarily win the war."

Indeed, Hopkins, while adopting an optimistic tone in his few remarks, had acknowledged to reporters Britain's desperate need for American aid. The correspondent believed that the president had dispatched his representative to Britain because "his own idea of the situation was neither complete nor sufficiently realistic," and, in fact, Hopkins returned with the grim news that nobody in America understood how bare Britain's cupboard was—in ships and aircraft, in weapons, in important elements of production like machine tools, in food and other supplies. Nor did many Britons understand how the American government worked, both formally and informally, with its separation of powers divorcing the legislature from the executive, and its proud territoriality. During the recent presidential campaign, Wendell Willkie had declared that if Roosevelt won, the United States would enter the war by April—and April was now only six weeks away. Surely, Britons thought, the president, the reelected head of the American government as well as chief of state, would be leading Congress into a declaration any day now.

Certainly Hopkins did not represent Roosevelt's only source of information about the situation of Britain, but, nevertheless, this lone ex–social worker had been assigned to take the measure of a whole country at war and to produce conclusions on which a national policy could be based. Here Hopkins's years as a New Deal administrator, dealing with millions of people and dispensing billions of dollars, and his practical political experience of course counted for a great deal. He had come back from Britain more of a partisan than perhaps might have been expected by anyone who had not been exposed to the Churchillian force (and, said General Ismay, "he had got right inside Churchill's mind"), but he had succeeded in his unlikely mission: he brought with him the essential news Roosevelt had hoped for—not that with American help Britain could win the war, whatever the prime minister might say about finishing the job, but that with American help Britain could survive; Roosevelt could bet on Churchill to stay in the ring. The help, however, was of vital importance.

Not only did Hopkins's reports all say so, but a prominent American military analyst, looking from his own point of view, saw the same picture. While the British Empire with its 500 million varied peoples might seem far more formidable than its enemies—noted the commentator—this empire, rather than closely knit, sprawled across the globe, united only by trade and linked only by sea; most of its land remained undeveloped, and most of its population could not be looked to for troops. Hence the 46 million people of the United Kingdom must bear the main burden of the war effort, and the necessary material must come from its own factories—and from the United States. That constituted the basic fact. On the other hand, Germany with its 80 million people had a good supply of fighting men and a steel industry that could produce twice as much as Britain's. The British could not come close to putting in the field even fifty trained divisions, compared with Germany's 250, half of these crack combat outfits. Britain simply was not big enough to "finish the job."

The Monroe Room, on the second floor of the White House, had seen many historic events, including President McKinley's signing of the treaty ending the Spanish-American War in 1898. This Monday morning saw it serving as the site of Eleanor Roosevelt's weekly press conference, with some forty newspaperwomen on hand, when a new factor entered the equation. Looking out through the open door, reporters glimpsed a male figure, clad in an old blue-and-white bathrobe, strolling by. This figure apparently heard their voices at the same moment, took a quick look into the room, then dived across the hall to take refuge in the suite King George and Queen Elizabeth had occupied during their visit in 1939. There Harry Hopkins remained until somebody closed the Monroe Room door; the president's adviser then felt able to continue his post-breakfast walk from the president's study back to his own room.

That afternoon, while the president and Hopkins, now fully dressed, sat in conference with Morgenthau, Stimson, Knox, Secretary of Agriculture Claude Wickard, and Harold Smith, the director of the budget, events were stirring on Capitol Hill. This conference, Steve Early told reporters, represented the beginning of a series of meetings to make arrangements for administering lend-lease, "when and if" the bill passed; then, biting his tongue, Early hastily had another go at the sentence, this time omitting "and if."

The time had now come for the U.S. Senate to take center stage. Under the supportive guidance of Senator Walter George of Georgia, chairman of the Foreign Relations Committee, the lend-lease bill had emerged from the committee virtually intact; the House had added a few amendments to the administration's original bill, largely for the sake of self-assertion, and the Senate committee had made its own revisions to those. Just the day before the committee's action, in a curious and total turnaround, Thomas E. Dewey had astounded the Republican faithful at a Lincoln Day dinner by expressing his support for the bill, as amended by the House; the *Chicago Tribune* charged him with "betrayal" of the party. And the officially most prominent Republican, Wendell Willkie, had rushed home from his overseas tour, he said, "to do anything I can to help Britain in her fight for freedom." For him, the *Tribune* produced such characterizations as "Quisling," "barefaced fraud," and, worst of all, "New Deal Democrat."

Eager at this point not simply to avoid any conflict but to win the widest possible support for lend-lease, the president had proved flexible on changes to the bill. Now, while FDR held his planning meeting at the White House, Alben Barkley of Kentucky, the majority leader, opened the debate on the bill by telling his assembled colleagues in the Senate chamber, "There is but one way to stop a conqueror. That way is to defeat him." In what a reporter called "as eloquent an address as has been heard in the Senate in many months," Barkley went on to discuss the thinking behind the lend-lease bill—to bring about the defeat of Hitler through aid to Britain and her allies, even at the risk of war for the United States.

The galleries, noisy with demonstrations at times, fell into a hush as Senator Claude Pepper of Florida declared, "Call it war or do not call it war. Lay it down as a premise: America will not let England fall to Hitler." And a while later, following the remarks of these Democratic allies of the administration, Senator Warren Austin of Vermont, assistant Republican leader and a general sympathizer with FDR's foreign policy, fended off attacks by noninterventionists, peaking with his reply to Senator Homer T. Bone of Washington, who stuck with the thought that passage of the bill might lead to war. Could Austin think of anything worse than "bloody war"?

"Oh, there are much worse things than war," Austin replied in a measured tone. "A world enslaved by Hitler is worse than war. It is worse than death." Then he stepped into the center aisle of the chamber and shouted to the senators and the galleries, "If it ever becomes necessary for us to fight, we will fight!" The galleries exploded, with cheers predominating over boos.

In the days that followed, opponents of the bill had their full say. On Thursday, North Carolina's baroque Senator Robert Reynolds, declaring his intention to speak for five hours, with a sob in his voice attacked the bill on the standard ground that it represented "a step toward war." It was designed to preserve the British Empire "without consideration for the preservation of the United States." But after two and a half hours, the senator surprised his listeners by yielding the floor; he was suffering, Barkley explained, from "an unexpected attack of brevity."

In another kind of surprise, Reynolds's traditionally antiwar North Carolina colleague, Josiah Bailey (the senator who in the commerce confirmation hearings had questioned Hopkins about his devotion to FDR's policies), defied doctor's orders by rising to deliver a stirring speech in support of the bill. "Intervention is not necessarily war," the senator declared, but he was ready if it did mean war: "I think it might be well for Mr. Hitler and Mr. Mussolini and the war party in Japan to know that there is a country in the world that will not stop short once the gage of battle is thrown down." The galleries warmly applauded these sentiments.

In general, opponents talked about war and dictatorship (American, not German), while supporters emphasized the importance of central authority and organization for aiding Britain. This fitted Roosevelt's determination to concentrate on the practical and concrete, not on discussion of long-range policy—indeed, the last place he wanted to go.

The threat of real trouble arose when the supposedly good intentions of Senator James F. Byrnes of South Carolina, a friend of lend-lease, led to an amendment that would restrict the president's freedom to transfer war goods—one of the primary aims of the lend-lease concept. If the change were adopted, said Stimson, it would "take the guts right out of the bill" by eliminating joint procurement. Matériel obtained through military appropriations could not be sent to Britain without specific congressional approval; civilian and military aid programs would be split. Roosevelt, laid up with influenza and perhaps with an attack of excessive caution in relation to the Senate, told his subordinates to work it out, and one of Morgenthau's invaluable staff members, Edward Foley, devised a clever compromise that preserved the president's essential freedom. General Marshall, whose advisers had originally harbored some fears about what lend-lease might do to the U.S. Army, now gave strong support to the bill because the program would force the coordination of military production. The general spoke both in a closed committee session and in a March 4 meeting with Democratic leaders arranged by Stimson; the senators, thought the secretary of war, "evidently don't know much about the whole situation."

The bill's proponents had to head off another move—an effort to put specific limits on the countries that could receive aid. Only Britain, China, and Greece should be on the list, said the backers of this idea; otherwise, the president could even go so far as to send aid to Russia. Indeed. With that problem solved, and a few other attempts at restrictions defeated, the Senate on March 8, almost two months after Congress had received it, passed the bill; after the House accepted it in its new form, the president signed the lend-lease act into law on March 11. The next day, moving to turn authorization into appropriation, FDR asked Congress for $7 billion to put the program into effect. With the days of debate now over, the legislators moved quickly to supply the money. From London, Winston Churchill hailed the act as "a new Magna Charta."

Looking back, without a trace of nostalgia, to the failure of the London economic conference in 1933, FDR's old brain truster Raymond Moley recalled the collapse of international credit and the hostilities attendant on attempts to collect debts represented by monetary values. The great scope of Britain's needs now made the new idea of trading goods "without the mediation of money" not only a great challenge but a great opportunity. Though Moley no longer sailed aboard the New Deal ship, in this great engagement he supported his old skipper.

It would take time for the lend-lease appropriations to turn into tools of war, but as Lord Halifax had observed in conversation with members of Congress, the act would have immediate impact because now, with unlimited supplies in view, Britain could throw all her resources into defense against invasion. Roosevelt had acquired the best weapon he could get to back up his bet on Winston Churchill—to keep Britain in the fight until, on another day, some other great and perhaps decisive development should turn up. He would hope for it and look for it, whatever it might be. Having risen above his infirmity to become the first paraplegic known in world history to be chosen as a head of state or government, FDR could fairly be ranked as the greatest optimist in American political annals. With the passage of the Lend-Lease Act, he could have the satisfaction of seeing his popularity, as reported by a Gallup poll, stand at the highest point it had yet reached in the five or six years since polling had become popular: 72 percent.

The president surrounded himself with full interventionists—friends and subordinates impatient for direct U.S. participation in the war. FDR defined intervention in his own way, but he allowed his associates to believe what they wanted to believe. Some of them thought they knew what the Boss was thinking; others knew they did not know.

Of all the high-level officials involved during the preceding months in efforts concerning aid to Britain, Henry Morgenthau had been the most active, and now that lend-lease had become law the secretary hoped to keep a strong hand on the program. In late February, however, the president had decided to create the Advisory Committee on Lend-Lease, made up of Morgenthau, Hull, Stimson, and Knox—representing the diplomatic, military, and financial interests that would be involved. Harry Hopkins, FDR told the others, would serve as executive secretary of the committee, and each of the four departments was to lend a staff member to Hopkins to help get the great new project moving. Stimson had suggested this arrangement, with the important difference that he had proposed Major General James H. Burns for the post given to Hopkins; though the president decided otherwise, the general would nonetheless remain in prominent association with lend-lease. The press immediately nicknamed the arrangement the "Plus Four," the Plus being Hopkins (and Plus Fours being big, billowy golfing knickers popular in the 1920s). In characteristic style, Roosevelt depicted Hopkins in this role as a bookkeeper, keeping track of lend-lease money. Whether he recalled it or not, FDR had applied the same innocuous description to Hopkins at the launching of the WPA, and it had proved woefully inadequate. Since the four Cabinet secretaries would hardly be functioning as active heads of the new agency, no one could mistake Hopkins's real role. His staff would come largely from the President's Liaison Committee, the group set up in 1939 to coordinate sales to Britain and France, and most of the work would be carried out through existing departments and agencies. FDR's announcement ended one bit of popular speculation, which had envisioned the job going to Wendell Willkie, who had maintained such popularity since his defeat as to invite all kinds of rumors. Some imaginative pundits even saw Willkie as a possible Democratic presidential nominee in 1944: after all, many Republicans had read him out of their party and some had never considered him a true member in the first place.

Though the president did not place Morgenthau's Treasury Department in charge of lend-lease operations, he did ask the secretary to perform the chore of negotiating a formal "quid pro quo" agreement with the British for the matériel that would be transferred to them. Even if few who had attended FDR's December 17 press conference believed that "lease" and "lend" really meant that when peace returned, the recipients of war materials would be expected to return any that had not suffered from explosion or other damage, Morgenthau's staff produced a draft declaring that any "defense articles" that were "used up, worn out, destroyed, or otherwise rendered incapable of effective use" would be replaced by similar items of equal value. The draft did authorize the president, if he chose, to substitute other types of repayment. More in tune with the actual march of events, however, a statement in a March 5 letter from Morgenthau to the president commented: "With the signing of the Lend-Lease Bill the period of cash-on-the-barrelhead will come to an end for the great bulk of foreign government orders in this country."

Not waiting for the bill to become law, Hopkins, knowing he would be serving at the center of things, had begun planning as soon as he returned from Britain. On his very first day back, he had made one highly important move.

16

"BY TEMPERAMENT, TRAINING AND EXPERIENCE"

The call from the White House came on Monday, February 17, and the next day saw Averell Harriman, "a man who wanted a world to conquer," sitting in the president's office. Curiously, he had not succeeded in the intervening hours in reaching Hopkins for a talk and hence had no clear idea of Roosevelt's intentions, but he felt safe in presuming that he would be going to England—even if he knew nothing more than that. In the conversation Harriman felt some surprise that the president seemed to take the mission for granted, speaking "as if it was mutually understood that it had been decided that I should go for some time past." So Hopkins had indeed come through, making good on the promise he had implied to his friend in their December telephone talk.

But FDR seemed "a bit foggy" in discussing what agency Harriman would work with in Washington, since the lend-lease organization had not yet been created. It would not be OPM (the production agency Harriman detested), the president assured him, nor would his mission come under the aegis of the State Department. He said, Harriman noted, that "I was to communicate with him on any matters that I thought were important enough." This made it plain that whatever the nouns and adjectives, the White House would run lend-lease and Harriman would be the London end of the operation. Well aware of FDR's discursiveness and his use of conversation as a kind of exercise in place of the mobility denied him by his infirmity, Harriman tried to be businesslike, pushing for details. Not many were forthcoming from the president, but, "rambling on as he does on many subjects, he was far more humble, less cocksure and more human than in any conversation I had with him since he was President." And, in fact, Roosevelt gave the mission all the definition an ambitious international operator like Harriman should need: "I want you to go over to London and recommend everything that we can do, short of war, to keep the British Isles afloat."

Having already realized that he had much to do to prepare himself for the job, Harriman made sure that FDR included the announcement of the mission in his press conference that afternoon. If people did not officially know about the assignment, he said, he would not be able to get the information he needed from anybody, including the army, the navy, and the British mission in Washington. The president was "rather amusing about titles," Harriman commented, an observation confirmed in the press conference, when, after infelicitously referring to the "Lend-Spend, Lend-Lease—whatever you call it— bill," FDR told the press about inventing a title for his representative: "[We] decided that it was a pretty good idea to call him an 'Expediter.' There's a new one for you. I believe it is not in the diplomatic list or any other. So he will go over as 'Defense Expediter.'"

Roosevelt might have added, had he wished, that Harry Hopkins had scouted out and taken the first steps in establishing a personal link between president and prime minister and that Harriman would now become, on the British end of the line, the custodian of the new relationship; Hopkins would serve the counterpart function in Washington. Roosevelt, Harriman later observed, wanted information to come to him directly, not filtered through bureaucratic departmental channels. (That wish would be particularly true with respect to the State Department, toward which FDR's aversion seemed almost genetic.) But Harriman considered Hopkins "responsible for the creative conception" of the need for a close relationship between Roosevelt and Churchill beyond the practices of traditional diplomacy.

Harriman eagerly set to work, applying the same "process of total immersion" to this new challenge as he had in the 1920s to polo. ("The great thing about Averell," a British friend would say, "was that everything he did he did bloody well. He was never sort of happy to be moderately good at anything.") Determined now to make the most of this great opportunity in London, he set out to see everybody who might conceivably supply him with useful information. With some relief, in view of the unorthodox, off-the-chart nature of his mission, he found Secretary of State Hull, while seeming tired and pessimistic, to be forthcoming, giving "not the slightest indication of any fear of complications" resulting from the special representative's independence from the State Department. Harriman also saw his old New Haven crew member Dean Acheson, who had just become an assistant secretary of state and who observed, somewhat disconcertingly, that he felt "completely in the dark as to the State Department's policy on every important question." (Much of this uncertainty related to the Pacific, where Japan continued to pose its own set of problems; Hull, Acheson said, would not take the lead in setting policy.)

Harriman encountered greater complexity in his talks with military and naval officers, the list including the top leaders—General Marshall, General Arnold, and Admiral Stark—and "as many assorted generals and admirals as he could collar" in the three weeks available to him. These discussions, bearing directly on weapons and matériel, involved the hard facts of the situation. In general, Harriman found, the officers understood the need to support Britain and stood ready to play their part in the effort. But they all felt in the dark, like Acheson at the State Department—they needed more information before they could make valid decisions about the disposition of munitions and supplies. Would a particular weapon have greater value in American or in British hands? Admiral John Towers, chief of the navy's Bureau of Aeronautics, might become willing to release Catalina patrol flying boats to the British for antisubmarine duty, for instance, but only if the Royal Navy had the bases and crews needed to operate them. "We are so short," an officer said, "that everything given up by the army and navy comes out of our own blood"; no surplus existed, and none would exist for many months. This view lent force to a point about the need for organization and coordination made to Hopkins by Philip Young, a Treasury staff member who came over to the lend-lease operation: "No person in the Army or Navy or the Maritime Commission is going to offer to release any materiel which might hurt the Army, Navy or Maritime commission although such a release might not in any way jeopardize the defense of the United States."

Because of the tight supply, Hopkins's report, with its historically evocative "fourteen points" listing British needs, had encountered rough going in the War and Navy departments; the officers felt that while he had presented these needs clearly enough, he had not accompanied the listings with proof. They also expressed doubts about the report simply because of its origin: it came from an amateur, not from a military expert. One lieutenant colonel, disturbed by thoughts of the Churchill–Hopkins intimacy, declared, "We can't take seriously requests that come late in the evening over a bottle of port."

An anguished memorandum from Hap Arnold to General Marshall told the high-level story in a more serious way. If the air force had to meet Hopkins's provisions, Arnold said in effect, that would be the end of it. By carrying out a "piecemeal reinforcement" of the British, in both planes and personnel, the Americans would violate

General Pershing's famous World War principle that Americans must fight in American units under American command; following Hopkins's provisions would simply wipe out the buildup of the air force. Though offering some concessions, Arnold declared that the United States essentially must decide whether it would function as a warehouse for the British or whether it was going to create an American air force. Failing the latter, Arnold said, General Marshall "should not accept the responsibility for the defense of our National Interest in the Western Hemisphere."

These talks, with such strongly held points, gave ample illustration of the distance, even the gulf, between Roosevelt's great and absolutely dominant priority, which went back to the September meeting two years before the crisis—keep Britain in the fight, regardless of almost all other considerations—and the natural and more orthodox aims of the military professionals. The interviews also gave Harriman what he needed to formulate a revealing definition of his mission, at least at first. "I must attempt to convince the Prime Minister that I or someone must convey to our people his war strategy or else he cannot expect to get maximum aid," he noted. "Without understanding and acceptance of his war strategy our military men will 'drag their feet.'" Harriman had made plain his own solid support of Britain in various recent public appearances—in a speech at the Yale Club in New York in which he observed that "the most fatal error would be half-hearted and insufficient help," and in a speech in Washington several days later in which he declared, "I have made my decision. I am not willing to face a world dominated by Hitler." But even high generals and admirals of this same persuasion might not find knowledge of Churchill's strategy wholly sufficient to defeat their objections. Without more information from London, nobody would be moved at all.

On Friday, March 7, Averell Harriman, making a farewell call on the president, had an encounter with one of the more curious aspects of the Roosevelt White House. Ungrateful as it might seem to say so, the presidential speechwriter Robert Sherwood once observed, "the White House cuisine did not enjoy a very high reputation"; he cited as one of the reasons a frequently served salad, "which resembled one of the productions one finds in the flossier type of tea shoppe: it was a mountain of mayonnaise, slices of canned pineapple, carved radishes, etc." FDR never touched this period piece; he would merely look at it and murmur sadly, "No, thank you." In general, the cuisine appears to have been as predictable and unimaginative as the regular weekly offerings at an old-time boarding house. A few years earlier Roosevelt had mounted a food rebellion, announcing that "the kitchen had better not send him any more liver for a while and he [was] also getting pretty tired of string beans." A *New York Times* reporter had sympathized with FDR, commenting that "any man might rebel against being served salt fish for luncheon four days in a row." The president had even taken to brewing his own breakfast coffee in his bedroom. The housekeeper, Henrietta Nesbitt, an acquaintance of Mrs. Roosevelt's from Hyde Park, ran the kitchen under the eye and firm budgetary control of the first lady, who, despite her husband's protests, seems to have found the meals perfectly satisfactory and to have taken almost grim satisfaction in the austerity. Bitter coffee bothered her not at all.

Harriman's visit included lunch at the president's desk, a standard arrangement for noontime visitors. "An extraordinary meal," he recorded with considerable awe. "Spinach soup—didn't taste bad but looked like hot water poured over chopped up spinach! White toast and hot rolls. Main dish—cheese soufflé with spinach!! Dessert—three large fat pancakes, plenty of butter and maple syrup. Tea for the president and coffee for myself." Harriman took special note of the meal, he said (but how could he not?), because, since the president was just recovering from his much-discussed cold, it struck him as "the most unhealthy diet under the circumstances," although one can hardly imagine any circumstance in which such a collation could be considered salubrious. In what Harriman regarded as the crowning point, however, the president had matters of diet on his mind. Expressing his concern about the increasing need of the British for vitamins, proteins, and calcium, he asked his new envoy to look into the British food situation. Since the president seemed tired and mentally stale, however, Harriman felt that the interests of Britain could best be served by fortification of FDR's own diet.

Summing up his feelings on leaving Washington, Harriman, much concerned about maintenance of the shipping lifeline to England, felt that the president had not faced the reality that without strong American intervention, German submarines might well succeed in cutting it. Harriman saw that FDR hoped that U.S. material aid would keep Britain going, but he also felt that this aid might arrive too late. This particular talk brought Harriman to a useful observation. "Lack of understanding of what the President means when he nods or says 'yes' has led to much bitterness on the part of certain types of business men who assume they have the agreement of the President when all they have really is an indication that the President is not prepared to argue the point with them." He blamed the caller, Harriman said: "it is so obvious that it is simply the President's pleasant way of dodging a discussion which he does not care to enter into."

Hopkins, said Harriman, "is the one man in official position who appears to be ready to force a decision for decisive action on every front"; he felt optimistic about the possibilities for lend-lease with his friend in charge. Having spent most of his evenings in Britain with Churchill, Hopkins was "so impressed by the decisive and quick action of the British Prime Minister that he wants to see this quality developed in the President, to whom he is so devoted."

Like Hopkins, Harriman received a "special faith and confidence letter" (which the stenographer forgot to date) from the president, this one stating that the special representative, with the rank of minister, would act in Great Britain "in regard to all matters relating to the facilitation of material aid to the British Empire." Roosevelt never liked to give precise orders, Harriman commented; "the most he gave was the direction of his mind." But he clearly wanted a direct contact and the "undiluted words" of Churchill; one reason for bypassing the State Department, Harriman shrewdly noted, was that the president "did not want to share his confidences until he was ready." The president had told the press straight out that he did not know and did not care "what Mr. Harriman's relation to the embassy in London would be; nor was he interested in the question as to whom Mr. Harriman would report [to]."

Whatever questions the new special representative might have, the *New York Times* editorialists had no problem finding a purpose for his mission. "The efficient functioning of the 'arsenal of democracy' calls for close coordination and exchange of information between the Administration and defense officials here and those in the front line of the fight in Britain," said the *Times*. "Britain herself has already found it wise to send to this country a number of her ablest men to maintain liaison with our Government and with the work of armament production. The need for having a corresponding arrangement on behalf of the United States is clear." The *Times* also considered Harriman an ideal choice for the job—"by temperament, training and experience."

On March 10, the day before FDR signed the Lend-Lease Act into law, Averell Harriman became the second presidential special representative of the season to board a Pan-Am Clipper at LaGuardia and head for England. He did not take his wife along with him on this new kind of mission. Since she suffered from glaucoma and needed the regular attentions of her doctors, an air trip to England was not deemed advisable, even if she otherwise had been inclined to go. In any case, her inability to be on time for appointments, Marie said, disqualified her from being of much use as an expediter. Besides, the marriage had developed some of the kinds of sex-related complications common in the Harrimans' world.

Roosevelt's expediter did, however, make the trip with a constant companion, his indispensable personal secretary at the Union Pacific or anywhere else he was wanted, Robert Meiklejohn, an honors graduate of Williams, who had always found his boss a study. When an employment agency sent him to Harriman's office in March 1937, the interviewer, he said, "turned out to be my predecessor, who wanted to get out, but Harriman wouldn't let him out until he got somebody else." So the prospective new secretary was checked out by a man eager to find a replacement for himself; remarkably, Meiklejohn passed muster. Harriman's "idea of delegating authority," Meiklejohn said, "was to abandon a person in a job completely"—something like the FDR approach Harriman in his turn found a bit perturbing. When originally hired, Meiklejohn recalled, he had traveled by train with his new employer from New York across the country to Sun Valley but had received no explanation of his duties and had spoken with the boss no more than five minutes on the whole trip, though they shared a private car. The new resort offered unusual perquisites, however: "I used to do gigoloing at Sun Valley—they always had more women than men guests and so I would go dancing with them and take them around."

Certainly Harriman never talked with his aide in a personal way. "Goodness knows how many thousands of hours I spent alone in his company," Meiklejohn said, "yet I don't know any amusing anecdotes about his private life. But he is a gentleman, very sincere, very hardworking." With respect to the mission to England, "he told me one day that we were going. I had only about a week to wind up in Washington and nobody to turn the old job over to." Harriman was not being inconsiderate, Meiklejohn said, "he just had no conception of what was involved." Since the boss did not flaunt a large retinue but prided himself on operating in a minimalist fashion, Meiklejohn had found himself commuting every week from New York to Washington "as a 'dollar a year' man on loan from the Union Pacific Railroad as virtually Mr. Harriman's entire personal staff in his several government jobs." Neither in government nor in his personal life did Harriman believe in spending a penny more than necessary on the help.

Also making the trip to Lisbon was Anthony J. Drexel Biddle, newly appointed U.S. ambassador to continental refugee governments (Belgian, Dutch, Norwegian, Polish) that had set up in London; this envoy had arrived accompanied by his wife and by thirty-four pieces of luggage, eleven other bags having made the trip a week earlier on the Dixie Clipper. Harriman also took ironic note of the presence of a Swiss gentleman, who, he said, wished to sell Oerlikon guns to both sides in the war. "I left feeling very much the adventurer," Harriman said later. "It was the first time I'd flown over the ocean, and I had a greatly exaggerated view of the dangers of living in a bombed city." The trip took five days, with three of them spent on the ground in Lisbon, waiting for the last-leg flight on the customarily overbooked KLM DC-3. In this respect the presence of Tony Biddle proved an irritant. Because he held the title of ambassador, he, together with his wife, got onto an early flight, while Harriman, a mere minister in rank though on a vital mission with every day now counting heavily, sat in Portugal "fuming at the foolishness of officialdom."

At 4:30 in the morning of Saturday, March 15, a gleeful Harriman called Meiklejohn to get him up and going; by 7:30 they were finally on their way to England, although the plane made a quick stop at Oporto to take on additional fuel before heading north for the Bay of Biscay.

At about two o'clock, members of the crew in effect blindfolded the passengers by blocking out the windows with wooden shades. Flying low, both to avoid any patrolling German aircraft and then, over land, to make sure that antiaircraft crews correctly identified the plane, the DC-3 landed at about 3:30. Since the flight did not always have the same destination, the passengers did not know they were at Bristol until they disembarked.

The president's special representative received a special welcome. A British officer came aboard and led him off, to be greeted by a modest honor guard and by an Anglo-American group including Churchill's aide, Commander Thompson. After a session in the airfield administration building, where Meiklejohn enjoyed tea and cakes while his boss talked with reporters, the party, which also included Herschel Johnson from the U.S. embassy, took seats on an RAF transport, which delivered them to a Bomber Command base. There the group split up, with Thompson escorting Harriman to Chequers, while Johnson and Meiklejohn stayed aboard and flew on to an airport on the outskirts of London. Accompanied by an embassy staff member, Meiklejohn registered at Claridge's (where the budget would not allow him to have a long stay) and began to look around his new home. Taken on a drive outside the city to see a thirteenth-century cathedral and some notable Roman ruins, he found himself more interested in the machine gun nests along the road, the tank traps, the cables strung overhead to snag airplanes or gliders attempting to land, and posts and ditches in open fields to accomplish a similar purpose.

Meanwhile, Thompson had led Harriman into immediate action with the prime minister. "We got to Chequers in time for dinner," Harriman said. "I was very excited, feeling like a country boy plopped right into the center of the war"—a thought that more logically might have come from Iowa's Harry Hopkins (and perhaps had) on his arrival two months earlier.

Recalling their first meeting, at Cannes in 1927, Churchill gave his visitor a warm welcome—as, in the circumstances, could hardly have surprised anyone—and Harriman graciously presented Clementine with a bag of tangerines he had brought her from Lisbon; he noted her "unfeigned" delight in this fresh fruit—a reminder of some of the inescapable austerities prevailing in British life, even at the top. ("Whoever the president had sent," said Churchill's daughter Mary Soames, "everybody here was going to bust themselves to get on with," even somebody difficult or abrasive; "it was immensely important to us how it all went." Fortunately, Hopkins and Harriman both represented "very remarkable personnel selection." The two, Mary thought, were "perfect for the times" and for the British officials with whom they would deal. "My papa," she said, "felt straightaway with Harry and equally with Averell that they could talk as friends and thrash out everything.")

After dinner, closeted with Churchill, Harriman had to bide his time while the prime minister discoursed on the war and discussed actions the United States might take. Then the American had his chance to make the move he had resolved on after his interviews with the military and naval officers in Washington. The American services had such great needs and such limited resources, he explained, that U.S. commanders would fight to keep what they had until they knew that the British could put it to immediate and effective use. "I told him Roosevelt's instruction," Harriman said, "and that I would have to have full information or otherwise I could be of no assistance to him."

"I welcome you as a friend," Churchill replied, "and any information you want will be given."

At the moment, Harriman as well as Churchill felt the most acute concern over what the prime minister had dubbed the Battle of the Atlantic. With the convoys coming to British ports losing about 10 percent of their ships, Harriman saw "how close they were to disaster in view of the fact that they imported about 50 percent of what they ate and almost all raw materials." Actually, Churchill could have pitched the matter more gravely; winter gales had held sinkings in January and February to sixty ships but now, with improving weather, the totals could reasonably be expected to rise. On the other hand, the British had a secret counter-weapon that Churchill could not have been expected to reveal to Harriman—the work of the cryptanalysts (the "code-breakers") at the so-called Government Code and Cipher School at Bletchley Park in Buckinghamshire; on the navy side these ingenious operatives attacked cipher messages produced by the Kriegsmarine's Enigma machines, which they were enjoying considerable success in reading. Yet Churchill would say with justice, "The Battle of the Atlantic was the dominating factor all through the war," not to be forgotten for a moment.

"You must get in touch with the Admiralty," Churchill told Harriman. "I have arranged for you to have an office there"—making his visitor surely the first foreigner to become a de facto member of the naval staff. (Though Harriman himself would spend little time in the Admiralty, a naval officer on his staff would cover the office every day.) The prime minister also brought his new American friend into the Battle of the Atlantic Committee, an arm of the War Cabinet whose existence in itself testified to the importance of the subject. In his final meeting with the president Harriman had suggested that American warships escort British convoys across the western Atlantic to Iceland, thus doubling the effectiveness of the Royal Navy's escort vessels. The president had seemed to think not. What if an encounter between a U.S. Navy ship and a U-boat brought on a state of war? No one would benefit, FDR said. Certainly his overall design did not call for the country's fate to be decided by random gunfire or torpedoes out in the North Atlantic.

But, he assured Harriman, he would move as far as American public opinion was willing to go. As an active interventionist, Harriman found this position unsatisfying, but he did not have the luxury of choice. The president, however, had not precluded making a move when he should decide that an exploding shell or a detonating torpedo would not bring on a war.

17

LINKING UP

During the evening of March 19 the prime minister provided a bit of special entertainment for his dinner guests, a group including Averell Harriman and Tony Biddle. When it became clear that the Luftwaffe was mounting a heavy raid on London, Churchill ordered tin hats for all of his guests and then took them up on the flat roof of the Air Ministry, to watch the antiaircraft fire as the bombs fell all around. It was the first time Jock Colville had met Harriman, and he noted how the prime minister's amusement at the spectacle "struck Averell as really very remarkable," but he thought that "Mr. Biddle was terribly upset by that. He didn't like standing on the Air Ministry roof. And I think Averell, who was no coward, was amused."

Following the pattern he had established with Harry Hopkins, Churchill immediately took Harriman into his personal circle, with country weekends and morale-boosting tours. On those excursions, he used surprise as his principal strategy of security, departing from London with just two bodyguards and making a sudden arrival in a town that had undergone heavy bombing. "He would always introduce me as the president's personal envoy," Harriman said, "to let the British people know that the Americans stood with them." It was not strictly necessary, Colville thought, but Churchill realized that "Averell counted very much as far as we were concerned in getting supplies and therefore the more he took Averell into his confidence, the better. And that was followed by the fact that he had really got to like Averell."

On Friday, April 11, at Swansea, in Wales, which had suffered a heavy attack just a few days previously, Churchill's party saw that the attackers had not left a single house standing in the town's center. The prime minister went straight to the waterfront and found himself closed in by a large crowd of dockers wanting to get close to their leader. This concerned the security men, since, as Harriman put it, "the dock workers were not a particularly well paid or contented group," and in any case the protective detail feared that their charge might be injured in the crush, but he simply called out, "Stand back, my man. Let the others have a chance to see, too." The crowd responded, leaving a space around the prime minister. He then delighted the people, and Harriman as well, by taking off his squarish bowler hat, putting it on the end of his walking stick, and hoisting it as a personal ensign. The crowd laughed and cheered.

The next day's schedule called for the prime minister to visit Bristol, where, as chancellor (ceremonial head) of the university, he would confer honorary degrees on Ambassador Winant and Australian prime minister Robert Menzies. "I'd like to give you a degree, too," Churchill blandly assured Harriman, "but you're not interested in that kind of thing." During the preceding night, as their train sat on a siding outside the city, the members of the party heard the explosions and saw the fires from a fierce Luftwaffe raid. In the morning the train pulled into the station, and the lord mayor led the party through the smoking hot ruins—"devastation such as I had never thought possible," Colville said. "Swansea was mild in comparison." The townspeople, giving Churchill what Harriman thought a particularly enthusiastic welcome, believed he had come in response to the raid and greeted him with shouts of "Here's Winnie!" Harriman found the spirit of the people "utterly amazing."

In the middle of the grim but in some ways inspiring scene, Harriman was amused to hear women shout, "There he is, dear old Winnie!" With Churchill walking a little way in front, Harriman remarked to General Ismay that the prime minister seemed particularly popular with the middle-aged women. Churchill, not out of earshot as Harriman had presumed, turned around and said, mock-brusque, "What did you say? Not only with the middle-aged women. With the young ones, too."

Harriman found the pageantry at the university particularly impressive, since the show went on as though no bombing attacks had occurred. Fires continued to burn in a building nearby, and beneath their robes, from which muddy boots protruded, some of the academics still wore the begrimed uniforms in which they had fought the night's blazes; swathed in scarlet, the prime minister presided over the ritual.

That evening, impressed by the spirit of the people, Harriman was further moved by what he saw as the spirit of Churchill. The prime minister had been facing the public all day long and now, back on the train, he said, with tears in his eyes, "They have such confidence. It is a grave responsibility."

Harriman went right to work in London just as he had in Washington, seeking out the facts from officials in a variety of ministries and bureaus, including Lord Beaverbrook, as minister of aircraft production, and Brendan Bracken, who against his own desires would soon yield to Churchill's wish that he shore up the Ministry of Information as minister (and enable it to assert itself in its fight with the Foreign Office for control of news). The focus was clear: in addition to Beaverbrook and Bracken, Harriman dealt with Ronald Cross, minister of shipping; Sir Andrew Duncan, minister of supply; Lord Woolton, minister of food; Hugh Dalton, minister of economic warfare; and Oliver Lyttelton, president of the Board of Trade. His mandate to keep the British Isles afloat meant keeping them supplied—having goods to send and getting them across the ocean in circumstances that had never existed before.

During his self-indoctrination time in Washington, Harriman had also arranged for his basic staff, which in his characteristic fashion he wanted kept as small, and as easy on the budget, as it could be to get the extremely complex job done. The special representative donated his own services, and Robert Meiklejohn had come on loan from the Union Pacific, as he had been in Washington. (As Meiklejohn saw it, "Mr. Harriman prided himself on keeping his staff to a minimum, mainly me.") Harriman's approach, and his own addiction to long hours, also meant that no member of the staff would ever find himself without plenty of work to do. Once, having at two o'clock in the morning assigned an aide a particular task, he phoned him at 7 a.m. to ask how the job was coming. Another time, striding out of the office at about 5:30 p.m., he declared over his shoulder, "I'm not coming back, so you can declare a half holiday." Few executives, noted a reporter, could "remain as imperturbable as Harriman under the petulant gaze of a stenographer who has a dinner date and is being kept late at dictation."

Harriman's own unusual working methods helped him achieve his minimalist desires. Gifted with a remarkable memory, he rarely needed to refer to the file on any particular activity or problem, and, like FDR, he kept no written record of meetings or conferences. Difficult as this approach could sometimes make life for his subordinates, Meiklejohn noted, it gave him great freedom of action. He could "take off on a moment's notice without staff or files to a meeting of momentous importance with all the relevant information stored in his head."

About a week after Harriman's departure from LaGuardia, two top assistants arrived in London. Harriman liked the fact that the services of Colonel George Alan Green, an Army Reserve officer on loan from the Yellow Truck & Coach Manufacturing Company in Michigan, cost him nothing. With Green came Edward P. Warner, a member of the Civil Aeronautics Authority and former assistant secretary of the navy for aviation. "Mr. Warner," said Steve Early, the president's press secretary, "certainly is an authority on the United States airplane industry." He added, more imaginatively, "Colonel Green might be called an automotive ordnance expert." The colonel was, in fact, vice chairman of the War Department's ordnance advisory committee. A statistician, Russell T. Nichols, came from Harriman's old bane, the Office of Production Management.

In London, in accordance with arrangements Harriman had made in Washington, the staff acquired three specialists: Commander Paul F. Lee, borrowed from the office of the U.S. naval attaché, on naval matters and ship repair (and as one of his responsibilities, he would keep an eye on the special office in the Admiralty); Brigadier General Millard F. Harmon, from the office of the military attaché, on air matters; and Lieutenant Colonel James L. Hatcher on production and engineering matters. The U.S. Maritime Commission lent Harvey Klemmer and A. C. Spencer to work on shipping questions. William Dwight Whitney, a New York lawyer who had come over to England at the beginning of the war and, rather singularly, happened to be a major in the Scots Guards, joined on March 29 as Harriman's executive assistant.

For the first few weeks the staff worked in the offices normally occupied by the U.S. consul general and his staff, in the embassy at 1 Grosvenor Square, in Mayfair. On April 15 the "Harriman Mission," as the operation became known for want of a descriptive name that could encompass its varied activities and interests, moved into its permanent home, a very large array of offices—twelve thousand square feet—on the second floor (American third floor) at No. 3 Grosvenor Square, an apartment building adjoining the embassy. Harriman's office suite occupied what had been an entire flat, but everyone else enjoyed ample space as well. Workmen broke through a wall to install a door connecting the mission with the embassy. As anything but an empire builder, Harriman created practical good will for his operation by making some of its space available to other agencies, many of which were always looking, sometimes desperately, for more room.

The thorough cooperation of the embassy staff, under its new chief John Winant, meant that Harriman could keep his infrastructure small; the embassy provided not only complete communication and coding facilities but bookkeeping and other services. (This kind of help was forthcoming even though Winant's "deep neuroticism," as one acquaintance saw it, led to various kinds of strange behavior, a notable and relevant example being his habit of turning up late at night at a friend's house, where he "would walk up and down the sitting-room, inveighing against some supposed slight he had received at the hands of the President or Averell Harriman.")

In the functioning of the mission, Harriman liked to emphasize that, while the members of the staff brought specialized knowledge from the various agencies that had supplied them, they had become members of the mission rather than representatives of their original organizations. At times, because of particular needs or aptitudes, they might find themselves doing work bearing no relation to the functions of these agencies. In line with the motif of simplicity, the mission's letterhead read: OFFICE OF W. A. HARRIMAN. Harriman maintained control of operations through his practice of allowing no messages to go to Washington without his approval, and, aside from a weekly coordinating meeting, he spent little time with staff members.

He explained his approach one day when a woeful Colonel Green came into his office. Harriman rarely saw him, the colonel complained. "Why the hell should I see you?" Harriman responded; he thought highly of Green's work: "I only call in men when I don't approve their messages." So what did Green want to talk about? Nothing, really, it seemed; the colonel simply sought a bit of reassurance. Harriman as expediter behaved toward Colonel Green exactly as Harriman the Union Pacific chairman had behaved toward Robert Meiklejohn.

Since London played continual host to U.S. special missions of various kinds, sent by various agencies and dealing with various branches of the British government, Harriman moved to prevent the chaos that could increasingly develop. All such missions, he decreed, would be headquartered at the Harriman mission and work under its supervision; supply activities thus would have the benefit of effective coordination and, beyond that, by coming under one central jurisdiction the special missions would be kept from developing policies that contradicted those of other missions. In the same vein, Harriman established ecumenical staff meetings that included senior members of any special missions and also representatives from established U.S. agencies in London, including the embassy itself. Before long, extending still further the intimacies of communication and liaison, Harriman arranged for a member of his staff to spend part of each day at the ministries with which the mission dealt, reviewing the messages to and from Washington; it was the best device he could contrive for overcoming the sometimes slow communication with the other end of the transatlantic link. FDR's term "expediter" proved to be an apt title and designation.

As quickly as he acquired and accepted statements of needs and problems, Harriman passed them on to Washington, mostly to Harry Hopkins; indeed, the lend-lease administrator soon found himself under a barrage of assessments and requests from London. Questions relating to shipping inevitably held a prominent place in the exchanges, and, whether by coincidence or otherwise, Harriman in an early message reflected the concern about nutrition in Britain expressed by Roosevelt during the carbohydrate-stuffed lunch the two had shared at the president's desk. "Of paramount consideration is shipping space and the protection of British shipping," Harriman wrote on March 24; the supply of food for Britain must be increased, and to save space "needed food values should be shipped in concentrated form," although depriving people of the kinds of food they were used to would likely hurt morale. Planners needed to call on their ingenuity, Harriman said, to economize the use of ships and to reduce the need for protecting the ships by minimizing the length of the trips British vessels made; for instance, the Americans could handle imports from the Pacific, releasing products of the same kind to be shipped to Britain from North Atlantic ports.

Three weeks later Harriman was asking Hopkins, "Are all departments doing everything they can to cooperate in saving weight in shipment to Britain?" Sticking to a subject, whatever it was, rigidly and relentlessly, represented Harriman at his most typical. Perhaps the most remarkable example of his devotion to one thing at a time came at a high-level conference, but not concerning a high-level issue, when the participants had to suspend the proceedings until Harriman, who had become focused on a fly walking across the table and had begun stalking it, finally did it in.

The food-shipping nexus sprang into the headlines at the end of May with the arrival of what was said to be the first American lend-lease food ship, loaded with four million eggs, 120,000 pounds of Wisconsin cheddar from Manitowoc, and one thousand tons of flour. The arriving vessel was greeted by Lord Woolton, the minister of food, together with Averell Harriman. A reporter noted the curious fact that the eggs, which came from Columbus, Nebraska, had made most of the land portion of their journey on Harriman's railroad. In reply to a message from Hopkins relaying the displeasure of the Department of Agriculture with the story's statement that this was the first food ship, Harriman conceded that in fact four others had arrived earlier, but the new arrival was played up because it was the first in the London area. "Such minor distortion of facts as was involved," Harriman said, "was employed for the purpose of bolstering morale here, especially with respect to cheese, of which there has been a deficiency which all the laboring classes have keenly felt."

The previous day Lord Woolton, who by common consent enjoyed almost dictatorial powers in his particular realm, had stirred up a different controversy by appealing in a press conference to the Americans to eat less so that they could send more food to Britain. Even if health was being maintained, he said, living involved more than the maintenance of physical life, including relief from an "unhappy and dull diet." Woolton, a notably successful entrepreneur but not a politician, had apparently given no thought to the way his plea for Americans to buy less food might be received by farmers and their spokesmen in Washington. "You should know the Department of Agriculture is greatly disturbed" over these remarks, Hopkins said. "Everybody here believes we can supply most British requirements with shifting of production to essential commodities, particularly dairy." If anybody was going to talk to Americans about rationing, Hopkins said, it would be the Department of Agriculture, not Lord Woolton. "The burden of this message," Hopkins said, "is to tell his lordship in a nice way to pipe down."

Woolton was planning a radio address to the women of America, but, Harriman assured Hopkins, this time he had agreed to give the Department of Agriculture the opportunity to clear his text. With regard to the "unfortunate 'creamless day' press conference," Harriman said, "I called his attention personally to the danger of such remarks." Happily, the London food shipment, he reported, had been "universally well received."

In a different kind of shipping problem, the British expressed great concern at the delays in turnaround in ports, caused by the methods of stowage practiced by American stevedores. One ship recently arrived from New York, Harriman told Hopkins, "was forced to shift an unbelievable number of times from ordinary discharging berth to the fixed heavy lift crane," with the result that unloading that should have been a matter of only ten days took seven weeks. Though the British had dispatched officials to the United States to help in this situation, Harriman doubted whether any real action would follow. What was needed, he said, was the visit to England of a team of two or three stevedores who could be taught the problems at the receiving ports and who could then return home and spread the word on methods of stowage that would conform to the needs. The situation, he concluded pointedly, was "receiving the personal attention of the Prime Minister."

A reply to this message soon came, via Hopkins, from Admiral Emory S. Land, head of the U.S. Maritime Commission. An old acquaintance from Harriman's World War shipbuilding days, Jerry Land, as he was known, kicked the ball straight back. The situation was a British affair, he said; the stevedores in question worked for the British Ministry of Shipping and under its supervision. "This problem," said Land with perhaps a trace of bureaucratic satisfaction, "seems to be one for adjustment between representatives of the British Ministry in the United Kingdom and representatives of the British Ministry in the United States." They should be capable of working out how a ship ought to be loaded to meet the "peculiarities of the facilities at the discharge port."

Harriman came back with a worldly-wise, statesmanlike reply. The Ministry of Shipping had in fact sent a special representative to the

United States and Canada, he told Hopkins and the admiral, but he had felt that more improvement could result from sending American stevedores to England to study conditions at the ports, because "our stevedores would be more apt to react favorably to their views than to those of British stevedores." Under normal conditions, as he knew from his own experience, a shipping company routinely sent its stevedores to study problems at receiving ports, and under the present abnormal conditions the practice seemed even more necessary. However, Harriman concluded, since Land had not responded favorably, perhaps they could keep the question open until the results of present British efforts became clear; meanwhile, perhaps Land could help the British in their efforts to correct stowage in all American ports.

Messages on subjects of all kinds—supplying machine guns to the Greeks, the degaussing (neutralizing the magnetism) of merchant ships, putting up oil-storage tanks in Iceland, the availability and allocation of .30-caliber ammunition, twin-engine versus four-engine bombers, and endless others—began to flow across the Atlantic, sending Hopkins's staff scurrying for answers and Hopkins himself pushing the appropriate branches of the Washington bureaucracy for the action he needed and, when necessary, explaining his own problems to Harriman. It was a case of two impatient men, an ocean apart, linking up and working with each other.

18

"IN A NIGHTMARE"

U nited States Army and Navy officers and civilian officials
concerned with defense matters, including relations with
the British, frequently and vocally fretted over the difficulty
of making plans in what seemed the absence of a national strategy.
The armed services could find professional contentment in sunshine
or in darkness, but working in twilight produced unease. The United
States had a strategic purpose, however. Like the purloined letter, it
sat out in the open for anyone to see: provide all aid to Britain short of
war. But skeptics insisted on looking past it.

In the summer of 1940, the army and navy chiefs had dispatched a
team of officers to London to see firsthand how well the British were
standing up to the long-heralded air assault now made possible by
the enemy's newly acquired bases on the other side of the Channel.
Encouraged by what they had learned, the officers returned to
Washington with ample notes on British views of strategy. Army
and navy planners then set to work to develop an American position
on strategy, arms production, and other relevant subjects. The most
striking result came in a document from Admiral Stark, who sought to
integrate the idea of a U.S. arms buildup with that of providing aid to
Britain (a version of the approach that won General Marshall's favor

for lend-lease); he described the aim of his paper as "arriving at a decision as to the National Objective in order to facilitate naval preparation." The gist of "Plan Dog," as Stark's most important recommendation became known, called for a strong offensive in the Atlantic together with a holding operation in the Pacific: "Germany first" became its shorthand designation. Using the paper as a basis and thrashing out details, the services and the State Department put together a plan that received general approval in a White House meeting on January 16; it made the key point that the United States must make every effort to continue supplying Britain, while standing on the defensive in the Pacific. (This meeting, as it happened, took place just one day after the House Foreign Affairs Committee began its hearings on the lend-lease bill.) The navy, the president said, must become prepared to convoy merchant shipping all the way to England.

As another consequence of Anglo-American discussions, when the *King George V* arrived off Annapolis in the last week of January she had aboard not only Lord and Lady Halifax but a delegation of British army and navy staff officers, shepherded by the military attaché in London, General Lee, who had made the trip to Scapa Flow with Hopkins on January 14. To avoid attracting the attention of congressmen and the press and other inquisitive types, the officers would wear civilian clothes and hope to disappear into the Washington mix as trade representatives or other typical and innocuous visitors to the capital. They could hardly hope to fool a reasonably perceptive isolationist, however, since in bearing, style, and ruddiness of complexion at least two of them almost cartoonishly exemplified the popular idea of high-ranking British officers.

The staff conversations proved to be a significant event. Known as ABC-1 (for first American-British-Canadian conference), they lasted from January 29 to March 27 and produced agreement in a number of areas, with the "Hitler first" concept serving as the undergirding principle. Most of the decisions could not become operational unless and until the United States became an active belligerent, but the talks "immensely facilitated the wise allocation of immediate resources in prudent preparation for such an evident possibility." When and whether that "possibility" would materialize depended on how effectively the president pursued his aims. One discordant note lingered from the talks. The British had nourished the unrealistic hope that the U.S. Pacific Fleet might take over the defense of Singapore, an idea opposed by the Americans on every ground and flatly rejected by Admiral Stark. Some of the Americans even balked at the whiff of imperialism and colonialism they sniffed in the proposal. Also to be sniffed was the scent of desperation, as the British compared their range of "imperial" commitments around the world with their limited resources.

Aside from that, the two democracies groped toward a framework of effective cooperation—the strategic counterpart of lend-lease and perhaps guide for it. For the time being, it was the best anybody was going to get. It was true that one day in late spring, talking about the war, FDR said to Morgenthau, "I may have to be pushed on this." But the president did not say how hard the push would have to be. An observation in May by Hopkins suggested a dawning understanding of what Roosevelt was about—that FDR was not, as Stimson and many others believed, simply drifting, waiting to be forced to act. Hopkins said, Morgenthau noted, that "the president has never said so in so many words, but he thinks the president is loath to get us into this war . . ."

From his inside track in the Admiralty, Averell Harriman became closely involved in all sides of British naval affairs. One cause he supported in his cables to Washington was the repair in American ports not only of merchant vessels but of warships. "Although requests were made through their mission in Washington," he said, "thanks to my telegrams we were able to get things done." The president confirmed this important and decidedly "unneutral" arrangement, as Harriman noted, in a telegram to the prime minister on April 4, adding the news that he was authorizing the building of fifty-eight more launching yards and two hundred more ships. Harriman set up with the British a system whereby his office would receive a list of ship repairs needed and then a decision would be made as to whether the parts should be sent by the British or made by the American shipyard involved. The shortcut this approach made possible produced quick results on such important warships as the torpedoed battleship *Malaya* and the dive-bombed aircraft carrier *Illustrious*.

To make up for losses in the North Atlantic, the Americans pulled two million tons of World War–era merchant ships out of mothballs and turned these vessels over to the British. Harriman credited Hopkins with creating this unorthodox arrangement. "There wasn't a thing we suggested," he said, "to which he didn't give serious thought."

The president came forth with another kind of help. At the beginning of the war in 1939, he had established the Neutrality Patrol, with the assignment of reporting and tracking any naval vessel of a belligerent power approaching the U.S. Atlantic coast. Now, not ready to authorize U.S. participation in convoys, as Harriman well knew, FDR picked up an atlas and in discussion with Secretary of War Stimson, one of the mandarins of interventionism, approached the problem another way—he would extend the patrol line eastward. At first the two talked about the twenty-fifth meridian, but as officially declared on April 24 the twenty-sixth meridian became the boundary, supplemented by a bulge that would include Iceland; in effect, the western hemisphere was expanding. The United States would take over the responsibility for antisubmarine patrol in the whole area westward of 26 degrees west longitude. On April 26 the fleet received orders to extend the patrol deep into the South Atlantic, to the twentieth parallel.

Events, however, were marching faster than decisions and policies. The sinking of almost half the ships in a convoy, on the night of April 3–4, convinced Admiral Stark that much more must be done, and in May the president declared a state of "unlimited national emergency," telling the world about the extension of the Neutrality Patrol and about Admiral Stark's substantive action of transferring an aircraft carrier and several other large ships from the Pacific to the Atlantic. The Atlantic Fleet, which had been established only two months earlier (in a move dividing the U.S. fleet between the oceans), came under the command of Admiral Ernest J. King, whom Stark had picked in faithful compliance with Roosevelt's order to give the two new commands to "the meanest SOB's in the Navy." (The Pacific Fleet went to Admiral Husband E. Kimmel.)

While the United States was making these moves, the British experienced a variety of disheartening disasters that raised serious questions for the Americans. Not only were U-boats destroying convoys, but German surface raiders seemed to work with impunity in the North Atlantic and even in the Indian Ocean. The effort to hold on to Malta was consuming aircraft and other resources at a rapid rate. British forces had been driven out of Greece, and the attempt to defend Crete turned into an embarrassing fiasco, with the Royal Navy suffering serious losses. ("By some error of judgment or lack of imagination," General Lee told Winant, "the R.A.F. withdrew all its planes. Even a few fighters would have wrought havoc amongst the German troop carriers.") For good measure, the battleship *Bismarck* sank the Royal Navy's beloved battle cruiser *Hood* in Denmark Strait, though, after a complex and arduous chase, an array of air and sea forces finally did in the German super-battleship. But was Britain really going to last, to hold on in the war? Churchill said so, of course, with all his eloquence, but so did Averell Harriman: aid to Britain would not be wasted. FDR's policy remained in force.

When it came to the effectiveness of American aircraft that had been supplied to the British, the discussion turned painful for Harriman. Getting little information out of Lord Beaverbrook, Harriman and his air officer, General Harmon, met for dinner with Air Vice Marshal Graham Dawson, who was concerned with preparing the planes for combat. How well was the P-40 performing? "There's only one trouble with the American airplanes," said Dawson. "They can't fight; they are utterly useless in combat"—in fact, "no goddam good." "This led," said Harriman, "to the first real discussion between the English and us about the defects of our planes." Dawson went on to propose, in a formal letter to Ambassador Winant, that Britain send a group of test pilots and ground engineers to the United States to give contractors the benefit of firsthand lessons drawn from fighting experience and thus prevent the "persistence of some faults" that had previously been identified. General Harmon advised Harriman to go slow, while he and colleagues worked out plans with Dawson to improve the situation. Harmon, said Harriman, "did a first-rate job in getting Washington to make the necessary changes, especially in regard to firepower."

Fully sensitive to the delicacy of his situation in relation to Winant, Harriman, as the personal representative close to the president's ear, carefully left diplomatic dealings to the ambassador and had little to do with the Foreign Office or Eden, the foreign secretary. Even Churchill got into the game, after Hopkins had passed on a complaint from the ambassador about being bypassed. "We'll have to be more careful," the prime minister told Harriman.

Churchill sometimes talked with Winant or Harriman before

sending Roosevelt a message accurately describing the seriousness of Britain's position. In a curious discussion one evening, Winant urged Churchill toward euphemism, saying that unvarnished bad news would depress the president. Harriman took exactly the opposite view (which presumably Churchill also held): the prime minister should make the situation as clear as possible. "I was serving the President," Harriman said, and his job was "to describe to him the desperate picture of Britain in that late winter and spring"—in particular, "the effect of the bombing on British production and devastating effect of the submarines on the supply lines. My important messages went to Roosevelt and Hopkins directly." In one of those messages, he told the president, "England's strength is bleeding. In our own interest I trust our navy can be directly employed before our partner is too weak."

Churchill and Harriman often argued about the telegrams to the president. Sometimes when he did not agree with the prime minister's draft, Harriman said, "he would attack me with great scorn. If you gave in, he paid no attention to your comments. But if you stood up to him, he'd pay attention." Harriman developed the approach of saying that he would like permission to bring up the subject again later. Then, next morning, Harriman would be summoned to Churchill's bedside. "Read this!" the prime minister would say, handing over a message revised in accordance with Harriman's suggestions. Well, Harriman would say, "I think this is all right."

To Marie Harriman, Averell wrote that he kept "trying to find words to convey the urgency to Washington so that they will wake up to the fact that 'Business as usual' is not possible if we want to be of help here." Altogether, he said, "it has been as if living in a nightmare, with some calamity hanging constantly over one's head."

At the Washington end of the transatlantic link, workers had hastily cleared seventeen rooms in the white marble palace of the Federal Reserve System on Constitution Avenue, fittingly enough a New Deal building project, to make way for the lend-lease staff, which at the beginning numbered thirty-five. Amid these splendors Harry Hopkins received the heavy flow of messages from Harriman, and increasingly from Churchill as well; the prime minister would come to regard Hopkins as "the most faithful and perfect channel between the President and me," treating him as a full partner. Once, in a despairing moment, he wrote: "I will be very pleased if you can give me any hope but you will know best whether there is anything else to do." (From Henry Morgenthau, often worried about maintaining his influence with his chief, came a discordant view of the transatlantic link. Speaking in a "triple confidential" conversation with three top associates, the secretary bluntly said, "You know this thing of going direct from Churchill to Hopkins to the President isn't so hot—I don't like it.")

In one of his earlier tasks (though it came surprisingly late for a bread-and-butter letter to a remarkable host), Hopkins wrote Churchill to express his gratitude for the hospitality shown him in England. In the letter he presented, almost in passing, a straightforward definition of his new job: "I have agreed to take on, on behalf of the President, a responsibility here for the promotion of the whole of our aid to Britain program and I am trying to avoid getting my mind cluttered up with any other problems." He also indicated fast progress on the job; he had already worked out a plan with Arthur Purvis to keep orders for Britain moving, and he was arranging with the Maritime Commission to get four million tons of new shipping. A further point: "All British purchasing requests are now routed through me." He was also, he said mysteriously, "on the trail of a Stilton cheese." Presumably, during his stay in England he had developed a liking for Stilton; he could hardly have been looking for one in America to send across the Atlantic to its homeland.

The nucleus of the lend-lease organization, as Hopkins explained in response to a request from Harriman, remained the group consisting of General Burns, Oscar Cox, Phil Young, and the others who had worked at Treasury on foreign-purchasing operations. Seeking to retain flexibility, Hopkins said, he had not encouraged a definition of functions that would "freeze it at the outset." Burns, Cox, and Young made up a team with no functional dividing lines, except that Burns was the executive officer, so appointed by the president. Decisions were made by consensus, but, Hopkins conceded, the situation called for a degree of specialization: Burns handled overall policy matters and high-level liaison work, Cox paid particular attention to legal problems, and Young had direct charge of operations—the handling of requests, coordination of departmental requests, supervising statistical reports, and, as Hopkins did not say, other bureaucratic responsibilities. The program, Hopkins assured Harriman, made "a constant and continuous effort to improve procedures, to cut red tape, and to expedite action." Completely converted to the role of wartime manager and fixer, Hopkins even expressed weariness at "complaints from those goddam New Dealers" who accused him of having deserted the faith. In compensation, a Republican corporation executive who came to help out in Washington said of Hopkins: "I can't escape the conviction that he has the clearest, coolest mind of anyone I have ever seen here."

Reference to the legal area accurately described Oscar Cox's professional concerns, but by no means the scope of his activities. Seeming to be working, or, at least thinking, twenty hours a day, Cox had ideas and produced memos in every field; it began to become apparent that in this big, husky Maine lawyer, Harry Hopkins had found his own Hopkins. (Cox would not have the role completely to himself, however. A Washington observer declared that "anytime Harry Hopkins wanted an odd job done, he would call on Averell, and Averell would somehow get it done," and Hopkins had plenty of work to go around.) Morgenthau had justly felt some pain at the loss of Cox and of Young, also a Treasury lawyer. According to Morgenthau, Hopkins had told the president he wanted to acquire Cox for his staff without identifying him as a Treasury man. "You're just Oscar Cox," Morgenthau said, adding that he had seen that happen before with Hopkins: "That's the way he works."

Continuingly prodded by Harriman, those operating the transatlantic exchange encountered stresses of various kinds, some of them amounting to growing pains. "Have received today substantial amount of data from OPM and other sources," Harriman wrote some weeks later, perhaps a bit more acidly than he intended, "that would have been most valuable had it been up to date." He had a fair point: some of the material he had received had been dispatched two months earlier, one batch even three months. Hopkins got right on to General Burns, who made arrangements to collect and collate statistical material for London and send it by courier and by air, not by steamer. Air communication across the Atlantic needed to be improved, Harriman said, but Hopkins noted the existence of various problems, particularly the availability of suitable aircraft. In any case, he suggested on May 6 that for the present Harriman not make a proposed trip home: "You are doing a very important job there and every time you accent something here some kind of affirmative action takes place." Until forthcoming important decisions were made in Washington, Hopkins said, Harriman ought to be in London.

The president's special representative, in fact, had many tasks and preoccupations in London, some of them not foreseen in FDR's charge to keep the British Isles afloat.

19

AT THE DORCHESTER

During a May weekend at Ditchley, Averell Harriman received an unusual and daunting assignment from the prime minister's wife. Clementine Churchill had become involved in an emotional tug-of-war with her seventeen-year-old daughter Mary, who had been accompanied to Ditchley by a suitor, a young man she saw as "entirely suitable"; her mother, however, did not share this opinion. It would have been "quite a grand marriage," Mary said in recollection, "and anybody would have thought that my mother would have been delighted." (Presumably so; the young man, aide-de-camp to a Canadian general, was the son of an eminently respectable peer who had served as governor general of Canada.) But the news of the engagement had not gone down well at all. Clementine considered Mary too young to know what she was doing, particularly amid all the uncertainty of wartime, and she had attempted to argue the point with her daughter.

Mary's father could offer no help in the crisis—he was occupied with the war, and at the moment with a particularly sensational aspect of it. That very weekend, Rudolf Hess, deputy Führer of the Nazi Party, parachuted onto a Scottish farm from a fighter plane he had piloted from Germany himself. What motives had sent this pioneer

Nazi figure on his startling, almost unbelievable flight? Had he been dispatched by Hitler, or had he come on some personal mission of his own? And was this night flier really Rudolf Hess? Who could, so to speak, vouch for him?

Shortly before the news came about the arrival of Hess, calls from London indicated that the Luftwaffe was attacking with particular intensity; the night's raid proved to be the heaviest of the Blitz, particularly to be remembered for the destruction of the House of Commons chamber—"blown to smithereens," as Churchill put it in a letter to his son, Randolph. When her husband was dealing with such questions, or even trying briefly to relax from them, Clementine did not wish to barge into the room and summon him forth to take part in an adolescent drama—at least, so Mary felt in retrospect. Clementine therefore turned to her American guest, saying, more or less, "Oh, Averell, for God's sake, I can't worry Winston, but do go and talk to the silly girl and try to get some sense into her head."

Responding dutifully, Harriman wrapped up in his coat and the two went out into a wet, muggy spring day for what proved to be a long walk around and between the hedges of Ditchley's French garden. Apparently saying nothing unusual but, nevertheless, all the right things, in his "rather sort of dull voice," Harriman calmed the excited girl. The combination of "Averell's worldly wisdom and his kind interest in my love life," she said, "worked the trick." Clementine definitely had reasons for concern about her children and marriage. Her eldest daughter, Diana, had been divorced a few years before the war began, and Sarah, the next daughter, was unhappily married to a truly unsuitable person, a comedian, and was headed for divorce. Randolph's drinking and his combative personality, and the behavior these characteristics created in combination, militated against his establishing a stable and serene relationship with anyone, but in any case he was now far away from the family circle, off in Cairo, serving as a press officer; his parents, however, treated Pamela very much as a daughter. As Hopkins had noted, she was the apple of Churchill's eye.

Quickly becoming the American of the entire Churchill family, Harriman developed another tie with Clementine. Long recognized as queen of the croquet lawn, the prime minister's wife found in Averell the only challenging opponent among all the weekenders; indeed, displaying no gallantry at all, Harriman in their first match proceeded to dethrone the queen. The two also battled at backgammon, as a personal friendship grew up between them.

During the night of April 16–17, London had reeled under the onslaught of a German bomber force estimated at more than four hundred; to Jock Colville it seemed the worst attack yet. The next morning he and another of the prime minister's secretaries walked around Whitehall in the sunshine, noting that London looked "bleary-eyed and disfigured"; the Admiralty had sustained heavy damage, and broken glass covered the streets. Along the Horse Guards Parade, Colville spotted two familiar figures, standing arm in arm or hand in hand, looking over the damage: the forty-nine-year-old special representative of President Roosevelt and the just-turned-twenty-one daughter-in-law of the prime minister.

London in the spring of 1941: an exotic city of people under attack, living defiantly and for the moment, a pressure cooker producing strange experiences for its inhabitants and certainly for Americans fresh from a country at peace. "During the war," said one, "there were all sorts of people having affairs with all sorts of people." "Unfortunately," said Colville, "there started a very special relationship between Averell and Mrs. Randolph Churchill."

During that same night of April 16–17, after Bob Meiklejohn heard the air raid sirens sounding, he borrowed a tin hat and headed for the roof of the embassy. He could hear bombers droning overhead and see fires already burning in a semicircle some distance away. For the first time he heard bombs on the way down, "more scary than actual explosions until one can form some impression whether or not they are near." He and the others did "a couple of tumbling acts," dodging bombs that actually fell blocks away. Soon as many as ten large fires were blazing around the city, accompanied by "amazingly big bomb explosions in the distance. It looked as if whole houses were sailing up into the air."

At about eleven o'clock, the Winants came up for a brief look. An hour later a huge bomb created a column of fire from an exploded gas tank at the Battersea power station on the Thames, and then Mayfair seemed to be getting more attention. A fellow watcher on the roof, onetime secretary to the former ambassador, thought a bomb might have hit his apartment building, and he and Meiklejohn left the roof and went to see. They found that the building behind the friend's flat had been demolished, and the friend's flat had lost its doors and windows, but, with bed intact, he decided he might as well retire for the night. Back at the embassy, at about three o'clock, with the huge raid continuing and the building shaking from bombs falling nearby, Meiklejohn went to the roof again. He was "met by the most amazing sight I have ever seen in my life," he said. "A whole section of the city north of the financial district was a solid mass of flames, leaping hundreds of feet into the air. It was a cloudless night but the smoke covered half of the sky and was all red from the fires below." Still more aircraft appeared overhead, dropping bombs into the fires. The attacks went on till five o'clock.

"Our first big London air raid," Meiklejohn called the night's activities, and the next morning, like Jock Colville, he took a walk to see the damage. He noted six to eight bombed buildings within a three-block radius of the embassy, and a time bomb embedded in front of the Woodstock Hotel. He took the ticking in stride.

As Averell Harriman later observed, "there was nothing like a Blitz to get something going." The "something" that Roosevelt's representative got going began during the great raid that had kept his secretary up most of the night. Of Mayfair's two leading hotels, Claridge's and the Dorchester, he had chosen as his residence the latter, on Park Lane facing Hyde Park. Though markedly indifferent to luxury and even to comfort, Harriman had, as it happened, picked the hotel that served as home for displaced elites from across the Continent and, as a modern, steel-framed building with heavy concrete between the floors, was thought by many to offer greater safety than conventional masonry structures. Even well-off Londoners moved in. "The socialites," said a reporter, "gathered in the Turkish bath." Even if you had to take refuge in a less substantial Mayfair hotel, Ed Murrow commented, if you were a retired colonel and his lady "you might feel that the risk was worth it because you would at least be bombed with the right sort of people."

On the evening of April 16, Harriman attended a dinner party at the Dorchester, and as the great raid grew in intensity the guests, in search of greater safety, trooped down to his rooms on the ground floor. The party continued for some time, and when it broke up Harriman had acquired a guest of his own. Pamela Churchill (aided by financial help from Lord Beaverbrook) was one of the many Londoners living in the Dorchester, and that exciting night she ended up alone with the American in his suite; to be sure, no one could argue that the ground floor did not offer greater safety than her room on an upper floor. They had met previously at Chequers, and Harriman of course already knew of her charms, and her possible usefulness, from Hopkins's description. Not a classic type, she was nevertheless "a tremendous beauty," a friend said, "all strawberries and cream, with great eyes." "Every man in London was attracted to her," a CBS correspondent declared. "She was honey drawing flies." (The disapproving Jock Colville was not so carried away. Having seen Pam at many dances in her teen years, he recalled that "she had no neck in those days.")

Averell certainly did not come onto the scene as a stranger to extracurricular beauties. During the 1920s, the decade in which he came closest to earning the playboy designation William Knudsen and other earnest executives gave him, he had attracted the interest of the tabloids by his relationship with Teddy Gerard, and shortly before coming to England he had been involved with the ballerina Vera Zorina, the wife of the choreographer George Balanchine. His stammering and mumbling never seemed to cause any problems in this aspect of his life. Looking enviously back to their younger years, a friend remembered being "very impressed with what beautiful women he had always had around him." Certainly, "the women loved him. He had a sort of melancholy personality, there was a little reserve, a little mystery, that drove the women mad. I used to kid him about it."

Pamela brought to the table an important something beyond physical charms: "She makes you feel," an acquaintance said, "she is absolutely interested in you and nobody else." And in Pam's eyes, Averell brought a great deal to the table besides his role in the war and his immense wealth. She had liked Hopkins, and the two had developed a sort of palship, but Harriman, though almost fifty, had the lean good looks of the sportsman he was. Neither, it appears, slept alone that night, and thus the prime minister's daughter-in-law acquired a tie to one of Roosevelt's two chief fixers to go along with her connection with Beaverbrook, who intermittently, at least, filled a comparable role. She would indeed be a repository of information, but she also could serve as a source and she had put herself in a position to play the fixer role on her own. A person close to Averell later characterized Pam as "a woman who wants to get from A to B, and she will damn well *get* to B."

Colville had asked Pam how long it took her "to get really, totally fed up with Randolph": less than a year, she told him. And by 1941 that year had passed. Of course, one could not blame her: "Randolph was always frightfully rude and offensive." Colville made no mention of his discovery to Winston or Clemmie, and he was sure they suspected nothing; they were too old-fashioned for that (surprising, perhaps, in view of the colorful sexual career of Churchill's mother). Hence, unless Clementine awoke some night to hear the patter of hurrying adult feet along one of the corridors of Chequers, she could hardly know what an unsuitable counselor Harriman made for a Churchill marital situation. But, as Colville reminded himself, Professor Lindemann liked to point out that men are naturally polygamous. The Prof perhaps did not feel it necessary to mention the frequent simultaneous occurrence of polygamous behavior and suspension of judgment. In the new affair, Pam made her own curious contribution to the cause of discretion. In order to leave no paper trail, if she and Averell both found themselves at Chequers on a particular weekend, she did not sign the guest book.

On Friday, May 16, Harriman's personal situation took a new and, as it proved, pragmatic turn. Kathleen, the younger of his two daughters, flew into Bristol and from there came by train to Paddington station. Harriman went off to meet her at 8:30, but Kathleen, a brisk and self-sufficient young woman, obtained a taxi so quickly that her father missed her and had to pursue her to the Dorchester. A graduate of Bennington, with much of the self-actualizing spirit that characterized the college's philosophy and its focus on life experience, Kathy, through an associate of her father's, had arranged a job with the International News Service—as fate would have it, the syndicate operated by the isolationist Hearst newspapers—and had come to London to see Ave (as she called him) and experience the excitement at the war's focal point. It turned out that she had come to see Pam as well, since they quickly became a threesome in the cozy confines of the Dorchester; Pam had left baby Winston in what seemed the permanent care of Lord Beaverbrook's staff at Cherkley.

Writing home about her new friend, Kathy commented on her many connections and her wisdom; indeed, "she was in on everything and it was a good way to find what the prime minister was about." Before long Kathy discovered one close connection she did not choose to report. She knew that her father had no reputation for marital fidelity, and in any case she considered the liaison no concern of hers—she was, of course, the daughter of Averell's first wife, not of Marie, who had a relationship of her own with the bandleader and pianist Eddie Duchin, Peter's father.

Just a week after Kathy's arrival, Harriman, weekending at Chequers with Churchill, was roused from sleep by a very excited prime minister, who was colorfully clad in a nightshirt and yellow sweater. The company had spent the previous evening waiting for reports from the Admiralty on the whereabouts of the German super-battleship *Bismarck* on its foray into the Atlantic. Finally, with no news, everyone had gone to bed, but now Churchill was declaiming to his American guest: "Hell of a battle going on." The battle cruiser *Hood* had been sunk—a grievous loss for the Royal Navy, as Churchill did not need to say. "Hell of a battle!" the prime minister repeated. In fact, the fight and the pursuit went on for three days, being brought to its climax after a decidedly unneutral American flier in a lend-lease PBY spotted the giant ship; an armada of ships and aircraft then combined to sink her. Harriman felt very much a part of the scene.

Kathleen and Pamela soon had arranged for the threesome to occupy a much larger suite in the Dorchester, and then Averell presented them with a country cottage. This move gave the group their own weekend place, allowing Averell to tone up by practicing the wood-chopping skills he had acquired at Groton, and baby Winston could join them. Before long Kathy and Pam, who had quickly become well known as chums, had discovered an available flat located, of all places, at 3 Grosvenor Square; with Averell away much of the time now, they said, Pam could move in and provide company for Kathy, who was serving as Ave's de facto social secretary. Kathy arranged to borrow furniture, and the ménage was born.

Kathy received an unusual indoctrination into basic London from the noted radio performer and wit Alexander Woollcott, one of the Long Island croquet gang whom she had disliked intensely. The inspiration for the central character in the play *The Man Who Came to Dinner*, Woollcott was "nasty," Kathy said; "he would reduce people to tears, women to tears, just for the joy of it." Despite her opinion of him, however, she agreed when Woollcott, visiting England, told her, "Put yourself in my hands for one week." He "took me around wartime London to all of the things that hadn't changed even though there was a war on—the prostitutes coming into court on Monday morning and things like that." As a reporter, Kathy proved to have a special value for Pam; through her, the prime minister's daughter met the elite group of American journalists based in London, and one in particular: Ed Murrow.

"Life is unbelievably social," Kathy wrote her sister Mary; people seemed to be afraid of being lonely and made sure to keep their calendars full. Though Harriman worked long hours, he and his daughter

kept busy socially during the week—Averell being the most prominent American official in London—and for the weekends they had
Chequers and Cherkley and the new cottage just a few miles away
from Beaverbrook's country seat. Kathy found Beaverbrook enjoyable,
though "he was something of a scoundrel and would use people," and
his idea of sport was "to surround himself with intelligent men, then
egg them on to argue and fight among themselves"; he and Averell
"got on famously." Clementine Churchill took Kathy into the family and had her down to Chequers even if Averell was away, but she
"always thought it was terrible that I was a reporter," Kathy said. Perhaps Clemmie had forgotten that, half a century earlier, her husband
had begun his literary career as a correspondent.

Being in England, up front in the war, had turned out to be as exciting as Kathy had imagined, and she was proving useful to her father.
Although she had not intended to make it a long visit, she decided to
stay around for more adventures.

20

ON HIS MAJESTY'S SERVICE

At the time Kathleen Harriman and Pamela Churchill staked their claim on the Grosvenor Square flat, Averell Harriman had departed on the kind of trip that definitely gave credence to their point about his absences. At the same time, it was unique.

Amid all the reverses suffered in early 1941—in Greece and Crete, in the Atlantic, and in North Africa (at the hands of a bold new German commander, Erwin Rommel)—the one theater in which British arms experienced success was East Africa. Victories over the Italians in the Somaliland and Eritrea and the capture of the port of Berbera, on the Gulf of Aden, on March 16 and then of Massawa, on the Red Sea, on April 7 brought important new possibilities. On April 11, President Roosevelt, as Oscar Cox had suggested to Hopkins, declared the Red Sea no longer a combat zone, thus opening it to American shipping previously banned from these waters by the Neutrality Act, which, almost strangely, continued in legal force.

Churchill had felt a need and seen an opportunity in this same area. Always concerned about threats to the Suez Canal and ready to run heavy risks to support British forces in Egypt (as in sending tanks from England when some of his leading advisers feared German invasion landings), the prime minister brought the commander in chief, Middle East, General Sir Archibald Wavell, up to date in a long message of June 4. President Roosevelt was sending two hundred light tanks beyond the number originally expected, Churchill said, and he intended to see that from now on all such American matériel went straight from the United States to Wavell's forces, cutting out transshipment in Britain. To help the general make the most of the increased aid he would receive, and to lighten his genuinely complex, area-wide responsibilities, Churchill would soon dispatch a political adviser (a "minister of state"), the amiable Oliver Lyttelton, along with an officer (as "intendant-general") whose true function, it appeared, would be to make sure that Wavell did what the prime minister wanted him to do.

In addition to British political and military support, Churchill said, he had asked Roosevelt to make Averell Harriman available, "because of the great mass and importance" of the new supplies. "It would be disastrous," the prime minister observed, "if large accumulations of American supplies arrived without efficient measures for their reception" and without commensurate plans for future handling. "Mr. Harriman enjoys my complete confidence," Churchill said, "and is in the most intimate relations with the President and with Mr. Harry Hopkins. No one can do more for you." That put it squarely up to the general, a much-admired officer in the British Army but a commander with whom the prodding, action-seeking Churchill had been increasingly losing patience.

In suggesting the mission for Harriman, Churchill had pointed out to Roosevelt the need to develop a base for receiving the flow of American tanks and aircraft and other supplies and for American personnel to instruct recipients in the use of them and to supervise maintenance. Harriman could make recommendations to ensure efficiency in these areas, and beyond that Churchill asked him to take a general look at the British Army's situation in relation to supplies and to make his own analysis of Britain's potential in the theater. Thus Harriman, who had arrived in Britain as Roosevelt's special representative, would now go out to the Middle East in a comparable role for Churchill, as if he were "on His Majesty's service" like the officers and civil servants with whom he would be dealing.

On Tuesday, June 3, when Bob Meiklejohn learned that his boss was planning a trip to the Middle East, he made a bid to go along and won Harriman's ready approval. Colonel Green and Brigadier General Ralph Royce (who had just replaced General Harmon on the staff of the Harriman Mission) would also make the trip as, respectively, ordnance and aviation expert. Meiklejohn, dismissed by Kathleen Harriman as a young man concerned only with his bookkeeping, lined up a reconditioned Catalina patrol bomber just converted to civilian use, arranged for permits that would allow the group to buy tropical clothes (very strict rules governed clothes rationing), and tended to other necessary chores; knowing his boss, he felt safe in disregarding a British general's advice to take his dinner jacket to Cairo. For his part, Harriman arranged for a reluctant General Lee to mind the store while he was away, and on Sunday the party took off for Lisbon.

During the inevitable stopover at the Portuguese capital, Harriman got off a note to Hopkins in which, almost wistfully, he expressed his pleasure at the availability of two-day-old New York newspapers; "in London," he said, "we jump for them if they are within a month." The direct contact with America brought about by the regular arrival of the Clippers created "an atmosphere and understanding that is completely lacking in London." The United States must set up "frequent direct service by air" with Britain "to get anything approaching full benefit of America's war effort." This declaration represented no passing fancy for Harriman; a month earlier, in a memo for Washington, he had listed it as the most important need, ahead of such items as repairing British ships in American ports or delivering more antiaircraft guns or tanks.

Harriman also told Hopkins that, after three months in London, he had concluded that Britain could not win the war without direct American intervention, at least with the navy and air force. "Every week America waits," he said, "the difficulties of the job when we do come in will be multiplied." He definitely did not realize that his *when* differed from the president's *if.* Their basic analyses did not differ, however: Britain could not win without American participation. How clearly either saw a further point is a question not easily answered— whether Britain might not win even with the United States as a full partner. The strategic situation that had developed in Europe during the 1930s and through 1940 may well have decreed a grim reality: the democracies could not defeat either of the two great totalitarian powers without the aid of the other one. General Lee made the point in his own fashion, saying that he could not see how "the British Empire can defeat Germany without the help of God or Uncle Sam. Perhaps it will take both." (Advocates of strategic bombing would not agree, to be sure.) In any case, Harriman expressed his worry about American complacency over the Battle of the Atlantic. He also expressed his concern over the news that sickness had forced Hopkins into bed. His friend must take care of himself, Harriman said: "You are the only man in Washington who has a grasp of the exigencies of the situation, the need for speed, and who gets things done."

At 7:45 in the evening of June 11, Harriman's flying boat left Lisbon on the first leg of the planned African grand tour, arriving at Bathurst, Gambia, a little over twelve hours later; the next stops were Freetown, Sierra Leone; Lagos, Nigeria; and Takoradi, Gold Coast. Harriman looked at Bathurst and Freetown from the point of view of their suitability as landing grounds for U.S. aircraft flown across the Atlantic. As always, he scrutinized everything close up and minutely, measuring and calculating distances and depths.

Tokoradi represented a special case. American planes, shipped knocked down from the factories, were assembled here at a secret plant and then flown across the continent, via Khartoum, to Cairo. The daily routine of the officers at Tokoradi represented something of a revelation for Meiklejohn. Taking note of the seven different occasions during the day that involved food and drink, consumed at a leisurely pace, he found it remarkable "that they get any work done at all." His boss nevertheless gave the Tokoradi plant a passing grade, but the service that delivered the assembled planes to Cairo did not fare as well—poorly organized, with two air commodores, RAF officials in Cairo, and the civilian British Overseas Airways Corporation all having a hand in the operation. (At Lagos, Meiklejohn noted, a number of bombers were held up because they lacked tires; at another stop, fighter planes sat idle because of the shortage of pilots.) Harriman's recommendation could not have surprised Churchill: "This ferry service should be put in the hands of one active, competent man with full power and supplied with the necessary equipment to make it an efficient operation."

The flights within West Africa were made in a twin-engine Lockheed Electra (the aircraft model identified with Amelia Earhart, who had disappeared in the Pacific just four years earlier), but now for the long ferry ride across the continent Harriman's team switched to another Lockheed model, the Lodestar (essentially an enlarged Electra). The trip had its complexities, from bad weather to short airstrips and lack of navigational aids; because they could not fly at night, they spent two-and-a-half days en route. None of these difficulties discommoded Harriman personally; not only indifferent to comfort, he paid little attention to heat, dust storms, or hostile insects, and, with his remarkable drive, never seemed to get tired.

Noting the wrecked planes they saw at every airstrip, the prime minister's observer had no trouble seeing why; even malaria played a part in the problems by crippling the work force. At this point in the survey, he had decided that the United States should take the responsibility for operating the ferry route.

In Cairo, General Wavell and his headquarters made a poor impression on Churchill's investigator, who reacted much as his secretary had done at Tokoradi. He later recalled his shock at the "luxury and complacence of British life in Cairo, as compared [with] London. There was no blackout. Food appeared to be in ample supply." The meeting took place in the context not only of the disasters in Greece and Crete but of a fresh defeat: just five days before, the British had launched an operation (Battleaxe) in the Western Desert to take out Rommel's armor, but it had already failed, and the attackers had retreated.

The group of high-living officers at Cairo headquarters included one who had a semiofficial mistress (the wife of a colonel) and a variety of other affairs and encounters—a young man who had quickly matched in Egypt the reputation for rowdy behavior he had long possessed in England. It seemed only right to his father that his son should become acquainted with Averell Harriman, the American expediter, agent of the prime minister and good friend of the son's wife. Accordingly, Randolph Churchill became an aide to the visitor during his stay in Egypt. The two went together on an inspection trip to Suez and two days later flew, with General Wavell, to Ethiopia, visiting ports on the Red Sea. They hit it off well. "I have been extremely impressed by Harriman," Randolph wrote his father, "and can well understand the regard you have for him. In ten very full and active days, he has definitely become my favorite American" —the standing, though Randolph did not know it, that Harriman also held with Randolph's wife.

As for Randolph, a surprising and redeeming side of his nature emerged. He was "not at all high hat," said Bob Meiklejohn, "and very pleasant company"; indeed, the young American saw Randolph as "very good natured"—a unique but honest opinion. For the jaunt with

Wavell and Harriman, the amiable Randolph borrowed Meiklejohn's notebook and even his pencil so that he could fill in as secretary.

"GHQ does not appear to be well organized," Harriman reported to the prime minister; "the telephone service is inexcusably bad and without a pre-arranged guide it is impossible to locate the room of even important officers." These and other more substantive observations and recommendations, however, came too late to help Wavell. Although the general was the theater commander in chief and not the army commander in the field, the latest failure proved to be the last straw for Churchill; Wavell was sent off to India, being replaced by General Sir Claude Auchinleck. The desert commander Churchill really needed, and probably wanted, was Rommel himself, who unfortunately served in the wrong army, though in what would prove a brief tenure "the Auk" would experience greater success than the prime minister realized.

Harriman examined Red Sea ports, railroads, and highways. Management of Egyptian railroads he found "lackadaisical," essentially the type of problem he saw everywhere, along with divided responsibilities, interservice bickering, and the need to make major improvements in communications systems. Characteristically, he called for direct air service, London to Cairo; having made much of the trip in low-flying, slow planes that invited enemy attack, he specified that the new service should be high altitude, with B-24s.

In view of the threat Rommel's advance posed to Egypt, including Cairo and even the Suez Canal, General Auchinleck immediately had to consider how to respond in case of disaster—withdraw up the Nile or move his forces across the canal. Since the new commander favored the latter, Harriman flew off in the Lodestar for a four-day trip to survey ports and installations in Iraq. For him, Auchinleck's choice was clearly right: the British must keep control of the oil fields. His recommendations included extending the railroad from Baghdad toward Syria and developing an alternative port to Basra, which was excellent but vulnerable to being isolated by mines, since an eighty-five-mile channel separated it from the Persian Gulf.

Because a mechanical problem delayed for a day the mission's departure for home, Harriman had the opportunity to end his Middle East tour on a pleasantly affirmative note. On July 10 he accompanied Auchinleck to a demonstration of U.S. light tanks, delivered straight from the factory and the first to arrive in the theater; the general responded to the show with enthusiasm. Then, having thus wound up the mission, Harriman and his team, homeward bound, took off in a Sunderland flying boat, with Malta as the first scheduled stop, a thousand miles away through skies watched by Axis fighters on both sides of the Mediterranean. This hazardous program definitely did not represent an example of the kind of fast, high-altitude service between Cairo and London that Harriman recommended in his report to the prime minister; the white-painted Sunderland, a flying if not sitting duck, flapped through the air at just ninety knots. Though it carried machine guns, it could put up little defense against fighter attack, and the pilot generally stayed no more than two hundred feet above the sea to avoid attracting the attention of the enemy. If danger arose, the defensive plan called for dropping down as low as fifty feet above the water. Since the approach to Malta had to be made after dark, as the Sunderland neared the embattled island the crew blacked it out by placing pie-shaped shields in the portholes. After an abbreviated stay, just long enough for a conference but not for sleep, the party left at two o'clock in the morning to get beyond the reach of Italian fighters before dawn.

Foul weather in southern England then delayed the travelers at Gibraltar for four days, and it was not until the early evening of July

15, after a ten-hour flight from the Rock, that they arrived at Plymouth. They had been away for more than five weeks. During this time they had seen exotic sights and experienced a variety of adventures, with Harriman even acknowledging a "boyish thrill" on flying over the Tigris and Euphrates rivers; he was returning to England with an array of recommendations calling not only for a higher level of performance by the British in Africa but for much greater American involvement in the whole theater. Churchill could hardly have asked for more from this second of the two influential Americans he had sought to make his own, and with Harriman his task had been easier: Hopkins had come first to inquire, Harriman had come to fight.

And now, during Harriman's absence in Africa, the war and the world had undergone a great transformation.

21

THE COLOSSUS FACTOR

In late February 1941, talking with several western reporters in Moscow, Sir Stafford Cripps declared his belief that Germany was going to attack Russia; he expected this invasion to come before the end of June. At the time, a series of treaties—nonaggression, friendship, trade—officially governed relations between the two powers, and the Soviet government, though nursing various complaints about some German actions, made every effort to live up to the arrangement between them, which called for a partnership in which the Russians were to supply the Reich with food, oil, and raw materials; in essence, Stalin wanted to keep the tiger tamed, or, at least, keep its fury directed elsewhere.

But what had led the British ambassador to his conclusion? It did not have the support of his own government's intelligence services, which presumed that the Russians and the Germans would settle their differences by negotiation, leaving Hitler free in the coming summer to attempt an invasion of Britain, if he should choose to do it. Most observers could not believe that, after Germany's experience in the 1914–1918 war, the Führer would create a major front in the East while still involved in a war in the West; after all, his policy of one at a time, both in diplomacy and in war, had served him supremely well up until now.

One likely source of Cripps's information was his colleague in Moscow, the American ambassador, and from there the trail led back to an enterprising U.S. diplomat, Sam Woods, assistant commercial attaché at the Berlin embassy. Woods had built up a close relationship with a disaffected Nazi official who had kept him briefed on Hitler's plans and had given him a copy of the Führer's directive for the Russian campaign. The Americans had handed this information, perhaps with some accompanying material from cryptanalysis, to the Soviet ambassador in Washington.

This, as it turned out, would represent only one of many American and British attempts to warn the Soviets of the danger they faced. Information from agents in Eastern Europe about troop deployments, construction of airfields, recruitment of Russian speakers into the German army, and an array of other items combined with diplomatic talk, which actually became a swelling chorus as the weeks advanced, to create a comprehensive picture. Then, in May, as Cripps's deadline came closer, the Ultra cryptanalysts at Bletchley Park began producing details concerning German dispositions that strongly indicated imminent invasion of the Soviet Union. It was, of course, not a certainty, and some felt for a time that the activities in the East amounted to a cover for a buildup in the West, with Britain as the target.

President Roosevelt, who believed the implications of all the information that had come to him, sent warnings to Stalin; Churchill, sharing this belief, made similar efforts. In all, western leaders made eighty-four documented attempts to warn Stalin; but all of these were dismissed as provocations, nothing more than vicious efforts to stir up trouble between Russia and Germany. (Stalin also brushed off similar reports from his own intelligence agents.) The Soviet dictator lived in a fearful mental state that required him to deny the possibility of imminent war, and faithfully, day after day, he continued to deliver the expected goods to his German partners.

On June 12, Stalin declared to a group of his generals: "I am certain that Hitler will not risk creating a second front by attacking the Soviet Union. Hitler is not such an idiot." And then, just ten days later, in the early morning hours, in a sudden great thunderclap the Wehrmacht exploded eastward, attacking Soviet forces on a thousand-mile front in the greatest land operation ever seen. In *Mein Kampf*, Hitler had written: "If the Urals, with their immeasurable treasure of raw materials, Siberia, with its rich forests, and the Ukraine, with its limitless grain fields, were to lie in Germany, this country under National Socialist leadership would swim in plenty." The Führer with his mighty forces had now, in Operation Barbarossa, entered into the active pursuit of his old dream, sometimes described as the drive for *Lebensraum* for the German people but having for Hitler almost a mystical meaning. He had also begun a process that could produce a transformation of the geopolitical situation: one of the great totalitarian powers had now gone to war with the other. But for how long? Opinions would vary.

On the day after the invasion, in the very different world of Washington, the tireless Oscar Cox presented Harry Hopkins with a definitive opinion on a critical question. The Soviet Union had served as Hitler's accomplice right up until yesterday, and communism ranked high on the list of evils for the great majority of Americans; certainly Stalin enjoyed little popularity on Capitol Hill. In this particular memo, Cox did not concern himself with such points but simply told his boss that "there is no doubt at all that aid can legally be rendered to Russia under the Lend-Lease Act." The act specifically stated that aid could be given to "any country whose defense the President deems vital to the defense of the United States." And both the House and the Senate had rejected amendments whose sponsors sought to specify the countries eligible for aid or to prohibit any possible aid to the Soviet Union. In its report, the Senate Foreign Relations Committee had summed up the issue: "Too few of us know the course which wars like those now in progress may take. In times so unpredictable, under a Constitution which authorizes it, a President should be trusted to use the responsibility imposed upon him adequately and swiftly to safeguard the best interests of this nation against dangers of which he, better than most, can be aware."

In another memo, Cox listed a series of points supporting a policy of aid to Russia, beginning simply with the principle that "we must keep our eye on the main objective—to see that Hitler is defeated." Hitler could become so bogged down and weakened in the fight against Russia that he could "never carry out his plan of world domination." Cox noted the clear, practical choice: "Whether or not we like Russia's internal and other policies, we will aid Russia, in our own national interest, to eliminate the far more immediate danger to our security from Hitler's already partially executed plans to rule the world."

Looking at all angles, Cox busied himself on the twenty-third in the preparation of still other material for Hopkins's use. In one memo he suggested that "the anti-religious part of the Nazi policy ought to be emphasized to prevent too many Catholics from getting confused into a policy of no support for the Russian fight." He was also collecting quotes from Hitler and other Germans about their views as to world domination, the need to acquire Russian granaries, and other relevant questions.

Whether to support Russia was one great question, but another loomed even larger: What good would it do? On the same day, June 23,

Secretary Stimson, wrestling with the question of the effect on U.S. policy of the new war, informed the president that General Marshall and his officers in the War Plans Division of the General Staff estimated that Germany would be "thoroughly occupied for a minimum of one month" and that the job might take as long as three months—that was all. If that calendar should hold, then the question of aid—production, allocation, delivery, and all the rest of it—would hardly possess even academic interest. Stimson did not seem to consider the issue worth further comment, but went on to discuss what actions the United States might take in the Atlantic theater during this period of German preoccupation with Russia. This followed Harry Hopkins's line of just a week earlier, when he had urged the president to turn the Neutrality Patrol into an armed escort service for American merchant ships, as a response to the sinking by a U-boat of an American freighter (the *Robin Moor*) in the South Atlantic. Roosevelt rejected the idea.

The British military experts essentially agreed with the Americans, though hedging their bet just a bit, seeing Barbarossa as leading merely to a temporary postponement of an attempted invasion of the United Kingdom. "It cannot be over-emphasized," they said, "that this is only temporary." The campaign might be over in three or four weeks; it might take longer. Behind these deeply negative western judgments lay such factors as Stalin's purge just a few years earlier of the Soviet officer caste and its leadership, which had cost the Red Army much of its brains and experience; the army's fumbling performance against Finland in the 1939–40 Winter War; and, in general, the fact that the Soviet government was "notoriously incompetent."

In London, turning his microphone over to the American foreign correspondent Vincent Sheean, who had traveled in Russia in earlier years, Ed Murrow suggested that his friend curb any optimism about the campaign in view of the experts' agreement on the hopelessness of the Russian cause. Ignoring him, however, Sheean declared on the air that the Red Army would hold out, "even though it should retreat to Irkutsk."

Broadcasting from Chequers, since the twenty-second was a Sunday, Churchill, castigating Hitler as "this bloodthirsty guttersnipe," promised to give "whatever help we can to Russia and the Russian people." As he said to Colville, "If Hitler invaded Hell I would at least make a favorable reference to the devil in the House of Commons." Though not forecasting the outcome of the fighting, the prime minister declared simply, "Any man or state who fights on against Nazidom will have our aid. Any man or state who marches with Hitler is our foe." And when he went to bed he said over and over how wonderful it was that Russia had "come in against Germany when she might so easily have been with her." But, of course, the Russians had not made the move of their own volition; they were like a big, heavy-footed prey animal, trying to avoid a predator but finding nowhere to run. (Churchill's promise to help Russia did not mean very much, General Lee commented. "They made the same promise to Poland, which was too remote for them to reach. Russia is even more remote than Poland was.")

And Roosevelt? In making his clear and direct case for aiding Russia, Oscar Cox had pointed out the likely areas of objection, political and religious, but Cox was not president of the United States. FDR would not have to yield to such objections, but he would have to take account of them. General Wood, the president of America First, declared, for example, that interventionists could hardly "ask the American people to take up arms behind the Red flag of Stalin." For many, the German attack came as welcome news because it alleviated fears of an assault on England and thereby made life simpler for the United States. A number of political figures, and not only isolationists, saw the war in the East as a useful development because it involved dictators and totalitarian ideologies in a deadly struggle with each other; one senator expressing such a view was Harry S. Truman of Missouri, though he added that in no case should the West help Hitler win.

For their part, interventionists could hardly pretend that the German attack had turned Stalin into a saint overnight, but they stressed Cox's point: Germany posed the far more immediate threat to American security. At the moment, however, even interventionists did not press for direct U.S. aid to Russia. The intellectual and emotional change was too great and had come too fast. Roman Catholic leaders preached and broadcast their anticommunism, as Cox had foreseen. The military leaders, with their pessimism about the outcome of Barbarossa, feared that American hardware sent to Russia would simply be seized by the Germans (the twin of the fear of a year earlier about the likely fate of American matériel sent to Britain). A Gallup poll taken two days after the attack showed only 35 percent support for the same kind of aid for the Soviet Union as the United States was giving to Britain; 54 percent of the respondents opposed it. As an example of existing attitudes, on the day that Gallup poll was taken the Illinois legislature adopted a series of acts barring from electoral ballots the Communist Party or any other group associated "directly or indirectly with communistic, Fascist, Nazi or other un-American principles." The *New York Times*, however, put the point not as "Help Russia" but as "Stop Hitler!"

In a press conference on June 24, the president spoke calmly and carefully. "Of course we are going to give all the aid we possibly can to Russia," he told the reporters; the United States would give material assistance to any country fighting Germany. He had not yet received a request for aid, however, and had no list of Soviet military needs, and he indicated that American help could hardly be effective unless the Nazi–Soviet war proved to be a long one. He spoke against the backdrop of dramatic Wehrmacht advances in these initial days. The president also declared that Britain would still have priority on American aid. But he could make immediate moves on behalf of Russia, including the release of Soviet funds that had been frozen and the decision not to apply the Neutrality Act to the Soviet–German war, which meant that American ships could sail into Russian ports. He also, more quietly, saw to it that talks began with the Soviets, in both Washington and Moscow, on military aid from the United States to Russia.

On Wednesday, July 16, the first day back in the office for the members of the Harriman mission after their African tour, they received the surprising news that the next day Harry Hopkins would be arriving at Prestwick airport, in southern Scotland. Rather than a comfortable but lamentably slow Clipper to Lisbon, Hopkins was flying the Atlantic in an austere B-24, on a route that symbolized Harriman's dream of an effective air link between Britain and the United States.

Hopkins's trip grew out of a long conversation with Roosevelt during the previous Friday evening. The time had definitely come, FDR had decided, to make arrangements for the long-anticipated meeting of the president and the prime minister, and the new Russo–German conflict had created a strategic situation, with implications not only in Europe but in the Middle East, that demanded high-level talk between the Americans and the British; FDR cabled the news to Winant. Hopkins spent the weekend in meetings with various members of his Lend-Lease team, dined on Saturday with Lord Halifax— he had developed an extremely cordial working relationship with his hopeless Tory—and on Sunday flew to Montreal and thence to Gander, Newfoundland, the air base from which lend-lease bombers set out for Scotland.

Harriman decided not to wait for Hopkins to arrive in London but to fly up to Scotland to welcome him and begin talking. He returned, with Hopkins in tow, in the middle of the afternoon of the seventeenth. The mission office had arranged accommodations for Hopkins at Claridge's, his old hotel, but—though he had been quite ill on the trip over—he drew on his remarkable drive to make an appearance at 10 Downing Street at about 5:30, bearing gifts of ham, cheese, cigars, and other bounty from the New World, most of which seems to have been for the prime minister, though Tommy Thompson received cigarettes.

Hopkins also carried notes for his own guidance from his talks with Roosevelt; three short items had the force of injunctions:

economic or territorial deals—No;
Harriman not policy;
no talk about war.

The Harriman reference simply meant the practice already in force, at least ideally: the realm of policy belonged to Winant, the ambassador, not to Harriman, the expediter. The last item is more provocative: Hopkins should not talk with Churchill about the United States entering the war, or better, perhaps, should not be talked by Churchill into talking about it. That subject Roosevelt reserved for himself; at the moment he did not discuss it at all.

The endless conversations that were to follow Hopkins's appearance at No. 10 began with a War Cabinet session that evening and, naturally, blended into a Chequers weekend for both Hopkins and Harriman. The chums Kathleen and Pamela were included, along with the regulars Brendan Bracken and Pug Ismay. (Kathleen was pretty, Colville noted, but "convinced of the superiority of the United States in all things." The next day they had an argument about *Citizen Kane,* for Jock a "deplorable American film.") The party steadily grew, becoming a true exaltation of luminaries: General Sir Harold Alexander, who then had a domestic command in England, came for lunch on Saturday; Ivan Maisky, the veteran Soviet ambassador, turned up for tea; the evening brought General Sir Alan Brooke, commander in chief of the Home Forces; Admiral Sir Dudley Pound, the First Sea Lord; and Colonel Robert Laycock, a pioneer Commando officer. (The group also included an air chief marshal, who would later cause a considerable stir by "running off" with, of all people, the wife of General Auchinleck.) On Sunday, Professor Lindemann, who had now become Lord Cherwell, came over from Oxford as usual, and also arriving for lunch was the popular American news commentator Raymond Gram Swing, who broadcast from New York for the BBC—a sort of reciprocal Edward R. Murrow. In the evening Clement Attlee, the Labour Party leader and deputy prime minister in the coalition government, and his wife came to dine and sleep. The talk this night went on until three o'clock, with Attlee and Harriman leading the brigade of yawners, when Hopkins finally succeeded in arguing Churchill into closing out his monologue and retiring. (On Harry's behalf, Clementine Churchill disapproved of these long sessions. Always worried about his frail health, she would try to persuade him to get more rest, tempting him with talk of the nice hot-water bottle she had placed in his bed.)

During the talks, arrangements were made for the coming conference of Churchill and Roosevelt, which would take place in early August in a Newfoundland bay, but much of the strategic discussion during Hopkins's stay concerned the Middle East. He brought news of the view of the American chiefs of staff that the British did not have the resources to defend the United Kingdom and simultaneously build up their forces in the Middle East. Churchill could not accept this judgment, and Harriman, whose trip to Iraq had been made partly in response to the beginning of Barbarossa and the consequent possibility of a German strike southeastward, strongly opposed it; Roosevelt in absentia seemed inclined to agree with the Churchill view, since it offered action against the enemy. In the talks the American representatives received an object lesson in British practice: while they felt free to differ among themselves in a joint session, they heard General Dill, who had strongly and consistently opposed Churchill's view on the Middle East, express the precisely contrary opinion when called on by the prime minister. As standard practice, the British did all their disagreeing behind closed doors, presenting a common front in meeting with allies. (A signal exception to the rule was sometimes offered by the mischievous Lord Beaverbrook.)

But what about the great issue, Russia? In truth, it was not yet recognized as such by most of Hopkins's hosts; in its fifth week the German advance rolled on and the Red Army, suffering titanic losses in men killed and men taken prisoner, gave ground and then more ground. Yet, despite Western negativisim, it still stood in the ring. Shortly after the launching of Barbarossa, the British had responded by dispatching a military fact-finding mission to Moscow, headed by Lieutenant General Mason Macfarlane. Now, having been in Russia almost four weeks, "Mason-Mac" expressed a degree of optimism, a sentiment shared by Cripps and the American ambassador, Laurence Steinhardt, but, as Steinhardt conceded, it was extremely difficult to get any idea of what was going on in the Soviet Union because of the suspicion and secretiveness that characterized all Russians in dealings with foreigners. The American military attaché, like almost all of the military officers, U.S. or British, expressed total pessimism.

Without some knowledge, not only of the actual situation on the ground but of Stalin's outlook and plans, the Americans and the British could make no reasonable plans of their own in relation to Russia. Just two weeks hence, the president and the prime minister would meet off Newfoundland; clearly, they needed much more information and insight into the Soviet situation, but at present they had almost none. Hopkins saw one answer: he would fly to Moscow and meet with Stalin, provided, of course, Roosevelt approved; he could then return in time to go with Churchill to the Newfoundland meeting. The United States had an ambassador in Moscow, and there was, of course, the military attaché, but these representatives generally found themselves facing the standard stone wall. On the other hand, Hopkins, as a high-level personal representative, could go to Russia as a substitute for the president himself, doing what the president would do if it were possible—just as he had done with Churchill. His going would indicate—and, indeed, dramatize—the seriousness of Roosevelt's purposes, and he could be received by Stalin accordingly. Replying on July 26, the president expressed hearty approval, adding, "I will send you a message tonight for Stalin." In that message, which duly arrived, Roosevelt gave his emissary his greatest credential: "I ask you to treat Mr. Hopkins with the identical confidence you would feel if you were talking directly to me."

On July 28, in a telegram to Stalin, Churchill gave full backing to Hopkins's mission. "I must tell you," he said, "that there is a flame in this man for democracy and to beat Hitler." More meaningful to Stalin than any democratic ardor, perhaps, was Churchill's identification of Hopkins as "the nearest personal representative of the president." He pointed out that when he had asked Hopkins for a quarter of a million rifles, "they came at once." Hopkins, said the prime minister, "is your friend and our friend," and "you can trust him absolutely."

After a farewell turn in the garden with Churchill to end this second Chequers weekend, and a "God bless you, Harry," Hopkins drove off with the Harrimans for Euston station, his destination being the naval air base at Invergordon, on the coast in northern Scotland. The party left Chequers in such a rush that Hopkins could not even stop by Claridge's, and just as the train was beginning to move, Ambassador Winant ran up with passports hastily scribbled by his Soviet counterpart, Ivan Maisky. (Hopkins's British friends apparently were the perpetrators of one particular offense, making off with a certain curly-brimmed and well-worn hat; Hopkins therefore departed from Chequers elegantly topped by a homburg stamped with the initials WSC.)

Aside from his other activities, Hopkins had just delivered a major radio address and now, after a train ride through the night, would be setting off on a recently inaugurated and hazardous route from Scotland around the North Cape of Norway to Archangel. Fittingly enough, he would fly in one of the PBY Catalina flying boats he had induced the U.S. Navy to release to Britain—which meant, however, that, like Harriman on his recent Mediterranean trip, he would be traveling on a slow, tempting target. He would sit in the tail gunner's blister.

Arriving at Archangel after a 20 ½-hour flight, Hopkins assured the captain, Flight Lieutenant D. C. McKinley, that he had passed a pleasant journey. That could not conceivably be true, McKinley thought, as he saw how tired Hopkins looked, but "this was an early indication of his determination to totally disregard personal comfort." Hopkins and his companions, two U.S. officers, then transferred to a Soviet plane for the flight to Moscow. En route, peering down at the vastness and density of the forests over which they flew, Hopkins decided that Russia would not be an easy country for anyone to conquer.

In a long talk with Ambassador Steinhardt, Hopkins described one of his purposes as simply being to learn whether the situation was as bad as the War Department believed. Steinhardt replied by making a point that seemed to have been overlooked by the military professionals in London and Washington: nobody who knew anything about Russian history could believe that the Germans were going to win an easy victory. Yet, at least for a few weeks, that had been the view held by both the British and the American staffs.

Hopkins met with various officials in Moscow, but the high point and essence of the trip came in two long conferences with Stalin. The Soviet dictator discussed the military situation not only candidly but in remarkable detail (which Hopkins efficiently captured in his notes), talking about deficiencies in his army and its equipment but also about positive points, and he pressed his visitor to expedite shipment of vital supplies. One item struck Hopkins with particular force: Stalin stressed the importance of aluminum. If he was giving a raw material rather than a finished product a high priority at this juncture, Hopkins decided, that meant that he expected the war to go on. At one point Stalin said, "Give us antiaircraft guns and aluminum and we can fight for three or four years." He also said forcefully, "They will never get to Moscow this year." Hopkins found himself agreeing. (Stalin might have spoken even more forcefully, and Hopkins's conviction might have run even deeper, had the two known that, within less than two weeks, the chief of the German General Staff would note somberly, "The whole situation shows more and more clearly that we have underestimated the colossus of Russia.")

Since the schedule required Hopkins to return quickly to Britain in order to join Churchill for the voyage to Newfoundland, he left Moscow on August 1. In a brief cable to Washington, he said, "I feel ever so confident about this front. The morale of the population is exceptionally good. There is unbounded determination to win."

Although pointing out in the detailed report he later produced that he used no source of information besides Stalin, Hopkins returned to the West fully convinced that the Soviet Union would not collapse under the German attack and that the Americans must hasten to provide aid.

"He looked very tired and ill when coming aboard," said Flight Lieutenant McKinley, but Hopkins had an even greater problem than usual because he had flown out of Moscow without the satchel containing the array of medicines he took every day. As he left the flying boat at Invergordon, McKinley and his crew "wondered if there was to be any rest for a man so obviously ill and yet showing unbelievable courage, determination and appreciation for the services of others. His was a noteworthy example of unparalleled devotion to duty."

On August 4, from the *Prince of Wales* as she set out on the transatlantic journey, Churchill reported to Roosevelt: "Harry arrived dead beat" but, the prime minister assured the president, was "lively again now."

With Hopkins away in England, FDR discovered that he had a new problem: presidential requests for information and orders for action normally handled with brisk efficiency were not yielding the customary results. Concluding that he needed a substitute Hopkins, particularly for one vitally important project, Roosevelt turned to an assistant, Wayne Coy, a young man from Indiana who had worked for Hopkins as a WPA official in the Middle West and was serving as liaison to the Office of Emergency Management. In a confidential memo to Coy, the president expressed his frustration that nearly six weeks after the beginning of the German invasion of Russia, "we have done practically nothing to get any of the materials they asked for on their actual way to delivery in Siberia." If he were a Russian, Roosevelt said, he would feel that he had been "given the run-around in the United States." He ordered Coy to get the Russian request list and with full presidential authority "act as a burr under the saddle and get things moving."

Indicating both his determination and optimism, FDR explained his plan to Coy. He had told the Russians, he said, that he was "dividing things into two categories—first, material which can be delivered on the Russian western front in time to take part in battle between September first and October first—and secondly, those materials which physically could not get there before October first." The point of the distinction was that after October 1, he and his advisers expected the Russian weather to limit active operations. "If Germany can be held until then," said the president, "Russia is safe until Spring." (Hopkins received the same analysis from Stalin.) The president closed the memo to Coy with a terse injunction: "Step on it!" (Coy proved an excellent ersatz Hopkins; within two days, he had picked up two hundred previously unavailable planes for Russia.)

The next day, FDR left Washington on the first leg of a secret trip that would take him to Placentia Bay in Newfoundland for the meeting with Winston Churchill—the conference that would become identified with the Atlantic Charter. Arriving before the British, the president had the pleasure of seeing his sons Franklin Jr. and Elliott, naval officers who had been detailed to join him for the occasion. In conversation with Elliott, FDR said, "I know already how much faith the PM has in Russia's ability to stay in the war." He snapped his fingers to emphasize the point.

"I take it you have more faith than that," Elliott said.

"Harry Hopkins has more," the president said. "He's able to convince me."

Hopkins's reports from Russia had confirmed the instincts that lay behind Roosevelt's grand design. The president had won his gamble on the British: something had indeed turned up.

POSTLUDE

I n talking with an interviewer some years after the war, Averell Harriman displayed an understanding of President Roosevelt that had eluded him while he was serving as FDR's expediter in London in 1941. During those months, Harriman continually hoped for FDR to lead the United States into full belligerency alongside Britain and then the Soviet Union as well. Like Henry Stimson and other strong interventionists, Harriman based his hope on the view that the president wished to enter the war but was letting excessive caution and fear of public opinion keep him from exercising the strong leadership the situation demanded. Years later, however, having had ample time for reflection, Harriman observed that FDR "had a horror of American boys going through what they went through in World War I and wanted to do everything we could to avoid our having to participate, and so he was ready to help the Russians as well as the British materially in so far as we were able to do so . . ."

On another occasion long after the war, Harriman expressed the belief that even if the United States should become fully involved, President Roosevelt "felt that if you kept the Russians in the war it might limit the extent to which we had to use our ground forces; our participation might be largely limited to naval and air cooperation." Neither Harriman nor Harry Hopkins had understood the point in 1941, although Hopkins sometimes had a glimmer of it, as in his remark in May to Henry Morgenthau that the president was "loath" to enter the war.

Winston Churchill, his own hopes of U.S. belligerency increasingly frustrated during the spring and summer of 1941, likewise did not see the point. (One day he grumped to a secretary, "The American Constitution was designed to keep the U.S.A. clear of European entanglements, and by god it has stood the test of time.") When the Germans unleashed Barbarossa on Russia, the prime minister believed that the danger posed by this expansion of the war increased the likelihood of full American participation. But in reality, for Roosevelt the new war in the East constituted the second great fact of the year, standing beside the creation of lend-lease; Hopkins's positive reports from Moscow showed that the president, with the aid of his two representatives, had won his game to keep Britain afloat. Churchill also had difficulty understanding that it was not blandishments of any kind but U.S. interest as he saw it that guided Roosevelt; the president's support of Britain had nothing to do with likes or dislikes, and it was not Churchill's actions that turned the United States into a full belligerent. In August, Anthony Eden expressed the fear that FDR not only intended to keep out of the war but to "dictate the peace if he can."

Chronically accused by fellow Americans of looking for a way to get into the European war, FDR in fact did not seize on opportunities even to sound bellicose, as in encounters in the Atlantic between U-boats and U.S. destroyers (including the sinking of the *Reuben James* on October 31). To the continuing dismay of his chiefs of staff, the president kept pushing the sending of arms and supplies overseas—where they could immediately join in the fight—right up until December and the Japanese attack on U.S. ships and installations in Hawaii. Contrary to a belief held by various conspiracy theorists, however, Pearl Harbor did not bring the United States into the European war, because the Axis treaty did not require Germany to come to the aid of Japan, since Japan had not been attacked. Nor did it bring the United

States into an existing great-power war—it created one in the Pacific. Four days later, however, Hitler resolved all questions by declaring war on the United States, thereby transforming America's nontraditional policies of 1941 into a properly traditional conflict. Right to the end, despite the criticisms of the skeptics, FDR had shown that he meant just what he said with his policy: "All aid short of war."

Roosevelt discouraged the keeping of records and minutes, and he died, literally intestate, just before the German surrender; whereas Churchill, the professional writer, went on to produce the great monument to the war, his towering six-volume history that established the terms of discussion of the subject and therefore has always had to be taken into account, accepted or challenged, by anyone speculating or writing in the field. Of the leaders of the three chief victorious powers, Churchill was the one who had his say, and he used his opportunity with famous eloquence. As time went on, however, his admirers and disciples were joined by revisionists of various kinds, and now readers can have any Churchill they want, from the greatest statesman since King Alfred to the stubborn politician who turned his country into a colony of the United States. But, whatever the point of view, the remarkable fact is that this man, always driven by the need for adventure, contrived for himself the supreme adventure of his time—and he made his two American friends part of it.

With Roosevelt, no one needed to wait for revisionism to arise. A wide range of options, from saint to devil, has been available for him all along, thanks to all the domestic political wars and, in part, to his unrivaled ability to mask his thoughts and feelings. But a reasonably objective observer must conclude that the president, if not operating on a precise plan, worked to a consistent design—a design he publicly declared—and his private "Keep the British Isles afloat" told the metaphorical truth. In the process, did his two agents become more Churchill's Americans than Roosevelt's? The prime minister did his best to woo and annex them, but the final record was clear: the agents went as far as the chief wanted them to go, no farther: aid, not war, always stood as the policy until the Japanese government created a new world context.

The president had devised his own personal variation on the concept of alliance, and the unique partnership that resulted grew into what has proved to be a permanent relationship—often vexed, sometimes derided from one side or the other, often puzzling to observers. At times, even as in Roosevelt's day, it eludes definition.

At the end of August 1941, Hopkins turned the direction of lend-lease operations over to Edward R. Stettinius, Jr., and, while keeping his hand in, devoted himself to his most effective role, as fixer, expediter, and troubleshooter for the president and, in many ways, as Washington representative of Churchill. He played an important part in high-level Anglo-American wartime conferences, evoking from the prime minister a special tribute. When Churchill wished to speak well of someone, he would say that the person had "the root of the matter in him"; thus Hopkins's impatience with equivocation won him the title "Lord Root of the Matter." In the summer of 1942, when Hopkins spoke of his plan to marry a New York fashion editor, Louise Macy, the prime minister grunted, "You're married to the war. That should satisfy you." Harry nevertheless went ahead, but his fragile health forced him into semiretirement in 1944, and though he made a partial comeback late in the year, even his incredible drive could not sustain him forever; he died in January 1946. Averell Harriman's daughter Kathleen summed up what may have been the secret of Hopkins's success in dealing with the great and mighty: "He was a very astute person. He knew how to get along with Churchill; he knew how to explain America's objectives. He was not personally ambitious, and that was the one thing that he had that other people didn't."

Harriman made trips to Russia with Beaverbrook and then Churchill, and he continued in his role in London until the late summer of 1943, when he reluctantly acceded to Roosevelt's command to go to Moscow as ambassador, where he remained, greatly helped by Kathleen, until 1946; he also had the counsel of George F. Kennan, the two men making an outstanding diplomatic team. In later years Harriman served as U.S. secretary of commerce, ambassador to Britain, European administrator of the Marshall Plan, governor of New York, and undersecretary of state. Characteristically, he had no hesitation about accepting the second-level State Department position—it kept him at the center of things, and for the Kennedy administration he negotiated the Laos neutrality accords and the Limited Test Ban Treaty in 1963; he also took part in the Paris peace talks on Viet Nam in 1968. In 1976, at the age of eighty-four, he represented presidential nominee Jimmy Carter on a mission to Moscow to talk about arms control with Leonid Brezhnev; still later, when he was past ninety, he met in the Kremlin with Yuri Andropov, Brezhnev's successor as Soviet general secretary. President Kennedy once said that with the possible exception of John Quincy Adams, Harriman "held as many important jobs as any American in our history." A few years earlier, commenting on Harriman's faithful and effective service in a variety of capacities for President Truman, some who knew the history of the preceding two decades called him "Truman's Hopkins." Part of his continuing effectiveness in difficult diplomatic situations, he believed, came directly from his independence and consequent willingness to take risks. "I've never really worried about whether I'd be fired or not," he commented. "Fortunately, I'm not dependent on my job to eat."

In Harriman's later years, his private life took a markedly colorful turn. His assignment to the Moscow embassy in 1943 had ended his affair with Pamela Churchill, who found consolation in a cozy series of relationships with Sonny Whitney's cousin John Hay "Jock" Whitney; Ed Murrow; and Murrow's boss, CBS chairman William Paley. When Randolph Churchill came home from the war, the couple divorced and Pam moved to Paris, where she switched from American to continental lovers, her friends and benefactors including the Fiat heir, Gianni Agnelli; a Rothschild; Aly Khan; and a Greek shipping tycoon, Stavros Niarchos. An American woman reporter in London described Pamela as "the only person I have ever known who could be described as a courtesan of high level."

In 1960 Pamela married Leland Hayward, an American theatrical producer and agent. A few months after he died in March 1971, fate put the widow at a Washington dinner party at which Averell was also a guest. Two months later they were married; the ensuing years, people said, were Averell's happiest; he died in July 1986, aged ninety-four. Pamela, however, still had another career ahead of her. As a prominent and influential Washington hostess she became a powerful figure in the Democratic Party, and in the administration of Bill Clinton she put the capstone on her remarkable, Atlantic-spanning life story by serving as American ambassador to France. She died in Paris in 1997, having achieved considerable popularity and winning a final bit of affection from her hosts because her parting thoughts were said to have been expressed in French.

NOTES

Abbreviations for sources of information, documents, interviews, and other materials: FDRL—Franklin D. Roosevelt Library; LC—Library of Congress; CAC—Churchill Archives Centre, Churchill College, Cambridge; AC—Abramson Collection. Two other sources, used for background but not quoted or explicitly cited, are the Kings College archives, University of London, and the Oral History Office, Columbia University Libraries.

In these Notes, initials are frequently used to refer to Harry Hopkins (HLH) and Averell Harriman (WAH).

PROLOGUE: CRISIS 1940

1. "For Americans": Simone, 19. Remainder of the paragraph from Simone, 20. (After the war. Simone [born Otto Katz] returned to Europe, where tragedy continued to follow him. A Communist, this journalist became an important editor in Prague, but in 1952, after a Stalin-inspired show trial, he and six other Jewish defendants were hanged.)

1. "as fighters": "French Front," *Life*, March 11, 1940.

1. "four Frenchmen": Saint-Jean, 25.

2. "We're sick": Saint-Jean, 22.

3. Quotes from Liddell Hart: Boothe, 73.

3. fortifications of a different type: Saint-Jean, 95.

4. U.S. officers quoted: Boothe, 173. George Kenney went on to become outstandingly successful in the war, serving as commander of the Far East Air Force and managing to maintain both his independence and a good working relationship with General Douglas MacArthur.

4. "The Germans are coming": Boothe, 223.

4. Liddell Hart and the role of armor: His failure to realize the impor-

tance of the tank was particularly striking because it contradicted his own earlier views.

5. "all the odious apparatus": Winston S. Churchill [hereinafter "WSC"], vol. 2, 118.

5. "I have noting to offer" and "wage war": WSC, vol. 2, 25.

5. "New World": WSC, vol. 2, 118.

6. White House telephone hours: The authority for this astonishing statement is Joseph P. Kennedy, in Amanda Smith, 479.

1: MONEY FLIES

7. "one of the darkest": Allan Nevins, introduction in Lippmann, viii.

7. "cheerfulness and wit": Bryson Rash, quoted in Goldfarb Marquis, "Radio Grows Up," *American Heritage*, August–September 1983.

8. "jackasses": Brendon, 81.

8. "time for the state itself": Rauch, *Roosevelt Reader*, 64.

9. "I would love it": Sherwood, 32.

10. "restless, electric": "Harry Hopkins," *Fortune*, July 1935 [hereinafter "*Fortune*, July 1935"].

10. "unworthy of Grinnell's": Sherwood, 17. The wording is Sherwood's.

10. "I've liked New York" and following quotes: Geoffrey T. Hellman, "House Guest: Harry Hopkins," *New Yorker*, August 7 and 14, 1943 [hereinafter "Hellman"].

11. "really got exposed" and "an easygoing": Hellman.

12. "On what possible grounds": Sherwood, 24.

12. "I can hardly picture": Giffen, 10.

12. "given their differences": Giffen, 2.

12. "Sweetheart": letter, May 19, 1913, Giffen, 97.

13. "charming, sociable": Giffen, 9.

14. "a three-hundred-and-sixty": Hellman.

14. "Say, Jack" and following quotes: Sherwood, 29.

14. "Harry never had": Henry H. Adams, 38.

14. "He is a man": Hellman.

15. "He was indefatigable": *Current Biography*, 1941, 405.

16. "rendered utterly obsolete": *Fortune*, August 1935.

16. "rarely tactful": Marquis Childs, cited by Henry H. Adams, 52.

16–17. "a suggestion" and "some people": *Fortune*, August 1935.

17. Smith–Hopkins exchange: *Current Biography*, 1941, 405.

17. "People don't eat": Sherwood, 52.

18. "maintenance of existing": *New York Times*, July 2, 1933.

18. "President Roosevelt": *Daily Mail* [London], July 4, 1933, quoted in Feis, 238.

18. Roosevelt's statements: Rauch, *Roosevelt Reader*, 93.

19. "How on earth": Feis, 254.

19. Roosevelt quotes: Rauch, *Roosevelt Reader*, 94.

19. "only to the extent": Fest, 410.

19. "only Hitler's death": Mowrer, 216.

2: FRIENDSHIPS

20. "It was an emotional": conversation, Curtis Roosevelt and Alistair Cooke, October 20, 1993, oral history file, FDRL.

20. "Small, sensible": Peggy Bacon, "Facts about Faces: IV, Harry Hopkins," *New Republic*, February 13, 1935.

21. "On first glance": Jonathan Mitchell, "Alms-Giver," *New Republic*, April 10, 1935.

21. "a lanky, good-humored": *News-Week*, May 23, 1936.

21. "You know, I can hear": *New Republic*, April 10, 1935; partially quoted also in *Fortune*, August 1935.

22. "busy as a nurse": *New Republic*, April 10, 1935.

22. "almost faultlessly": Jonathan Mitchell, *New Republic*, April 10, 1935.

22. "The appeals for help": Eleanor Roosevelt, 172.

22. "All his working life": *Fortune*, August 1935.

23. "What were the people": Henry H. Adams, 54.

23. Roosevelt–Hopkins parallels from Hellman: August 7.

24. "simply behaved": Alistair Cooke, conversation with Curtis Roosevelt, October 20, 1993, oral history collection, FDRL.

24. "was like a giant spider": interview, AC.

24. "I just kept at it": E. J. Kahn, Jr., "Plenipotentiary," *New Yorker*, May 3 and 10, 1952 [hereinafter "Kahn"].

25. "When he started" and following quote: Josephson, 400.

26. Father's anger: WAH interview, December 3, 1984, AC.

26. "I think I am": Abramson, 73.

27. "You run": Abramson, 80.

27. "the secret": Josephson, 401.

27. "a bold and gifted": Josephson, 402.

27. "All my father's life": WAH interviews, October 12, 1984, and undated, AC; sentences rearranged.

27. "bright boys" and following quotes: Arnold Whitridge interview, AC.

28. "lackluster reputation": Harriman and Abel, 35.

28. Dean Acheson: holder of various high positions, including secretary of state in the Truman administration.

28. "before he could be fired": Harriman and Abel, 38.

28. "learned a great deal": Harriman and Abel, 36.

29. Judge Lovett's son Bob: Robert A. Lovett, like Dean Acheson a mandarin of the eastern establishment; one of the fathers of the independent U.S. Air Force and secretary of defense under President Truman.

29. "Harriman's dinner": Harriman and Abel, 48.

30. "to take every occasion": Harriman and Abel, 30.

31. "led me to conclude": Harriman and Abel, 31.

31. "the first really modern": Mrs. Robert A. Lovett interview, July 16, 1983, AC.

31. "a good, hard-shelled": Henry Brandon interview with WAH, *New York Times Magazine*, March 5, 1967.

3: "BRILLIANCE AND GLITTER"

32. "I pulled him back": WAH interview, October 12, 1984, AC.

32–33. Kitty's accident: The popular story came straight out of Horatio Alger: the two were said to have met when Averell saved her from a runaway horse.

33. "rather spectacular-looking": Allen Grover interview, AC.

33. "a wonderful old character" and following quotes: Rodengen, 48.

34. "was pretty rough": Dorothy Schiff interview, February 7, 1985, AC.

34. "out of his starched collars": Charles Collingwood interview, AC.

34. "My French": Kahn.

34. "buying Matisses": Mrs. Robert A. Lovett interview, July 14, 1983, AC.

35. "I am going": Giffen, 179.

36. "I can understand": Giffen, 207; following quotes, 205.

36. "dirty-rotten slums": Giffen, 208.

37. Hampstead Heath: Giffen, 210.

37. Observations on Hopkins: *Fortune*, August 1935.

38. "fine, discriminating intelligence": Raymond Moley quoted, Abramson, 242.

39. "I've had a lot more fun": Henry Brandon interview with WAH, *New York Times Magazine*, March 5, 1967.

39. "I think he liked Harry": John McCloy interview, May 13, 1983, AC.

39. "he might read": William Walton interview, September 28, 1983, AC.

39. "a secondhand building": Olive Clapper, 93–94.

40. "Hopkins attracts attention": "Alms-Giver: Harry L. Hopkins," *New Republic*, April 10, 1935.

40. "caustic good nature": *Fortune*, July 1935.

40–41 White-collar projects: Sherwood, 60–61.

41. "took all the heat": Franklin D. Roosevelt, Jr., interview by Diana and James Halsted, January 11, 1979, small collections, oral-history interviews, FDRL.

4: DARK AUTUMN

44. "bombastic utterances," "fairly glowered," Tully, 230

44. "The Spanish Civil War": Tully, 229.

45. "When an epidemic": Rauch, *Roosevelt Reader*, 191.

45. "war is a contagion": Rauch, *Roosevelt Reader*, 192.

45. "There is a solidarity": Rauch, *Roosevelt Reader*, 189–90.

45. "look-see": term quoted by Tully, 230.

45. "They are afraid": Freidel, 257.

45–46 "aroused in the financial": Allen, 310.

46. "Roosevelt is blamed": Brendan Bracken, in Lysaght, 152.

47. "treating a department": Percy, 17.

47. "it is always best": One of Chamberlain's most famous observations; cited by Reynolds, *The Creation*, 16, from Feiling (UK edition), 25.

48. "with a very quick": Eden, 625.

48. "in the nature of a douche": Sumner Welles quoted, Eden, 626.

49. "an ornate example": *Fortune*, August 1935.

50. "treading a very dangerous": PSF, Gt. Britain (Keynes folder), FDRL.

50. "businessmen have a different set": Letter of February 1, 1938, Moggridge, 607.

51. "improved equipment": *Time*, May 11, 1936.

52. nobody associated with the Union Pacific: author's rephrasing of a point made by Abramson, 221.

52. "as hard as I know how": Kahn.

52. "a big rodeo": WAH to HLH, July 30, 1937, Hopkins Papers, FDRL.

53. "frank and full discussion": WAH to HLH, March 3, 1937, Hopkins Papers, FDRL.

53. "What would you think": WAH interview, AC. (The aide, Tommy Corcoran, later liked to say that he gave Harriman a nudge toward Hopkins.)

54. "This support": WAH interview, AC.

5: TERROR IN THE AIR

57. The passivity of the French: see, for example, Reed, *Disgrace Abounding*, 134–35.

57. "After all": Lord Lothian, quoted in WSC, vol. 1, 196–97.

57. "The Tragedy": FDR to Daisy Suckley, March 8, 1936, Ward, 69.

57. Arthur Harris: This officer went on to become one of the war's principal advocates of strategic bombing and, as "Bomber" Harris, chief of the RAF's Bomber Command, perhaps the leading practitioner.

58. "I was shocked": Bullitt to president, May 12, 1938, PSF—Bullitt, FDRL.

58. "never heard the Adolf": Shirer, 126–27.

61. "It is probably impossible": Toynbee, October 14, 1938; punctuation slightly altered. Letter in author's collection.

61. "Hitler was not bluffing": Marc A. Rose, "Hitler's Aerial Triumph," *Reader's Digest*: March 1939. This statement demonstrates just how thoroughly Hitler's "bluffing" succeeded.

63. "The President is expecting": Monnet, 118.

63–64. Monnet background: Bullitt to president, September 28, 1938. PSF—Bullitt, FDRL.

64. "old patrician mansion": Monnet, 118.

64. "we were talking": Monnet, 119.

65–66. November 14 meeting: see Parrish, *Roosevelt and Marshall*, 16–18.

66. "The President was under": Jackson, 80–81.

6: THE CAUSE OF SOLIDARITY

67. "the Army and the Navy": this conversation from Parrish, *Roosevelt and Marshall*, 92–93.

68. "a third-rate power": quoted in Miller, 443.

68. "trouble with his legs": Robert Hopkins, in Sherwood, 119.

69. "You always had the feeling": interview with Franklin D. Roosevelt, Jr., by Diana and James Halsted, January 11, 1979, small collections, oral history interviews, FDRL.

69. "wave of perverse optimism": WSC, vol. 1, 342.

69. "settling down" and "jitterbugs": Mowat, 637.

69. "a golden age": Mowat, 637, and WSC, vol. 1, 342.

70. "prudently but relentlessly" and following sentence: Monnet, 122.

70. Chamberlain's appearance: Nicolson, 393. In the second sentence, "is" is omitted.

70–71. "In the event": quoted, WSC, vol. 1, 345–46.

72. "they did not believe": Stettinius, 20.

72. "in this hemisphere": "Shall We Send Our Youth to War?" *Reader's Digest*, September 1939.

72. "resulted in at least 15 dictatorships": "Mr. Con" in debate: "Should We Act to Curb Aggressor Nations?" *Reader's Digest*, March 1939.

72. "If we enter": Hixson, 101.

72. "we are already engaged": "The Nation's Columnists Debate on War and Peace," *Reader's Digest*, June 1939.

73. "master word-painter": *Time*, July 31, 1939.

74. Garner quotes: *New York Times*, July 20, 1939.

74. "Who could have imagined": Major General H. L. Ismay, quoted in Parkinson, 184.

75–76. FDR speech quotes from Rauch: *Roosevelt Reader*, 222–26.

76. "some kind of malnutrition": Hellman, August 14, 1943.

77. "It was good to see you": Sandburg to "Friend Hopkins," December 3, 1939, Hopkins Papers, FDRL.

7: "SEND FOR HARRY!"

78. All quotes in the first paragraph from Bullitt to the president, September 8, 1939, PSF, FDRL.

78. "engaged in some rather doleful": Jackson, 79.

79. "Roosevelt knew how": interview with James Rowe by Thomas Soapes, July 12, 1978, Eleanor Roosevelt Oral History Project, FDRL.

79. "Our acts must be guided": *Time Capsule/1939* (New York: Time-Life Books, 1968), 24.

79. "almost literally walking": Roosevelt to Lord Tweedsmuir, quoted in Miller, 441.

81. The Phony War: Appropriately enough, it was Senator Borah, the war skeptic, who contributed the name.

81. "oysters, lobsters": Parkinson, 262.

81. "As much American": Stettinius, 21.

82. "I'll find the money": Monnet, 131.

82. "So far as France and Britain": Stettinius, 23.

82. "The ineptitude of the government": Spears, vol., 1, 115.

83. "was convinced that he was erratic": Spears, vol. 1, 19.

83. "the latest and the greatest": advertisement poster for Churchill lecture, 1900.

84. "half-naked fakir": Like many well-known phrases, this one is a condensed version of the original. In 1930, speaking of a meeting between the viceroy of India and Gandhi, Churchill said robustly: "It is alarming and also nauseating to see Mr. Gandhi, a seditious Middle Temple lawyer, now posing as a fakir of a type well known in the East, striding half-naked up the steps of the viceregal palace . . ."

On this point see, e.g., Geoffrey Best, *Churchill: A Study in Greatness*, London: Hambledon and London, 2002.

84. "I believe in Winston's": Lord Derby, James, 205.

84. "I think he has very unusual": Andrew Bonar Law, James, 205.

84. "I like things to happen": James, 205.

85. "Do you know": Boothe, 247.

85. Lady Astor: Kennedy, 422.

86. Churchill *must not speak first*: Bracken Project interview notes, CAC.

86. "it was clear": WSC, vol. 1, 663. Churchill mistakenly puts this pivotal meeting on May 10.

86. "I suppose Churchill": Harold Ickes, *The Secret Diary*, vol. 3, 176. In the published version, Ickes omitted the second half of the sentence.

87. FDR "discovered": Marquis Childs, "The President's Best Friend," *Saturday Evening Post*, April 19, 1941 [hereinafter "Childs"].

87. "Send for Harry!": Turner Catledge, "It's 'Send for Harry,'" *New York Times Magazine*, March 16, 1941.

87. "a charming, charming person": Franklin D. Roosevelt, Jr., interview by Diana and James Halsted, January 11, 1979, small collections, oral-history interviews, FDRL.

88. What surprised "some of us": Eleanor Roosevelt, 173.

88. "Franklin had changed Hopkins": Parks, 76.

88. Bullitt statements: Bullitt to secretary of state, May 14, 1940. PSF—Bullitt, FDRL.

89. "France can continue": M. Reynaud to President Roosevelt, June 14, 1940, FDRL.

8: DECIDEDLY UNNEUTRAL ACTS

90. "proof against British wiles": Kennedy quoted in Amanda Smith, 224.

91. "There is no doubt": Kendrick, 218.

91–92. Meeting with Churchill: Kennedy quoted in Amanda Smith, 425.

92. "the most dynamic individual": Kennedy, 426.

92. "I have nothing to offer": WSC, vol. 2, 25–26.

92. "like rabbits": *Time Capsule/1940* (New York: Time-Life Books, 1968), 69.

93. "The Dunkirk episode": Ponting, 92.

93. "wars are not won": WSC, vol. 2, 115.

93. "the greatest British": Ponting, 92.

93. "outlive the menace": Sperber, 155.

93. "We shall never surrender": WSC, vol. 2, 118.

93. "There was a prophetic quality": Sperber, 155.

94. Quotes from Tennessee and Massachusetts: Parrish, *Roosevelt and Marshall*, 132.

94. "German victory": Alsop and Kintner, 82a.

95. "The voice and force": WSC, vol. 2, 24.

95. "The President was not": Jackson, 74.

96. "You cannot pick our bones": Stettinius, 31.

96. "If members of the present administration": Loewenheim (May 20), 97.

97. "Never cease to impress": June 28, WSC, vol. 2, 228.

98. "I do not want to run": quoted in Freidel, 328.

99. "Mr. President": Loewenheim, 107.

100. FDR–Jackson conversation: Jackson, 86.

101–102. "obviously was not happy": Jackson, 88.

102. "It is understood": quoted in Jackson, 89.

102. "But what Winston can't get": Jackson, 90.

102. "seeming to make a 'Yankee trade'": Arthur Krock, *New York Times*, November 24, 1940.

103. "the President never entertained": Jackson, 91.

103-104. "the President is not considering": *New York Times*, August 18, 1940.

104. "How many Americans": *New York Times*, August 19, 1940.

104. James Madison: quoted in *Time*, September 2, 1940.

105. "would never be turned over": Jackson, 90.

105. draft agreement: Cordell Hull to HM ambassador, undated, PSF, safe file, Great Britain, FDRL. The use of the plural verb in "the United States Government wish" makes plain which country's drafters produced the basic document.

105-106. FDR on the islands: Jackson, 100.

106. "a decidedly unneutral act" and following quote: WSC, vol. 2, 404.

9: THE POLITICAL CALCULATING MACHINE

107. "Well, boys": Dallek, 252.

107. "planes, munitions": *New York Times*, November 24, 1940.

109. "I shall drag the United States in": Gilbert, *Churchill and America*, 186.

109. "Do not underestimate England": WSC, vol. 1, 223.

110. "the special sting": Percy, 33.

111. "irresistible and inimitable": Jackson, 136.

111. "I didn't know": Parrish, *Roosevelt and Marshall*, 162.

112–113. Quotes from Churchill letter: Loewenheim, 122–23.

113. "political calculating machine": Morison, 29.

113. "mere grandiloquence" and "hard fact": Parrish, *Roosevelt and Marshall*, 162.

113. Description of the machine: Morison, 29.

114. FDR–Morgenthau: Morgenthau, presidential diaries, December 17, 1940, FDRL.

114–116. Press conference quotes: Rauch, *Roosevelt Reader*, 268–71.

116. "There were probably very few": Sherwood, 225.

10: "REPOSING SPECIAL FAITH AND CONFIDENCE"

117. "Americans are being very tiresome": Dilks (December 27), 344.

118–119. Speech quotes from Zevin (December 30, 1940), 247–58.

120. Churchill to FDR on Eire: Gilbert, *Winston S. Churchill*, vol. 6, 938 (footnote).

120–121. Roosevelt–Hopkins conversation: Sherwood, 230, based on notes made by FDR's secretary, Marguerite "Missy" LeHand.

121. president "wished to discover": Davis and Lindley, 173.

122. "Harry had a very clear mind": Franklin D. Roosevelt, Jr., interview by Diana and James Halsted, January 11, 1979, small collections, oral-history interviews, FDRL.

122. "capacity to get inside" and following quote: Childs, *Saturday Evening Post*.

123. Hopkins–Early conversation: Childs.

123. "Did you say that, Boss?" and "I'm not going to hang around here": Henry H. Adams, 199.

123. "He's just going over": press conference, Sherwood, 231.

124. "An Iowa farmer": Sherwood, 37. Hopkins wrote the short poem containing these lines in 1928, while trying to deal with the crisis in his marriage. He also managed to make a populist economic point: "Iowa tends its corn like a slick banker watches a ticker tape."

124. "Churchill *is* the War Cabinet": Monnet, 166.

124. "Roosevelt's alter ego": Monnet, 165.

125. "I suppose Churchill" and following quote: Sherwood, 232.

125. "Reposing special faith": Roosevelt to Hopkins, January 4, 1941, Hopkins Papers, FDRL.

125. Harriman in the hospital: WAH to Whitney, April 9, 1940, Harriman Papers, LC.

126. "Goddammit, the rest of us": William Bundy interview, quoting Dean Acheson quoting Robert Lovett, AC.

126. On Reynolds Metals: WAH reminiscence, October 12, 1953, AC.

127. "I've met Churchill": Harriman and Abel, 10.

127. "I will be back": reported by several newspapers.

128. "There is no chance": *Washington Star*, January 6, 1941.

128. Hopkins "flushed": *New York Journal-American*, January 6, 1941.

128. "appeared ruffled": *New York Sun*, January 6, 1941.

128. "social trends in England" and following quote: *New York Journal-American*, January 6, 1941.

11: "A SMILING GENTLEMAN"

130. "unattractive to women": Whelpton interview, August 30, 1977, Bracken Project, CAC. See also Tree, 111.

130. "clumsy and uncouth": Driberg interview, April 10, 1972, Bracken Project, CAC.

130. "I've taken the trouble": Tree, 110.

131. "a romantic and ardent": Bracken folder, December 18, 1972, CAC.

131. Positive description of Bracken: Colville, *Winston Churchill and His Inner Circle*, 61.

131. "Who?": Sherwood, 234.

131. Hopkins as Sunday-school teacher: Tree, 145.

131. "Necessarily there are many intangibles": *Washington News*, n.d.

132. Bracken on Hopkins: Bracken to Swope, January 16, 1939, Hopkins Papers, FDRL.

132. Following letter: Bracken to Hopkins, March 13, 1939, Hopkins Papers, FDRL.

133. "arrangements were made": Sir Eustace Missenden, undated letter to the *Sunday Times*, in Sherwood, 235.

133–134. exchange between Hopkins and Bracken: Sherwood, 235.

134. "the intense relief": Missenden, quoted by Sherwood, 235.

134. "Here is a man": Leutze, 201.

135. "quiet, unassuming": Leutze, 216.

135. "intensity of Harry Hopkins' determination": quoted, Sherwood, 235–36. Following sentence, page 236.

135–136. Hopkins on Eden: H.L.H. Personal for FDR. January 10, 1941. Hopkins microfilm, FDRL.

136. "Seems simple": Dilks, 348.

136. Hopkins on Halifax: Personal for FDR.

137. Bracken: In his handwritten notes for this day, January 10, Hopkins refers to Bracken as "Brackett."

137. Meeting with Churchill: All of Hopkins's quoted observations that follow come from his notes.

138. "I did not think it right": Loewenheim, 119.

139. Pamela anecdote: Pamela C. Harriman, "Churchill's Dream," *American Heritage*, October–November 1983.

140. "Thus I met Harry Hopkins": WSC, vol. 3, 23.

140. "The President is determined": Hopkins quoted by WSC, vol. 3, 23.

141. "to describe Roosevelt": William Phillips quoted in Miller, 350.

141. "the most complicated": Perkins, 3.

141. left hand–right hand: quoted in Miller, 351. Miller gets full credit for the brilliantly chosen adjective "prismatic," which the present author has borrowed.

141. Hopkins "no doubt was being subjected": Leutze, 218. The following description of the conference with British reporters comes from this source, 218–19.

142. "tapping the arms" and following quotes about the American press conference: *New York Times*, January 11, 1941.

142. "with the suave, toothy, and inane grin": Leutze, 219.

143. "how wide an acquaintance": Kendrick, 258.

143. "I'm a reporter": Kendrick, 257.

12: "THE PERFECTION OF HUMAN SOCIETY"

144. "when the moon was high": Tree, 131.

144–145. Churchill's request and Tree's reply: Tree, 131.

145. "a welcoming quality": Tree, 48.

145. "antiquated armoured car" and "no complaints": Tree, 132.

145. "high moon or no": Tree, 133.

146. "so far as we were concerned" and following quotes: Lord Norman-brook in Wheeler-Bennett, 26.

146–147. The discussion of the London dinner and the English country house: Henry Adams, 200–203.

147. "he can get along": Turner Catledge, "It's 'Send for Harry,'" *New York Times Magazine*, March 16, 1941.

147. "Mr. Hopkins arrived": Colville, *The Fringes of Power*, 332.

148. Duke of Windsor and Wenner-Gren: Unsigned memorandum, January 13, 1941, Chartwell Papers, CAC.

148. "it would be better": Colville, *The Fringes of Power*, 333.

149. Churchill remarks: Chandos, 165.

149. "in a remarkable contrast": Colville, *The Fringes of Power*, 333. "exaggerating his American drawl": Chandos, 165.

149. Hopkins's reaction: Accounts disagree on some details. The present version is synthesized from Sherwood and Colville, who deny some of the points even while making them, and Chandos, who gives a straightforward account.

150. "a sophisticated outsider": Jenkins, 648.

150. "Hopkins quickly acquired": Jenkins, 648.

151. "It was in this room": Tree, 42.

151. "Churchill was not": Normanbrook in Wheeler-Bennett, 26.

151. to guard the gold: Colville, *The Fringes of Power*, 334.

152. "I think": Colville, *The Fringes of Power*, 335.

152. "less rhetorical": Normanbrook in Wheeler-Bennett, 26.

153. "Here was one": Sherwood, 242.

153. "whether the reports": Colville interview, AC.

153. "the danger of rash" and other quotes in this paragraph: Colville, The *Fringes of Power*, 122.

153. A new Winston Churchill: These quotes from Ian Jacob, "His First Hour," *Atlantic*, March 1965.

154–156. Hopkins messages to president from Hopkins Papers, FDRL.

13: "WHITHER THOU GOEST"

158. "I am most grateful": WSC, vol. 3, 25.

159. "they strike me": quoted in Thorne, 97. Percy himself was mentioned as a possible choice for the Washington embassy, along with, incredibly, the Duke of Windsor.

160. Ismay and Hopkins: Ismay, 215.

160. "I shouldn't stay there": Ismay, 216. Accounts of this near-misadventure vary somewhat; Ismay's seems the most authoritative.

161. Churchill speech: *Daily Mirror* [London], n.d., Hopkins Papers, newspaper file, FDRL.

161–162. Hopkins's remarks: quoted in McJimsey, 141.

162. "the final stage": Stettinius, 71.

163. "a mere majority": Stettinius, 72.

163. Gerald Ford, Potter Stewart, Kingman Brewster: These young activists went on to become, respectively, president of the United States, associate justice of the Supreme Court, and president of Yale.

163. Comments on the "Great Debate": Cole, 10.

164. Hoover comments: press statement issued in New York on January 10, 1941. All other quotes (including from the *Plain Dealer*) from the *New York Times*, January 11, 1941.

165. Hutchins and Conant quotes from Stettinius, 75.

165. "No bill like it": *Time*, January 20, 1941.

165. Hamilton Fish: Parrish, *Roosevelt and Marshall*, 166.

165. Morgenthau comments: Morgenthau presidential diaries, December 31, 1940, FDRL.

166. "fervent hope": Johnson, 565.

166. "at last the Democracies": Johnson, 565.

167. Hopkins "really a charming and interesting man": letter, January 19, 1941, [Eric] Seal papers; quoted in Gilbert, *Winston S. Churchill,* vol. 6, 992. Seal described the telephone call to his parents.

167. "on a cold, dreary morning": Hopkins memorandum, January 25, 1941, Hopkins Papers, FDRL.

168. Letters concerning Hopkins: copies in Hopkins Papers, FDRL.

170. "little touch of Harry in the night": Sherwood, 250. One of the editors present produced this Shakespearean allusion.

170. Hoover report: J. Edgar Hoover to Major General Edwin M. Watson ["Pa" Watson], FDR's close aide, February 12, 1941, Hopkins Papers, FDRL.

14: "THE ALL-SEEING EYE"

171. "Mr. Churchill himself": *Daily Express,* February 8, 1941.

171. "There goes the bloody" and following quote: Colville, *The Fringes of Power,* 341.

172. "delicious-looking": Ogden, 125.

172. "kittenish eyes": Amory, 154

172. "very friendly disposition": Amory, 147.

172. "in the nature": Amory, 149.

174. "gigantic": Colville, *The Fringes of Power,* 341

174. "It is better": Colville, manuscript diary, 122, CAC.

175. "hustling tour" and following quotes: *Times* [London], February 1, 1941.

175. "He gets on": letter, Eric Seal, February 2, 1941, quoted in Gilbert, *Winston S. Churchill,* vol. 6, 999–1000.

176. Precedent-setting third inauguration: In the postwar years, under Republican impetus, the United States adopted a constitutional amendment that, with one technical exception, limits a president to two terms.

176. Willkie "is truly helping" and following FDR quote: WSC, vol. 3, 26.

176. "I shall have it framed": president from former naval person, January 28, 1941, Hopkins Papers, FDRL.

176. "were an inspiration": WSC, Vol. 3, 28.

177. The account of Hopkins's lunch with the king and queen comes from his London diary: Hopkins Papers, FDRL.

177. FDR on the king and queen: Ward, 131.

177. "I've just seen": Eleanor Roosevelt, 195.

178. Sir John Dill: At the time General Dill was chief of the Imperial General Staff. After Pearl Harbor, having been succeeded by General Sir Alan Brooke, Dill served with great effectiveness on the Combined Chiefs of Staff in Washington, where he developed a close friendship with General Marshall.

180. Hopkins's reports to FDR are found in Hopkins Papers, FDRL.

180. "relatively remote": Stafford, 53.

181. "persevering in their preparations": president from former naval person, January 28, 1941, Hopkins Papers, FDRL. (Following Hopkins quotes from this source.)

181. intelligence decrypts had indicated otherwise: see, e.g., Stafford, 52–54.

182. "very kindly offered": cover letter for list of items required (illegible signature), January 27, 1941, Hopkins Papers.

182. "the necessary decision": Dalton to Hopkins, February 6, 1941, Hopkins Papers, FDRL.

182. "It is absolutely urgent": Hopkins to president and secretary of state, January 30, 1941.

182. "I have seen destroyers": Hopkins to president and secretary of state, February 3, 1941.

183. *Daily Express* article: February 8, 1941.

183. "very genial": Sherwood, 254.

184. Churchill's BBC speech: CAC.

185. "It has been a great pleasure": president from former naval person, January 28, 1941.

185. "He is an outstanding liberal": *Manchester Guardian*, February 11, 1941.

185. "Poker Face" and "Oyster": *Evening Standard*, February 11, 1941.

185. "Mr. Hopkins is an American": *Daily Telegraph*, February 11, 1941.

15: A NEW MAGNA CHARTA

187–189. Details of Hopkins's arrival: *New York Times*, February 17, 1941, and *New York Herald Tribune*, February 17, 1941.

188. "When Mr. Hopkins reports": *News Chronicle*, February 5, 1941.

189. "If he has any money troubles": Morgenthau presidential diaries, December 31, 1940, FDRL.

189–190. Winant in re Labour Party leaders: see discussion by David Reynolds, *International Historical Review*, August 1982.

190. "a democratic world": *Newsweek*, February 17, 1941.

190. "an example of the best": *New York Times*, February 8, 1941.

190. Hopkins's arrival in Washington: *Washington Post*, February 17, 1941, and *New York Times*, February 17, 1941.

191. American correspondent's analysis: William H. Stoneman, *Chicago Daily News*, February 13, 1941.

192. "he had got right inside": Ismay, 217.

192. prominent military analyst: Hanson Baldwin, *New York Times*, February 23, 1941.

193. Early with reporters: *Washington Star*, February 17, 1941.

194. "betrayal": *Newsweek*, February 24, 1941.

194. "to do anything I can": *Newsweek*, February 17, 1941.

194. "Quisling": *Newsweek*, February 24, 1941.

194. Opening of Senate debate: *New York Times*, February 18, 1941.

195. Senator Reynolds: *New York Times*, February 21, 1941.

195. "an unexpected attack": *New York Times*, February 23, 1941.

195. Senator Bailey: *Newsweek*, March 3, 1941.

196. senators "evidently don't know much": Parrish, *Roosevelt and Marshall*, 172.

197. "new Magna Charta": *Newsweek*, March 24, 1941.

197. "without the mediation": *Newsweek*, March 24, 1941.

199. "With the signing": Morgenthau to president, FDRL.

16: "BY TEMPERAMENT, TRAINING AND EXPERIENCE"

200. "a man who wanted a world": John McCloy interview, May 13, 1983, AC.

200. "as if it was mutually understood" and following quotes: Harriman, March 11, 1941, memorandum, Harriman Papers, LC.

201. "I want you to go over": Harriman and Abel, 3.

201. press conference: February 18, 1941, Harriman and Abel, 5.

202. "creative conception": Harriman and Abel, 14.

202. "process of total immersion": Harriman and Abel, 14.

202. "The great thing": Colville interview, AC.

202. "not the slightest" and following quote: Harriman, March 11, 1941, memorandum.

202. "as many assorted generals": Harriman and Abel, 15.

203. "We are so short": Harriman, March 11, 1941, memorandum.

203. "No person in the Army": Young to Hopkins, March 17, 1941, Hopkins Papers, FDRL.

203. "We can't take seriously": Harriman, March 11, 1941, memorandum.

203–204. Arnold memorandum for the Chief of Staff: March [no date], 1941. Hopkins-Sherwood Collection, FDRL.

204. "I must attempt": Harriman, March 11, 1941, memorandum.

204. Harriman speeches: Harriman and Abel, 5–6.

205. "the White House cuisine": Sherwood, 214.

205. "the kitchen had better not": White House Historical Association, Henrietta Nesbitt (www.whitehousehistory.org/ob_d.html.)

205. "any man might rebel": *New York Times,* quoted in preceding sentence.

205–206. Harriman's lunch with FDR: March 11, 1941, memorandum.

206. "Lack of understanding" and following discussion: Harriman, March 11, 1941, memorandum.

207. "the most he gave": WAH reminiscences, October 12, 1953, Harriman Papers, LC.

207. "what Mr. Harriman's relation": press conference, February 18, 1941, Harriman and Abel, 5.

207. "The efficient functioning": *New York Times,* February 20, 1941.

208. Meiklejohn information: interview, AC.

209. Meiklejohn as "a 'dollar a year' man": foreword, Meiklejohn diary, Harriman Papers, LC.

209. "I left feeling very much": WAH interview, AC.

209. "fuming at the foolishness": Harriman and Abel, 21.

210. "We got to Chequers": WAH interview, AC.

211. "Whoever the president had sent": Mary Soames interview, AC.

211. "I told him Roosevelt's instruction": WAH interview, AC.

212. "how close they were to disaster": WAH reminiscence, October 12, 1953, AC.

212. "The Battle of the Atlantic": WSC, vol. 5, 6.

212. "You must get in touch": Harriman and Abel, 22.

17: LINKING UP

214. "struck Averell as really very remarkable": Colville interview, AC.

214. "He would always introduce me": WAH reminiscence, October 12, 1953, AC.

215. "Averell counted very much"; Colville interview, AC.

215. "the dock workers": WAH reminiscence, October 12, 1953, AC.

215. "Stand back": WAH foreword to Pawle.

215. "I'd like to give you a degree": WAH reminiscence, October 12, 1953, Harriman Papers, LC.

215. "devastation such as I had never thought possible": Colville, *The Fringes of Power*, 373.

216. "Here's Winnie" and following paragraph: WAH reminiscence, October 12, 1953, LC.

216. "They have such confidence": WAH reminiscence, October 12, 1953, LC.

217. "Mr. Harriman prided himself": Foreword, Meiklejohn MS World War II Diary, LC.

217. "I'm not coming back": E. J. Kahn, Jr., "Plenipotentiary—II," *New Yorker*, May 10, 1952.

217. "remain as imperturbable": "Plenipotentiary—II."

217. "take off on a moment's notice": Foreword, Meiklejohn MS World War II Diary, LC.

218. Steve Early: *New York Times*, March 8, 1941.

219. Winant's behavior: Tree, 157.

220. Colonel Green's complaint: Harriman and Abel, 60.

221. "Of paramount consideration": WAH for HLH, Harriman Papers [food and food shipping], LC.

221. "Are all departments": HLH from WAH, April 18, 1941, Harriman Papers [shipping priorities], LC.

222. "Such minor distortion of facts": WAH to HLH, June 5, 1941, Harriman Papers, LC.

222. "unhappy and dull diet": Woolton quoted in *New York Times*, May 31, 1941.

222. "You should know": HLH to WAH, June 4, 1941, Harriman Papers, LC.

223. The stevedore problem: Harriman to Land and Hopkins, April 10, 1941, Harriman Papers [stevedore mission], LC.

223. Land's reply: April 18, 1941, Harriman Papers [stevedore mission], LC.

223–224. Harriman's reply to Hopkins and Land: April 25, 1941, Harriman Papers [stevedore mission], LC.

18: "IN A NIGHTMARE"

226. "arriving at a decision": Parrish, *Roosevelt and Marshall*, 195.

226. Plan Dog: i.e., the fourth—D—plan drafted by the admiral and his staff.

227. "immensely facilitated": quoted in Leutze, 235–36. For details of the talks, see Watson, 374–80.

227. "I may have to be pushed": Morgenthau, presidential diaries, FDRL.

227. "the president has never said": Morgenthau, presidential diaries, May 14, 1941, FDRL.

227–228. Repair of British ships: WAH reminiscence, October 12, 1953, Harriman Papers, LC.

228. "to make up for losses": Harriman and Abel, 58.

229. "Unlimited national emergency": FDR declaration in a speech on May 27, 1941.

229. "Meanest SOB's": Love, vol. 1, 628.

229. "By some error of judgment": Lee to Winant, May 27, 1941, Hopkins Papers, FDRL.

230. "There's only one trouble": WAH reminiscence, October 12, 1953, LC.

230. "no goddam good": Harriman and Abel, 58.

230. "This led": WAH interview, October 12, 1953, LC.

230. "persistence of some faults": Dawson to Winant, March n.d., 1941, Harriman Papers, LC.

230. Harmon "did a first-rate job": WAH reminiscence, October 12, 1953, LC.

230. "We'll have to be more careful": Harriman and Abel, 26.

231. "I was serving the president": WAH reminiscence, October 12, 1953, Harriman Papers, LC.

231. "England's strength is bleeding": WAH to the president, April 10, 1941, PPF, FDRL.

231. "he would attack me": WAH interview, AC. See also Harriman and Abel, 26.

231. Harriman to Marie: May 6, 1941, AC.

232. "the most faithful": WSC, vol. 3, 22.

232. "I will be very pleased": WSC to HLH, August 29, 1941, Hopkins Papers, FDRL.

232. "You know this thing": Morgenthau, presidential diaries, March 1, 1941, FDRL.

232. "I have agreed to take on": HLH to WSC, March 19, 1941. Sherwood, 265.

233. "freeze it at the outset": HLH to WAH, July 1, 1941, Hopkins Papers, FDRL.

233. "complaints from those goddam New Dealers": Sherwood, 280.

233. "I can't escape the conviction": James S. Knowlson, quoted, Sherwood, 288.

233. "anytime Harry Hopkins": John McCloy interview, May 11, 1983, AC.

234. Morgenthau on Cox: presidential diaries, March 1, 1941, FDRL.

234. "Have received today": Hopkins from Harriman, June 26, 1941, Hopkins Papers, FDRL.

234. "You are doing a very important job there": Hopkins to Harriman, Hopkins Papers, FDRL.

19: AT THE DORCHESTER

235–236. Mary and Averell: Mary Soames interview, AC.

236. "blown to smithereens": WSC to Randolph, June 8, 1941, CAC.

237. "bleary-eyed and disfigured"; Colville, *The Fringes of Power*, 375.

237. "During the war": Kathleen [Harriman] Mortimer interview, AC.

237. "Unfortunately": Colville interview, AC.

238–239. Meiklejohn and the air raid: World War II Diary, April 16, LC.

239. "there was nothing like a Blitz": Kathleen Mortimer interview, AC.

239. "The socialites": Helen Fitzpatrick Millbanks interview, AC.

239. "you might feel that the risk was worth it": Kendrick, 248.

240. "a tremendous beauty": Charles Collingwood interview, AC.

240. "Every man in London": Larry LeSueur interview, AC.

240. "she had no neck": Colville interview, AC.

240. friend "very impressed": John McCloy interview, AC.

240. "She makes you feel": Donald Klopfer interview, AC.

241. "a woman who wants to get": Peter Duchin interview, AC. Pamela liked to say that she met Averell at a dinner party given by Emerald Cunard, but on the date in question (March 19) Harriman was dining with the prime minister and watching bombs fall on London, as described in Chapter 17.

241. Colville on Randolph: Colville interview, AC.

242. "she was in on everything": Kathleen Mortimer interview, AC.

242. "Hell of a battle": Harriman and Abel, 33–34.

243. Alexander Woollcott: Kathleen Mortimer interview, AC.

243. "Life is unbelievably social": Abramson, 313.

244. "he was something of a scoundrel": Kathleen Mortimer interview, AC.

244. "to surround himself": Kathleen quoted in Harriman and Abel, 61.

244. Beaverbrook and Averell "got on famously": Kathleen Mortimer interview, AC.

244. Clementine "always thought it was terrible": Kathleen Mortimer interview, AC.

20: ON HIS MAJESTY'S SERVICE

246. Churchill message to Wavell: June 4, 1941, Chartwell Papers, CAC.

247. "in London" and all following quotes to Hopkins: WAH to HLH, June 10–11, 1941, Harriman Papers, LC.

248. "the British Empire": Leutze, 302

249. remarkable "that they got any work done": Meiklejohn, World War II Diary, June 15, 1941.

250. "luxury and complacence": Harriman and Abel, 65.

250. "I have been extremely impressed": quoted in Ogden, 139.

250. Meiklejohn on Randolph: World War II Diary, June 23 and June 26, 1941, LC.

251. "GHQ does not appear to be well-organized": Harriman report to Churchill, "Observations on the Middle East," July 16, 1941, Harriman Papers, LC.

253. "boyish thrill": Harriman and Abel, 70.

21: THE COLOSSUS FACTOR

254. For a good look at the intelligence background of the German invasion, see Hinsley, vol. 1, chapter 14.

256. "I am certain": Berthon and Potts, 76, quoting Conrad Black, *Franklin Delano Roosevelt: Champion of Freedom*, 2003.

256. *Mein Kampf* quote: Parrish, *Simon & Schuster Encyclopedia of World War II*, 586.

256. "there is no doubt at all," including the quotations from the act: Cox to Hopkins, June 23, 1941, Hopkins Papers, FDRL.

257. "we must keep our eye": Cox to Hopkins, June 23.

257. "the anti-religious part of the Nazi policy": Cox to Hopkins, June 23.

258. Germany would be "thoroughly occupied": Stimson to the president, June 23, 1941, Hopkins Papers, FDRL.

258. "It cannot be over-emphasized": quoted in Sherwood, 304–305.

258. "notoriously incompetent": *New York Times*, June 16, 1941.

259. "even though it should retreat": Kendrick, 266.

259. "If Hitler invaded Hell": WSC, vol. 3, 370. Actually, Churchill is here quoting Colville quoting him. Also curiously, Churchill made the comment to Colville during the evening before the Germans launched their attack on Russia; he, like Roosevelt, expected the invasion, even if Stalin did not.

259. Russia had "come in against Germany": Colville, *The Fringes of Power*, 406.

259. "They made the same promise": Leutze, 316.

259. "ask the American people": quoted in Herring, 6.

260. "Help Russia": *New York Times*, June 26, 1941.

260. "Of course we are going": quoted in Freidel, 374.

261. Hopkins's memorandum of his talk with FDR is in Hopkins Papers, FDRL.

263. Jock Colville and Kathleen: Colville, *The Fringes of Power*, 415–16.

263. Alexander: later commander in chief in the Middle East and Allied supreme commander in the Mediterranean; Brooke succeeded General Dill as chief of the Imperial General Staff, the post in which he served for the remainder of the war. Attlee: postwar prime minister.

265. "I will send you a message": quoted in Sherwood, 318.

265. "I ask you to treat": quoted in Sherwood, 322.

265. "I must tell you": prime minister for M. Stalin, July 1941, CAC.

266. "this was an early indication": McKinley, "Flight to Archangel," Hopkins Papers, FDRL.

267. "Give us antiaircraft guns": Hopkins report, quoted in Sherwood, 328.

267. "They will never get to Moscow": quoted in *Washington Times-Herald*, July 30, 1942.

267. "The whole situation shows": General Franz Halder, August 11, 1941, quoted in Murray and Millett, 125.

268. "He looked very tired" and following quote: McKinley, "Flight to Archangel."

268. "Harry arrived dead beat": Former naval person to president, August 4, 1941, FDRL. [In WSC, vol. 3, the message reads: "Harry returned dead-beat from Russia, but is lively again now." All such messages were paraphrased for security reasons.]

268–269. FDR memorandum to Coy: August 2, 1941, FDRL.

269–270. FDR and Elliott: Elliott Roosevelt, 22.

POSTLUDE

271. FDR "had a horror": WAH interview, AC.

271. Roosevelt "felt that if you kept": Harriman interview by Thomas F.

Soapes, February 2, 1978, Eleanor Roosevelt Oral History Project, FDRL.

272. "The American Constitution": John H. Peck, "The Working Day," *Atlantic*, March 1965.

272. "dictate the peace": Kimball, *The Juggler*, 14, from John Harvey, ed., *The War Diaries of Oliver Harvey* (London: Collins, 1978), 229.

274. "root of the matter": Churchill also applied the concept to General de Gaulle, once saying of him to a visiting French general: *"Mon ami, il a la racine de la matière dans lui."*

274. "You're married to the war": WAH, personal notes, June 30, 1942, Harriman Papers, LC.

274–275. "He was a very astute person": Kathleen Mortimer interview, AC.

275. Kennedy quote: *Time*, August 4, 1986. In the decades after JFK made that observation, Harriman, as we saw, went on to add numerous other "jobs" to his résumé.

275. "I've never really worried": WAH Henry Brandon interview, *New York Times Magazine*, March 5, 1967.

276. "the only person I have ever known": Helen Fitzpatrick Millbanks interview, AC.

BIBLIOGRAPHY

The vastness of the literature on the period during which the events figuring in this book occurred has called for the exercise of considerable bibliographic discipline. The following listing includes only books directly consulted in the preparation of the book.

All other materials—documents, interviews, memoranda, articles—are cited in full at the relevant points in the Notes.

Abramson, Rudy. *Spanning the Century.* New York: William Morrow, 1992.

Adams, Henry. *The Education of Henry Adams.* Boston: Houghton Mifflin, 1961 [original pub., 1918].

Adams, Henry H. *Harry Hopkins.* New York: Putnam, 1977.

Allen, Frederick L. *Since Yesterday: The 1930's in America.* New York: Harper, 1939.

Alsop, Joseph, and Robert Kintner. *Men Around the President.* New York: Doubleday, Doran, 1939.

Amory, Mark, ed. *The Letters of Evelyn Waugh.* New Haven, Conn.: Ticknor and Fields, 1980.

Begbie, Harold [A Gentleman with a Duster]. *The Mirrors of Downing Street.* New York: Putnam, 1921.

———. *The Windows of Westminster.* New York: Putnam, 1924.

Bennett, Gill. *Churchill's Man of Mystery: Desmond Morton and the World of Intelligence.* London: Routledge, 2007.

Berg, A. Scott. *Lindbergh.* New York: Putnam, 1998.

Berthon, Simon. *Allies at War.* New York: Carroll & Graf, 2001.

Berthon, Simon, and Joanna Potts. *Warlords.* n.p.: Da Capo Press, 2006.

Beschloss, Michael R. *Kennedy and Roosevelt: The Uneasy Alliance.* New York: Norton, 1980; Harper Perennial ed., 1987.

Blair, Clay. *Hitler's U-Boat War.* 2 vols. New York: Random House, 1996.

Blum, John Morton. *From the Morgenthau Diaries*. Vol. 2, *Years of Urgency, 1938-1941*. Boston: Houghton Mifflin, 1965.

———, ed. *Roosevelt and Morgenthau*. Boston: Houghton Mifflin, 1970.

Blythe, Ronald. *Age of Illusion: England in the Twenties and Thirties, 1919-1940*. Boston: Houghton Mifflin, 1964.

Bois, Elie J. *Truth on the Tragedy of France*, trans. N. Scarlyn Wilson. London: Hodder and Stoughton, 1941.

Bonham Carter, Violet. *Winston Churchill: An Intimate Portrait*. New York: Konecky & Konecky, 1965.

Boothe, Clare [Clare Boothe Luce]. *Europe in the Spring*. New York: Alfred A. Knopf, 1940.

Boyne, Walter J. *Clash of Wings: World War II in the Air*. New York: Simon & Schuster, 1994.

Brendon, Piers. *The Dark Valley*. New York: Alfred A. Knopf, 2000.

Brownell, Will, and Richard N. Billings. *So Close to Greatness: A Biography of William C. Bullitt*. New York: Macmillan, 1987.

Bullitt, Orville H., ed. *For the President, Personal and Secret; Correspondence between Franklin D. Roosevelt and William C. Bullitt*. Boston: Houghton Mifflin, 1972.

Butler, Susan, ed. *My Dear Mr. Stalin: The Complete Correspondence of Franklin D. Roosevelt and Joseph Stalin*. New Haven, Conn.: Yale University Press, 2005.

Casey, Steven. *Cautious Crusade*. New York: Oxford University Press, 2001.

Cecil, Robert. *Hitler's Decision to Invade Russia*. New York: David McKay, 1975.

Chandos, Oliver Lyttelton, Viscount. *The Memoirs of Lord Chandos*. London: The Bodley Head, 1962.

Chase, Stuart, in collaboration with Marian Tyler. *The New Western Front*. New York: Harcourt, Brace, 1939.

Churchill, Winston S. *The Second World War*. 6 vols. Boston: Houghton Mifflin, 1948-53.

Clapper, Olive Ewing. *Washington Tapestry*. New York: Whittlesey House/McGraw-Hill, 1946.

Clapper, Raymond. *Watching the World*, ed. Mrs. Raymond Clapper. New York: Whittlesey House/McGraw-Hill, 1944.

Cockett, Richard, ed. *My Dear Max*. London: Historians' Press, 1990.

Cole, Wayne. Charles *A. Lindbergh and the Battle Against American Intervention in World War II*. New York: Harcourt, Brace, Jovanovich, 1974.

Colville, John. *The Fringes of Power*. New York: Norton, 1985.

_____. *Winston Churchill and His Inner Circle*. New York: Wyndham Books, 1981.

Cowling, Maurice. *The Impact of Hitler*. New York: Cambridge University Press, 1975.

Dallek, Robert. *Franklin D. Roosevelt and American Foreign Policy, 1932–1945*. New York: Oxford University Press, 1979.

Danchev, Alex. *Establishing the Anglo-American Alliance: The Second World War Diaries of Brigadier Vivian Dykes*. London: Brassey's, 1990.

Davis, Forrest, and Ernest K. Lindley. *How War Came*. New York: Simon & Schuster, 1942.

Dilks, David, ed. *The Diaries of Sir Alexander Cadogan, 1938–1945*. New York: Putnam, 1972.

Dobson, Alan P. U. S. Wartime Aid to Britain 1940–1946. New York: St. Martin's Press, 1986.

Dutton, David. *Neville Chamberlain*. London: Hodder Arnold, 2001.

Eden, Anthony (Earl of Avon). *Facing the Dictators*. Boston: Houghton Mifflin, 1962.

Fedden, Robin. *Churchill and Chartwell*. n.p.: The National Trust, 1986 [rev. ed.].

Fehrenbach, T. R. *F. D. R.'s Undeclared War, 1939–1941*. New York: David McKay, 1967.

Feiling, Keith. *The Life of Neville Chamberlain*. London: Macmillan, 1946.

Feis, Herbert. *1933: Characters in Crisis*. Boston: Little, Brown, 1966.

Fest, Joachim C. *Hitler*, trans. from the German by Richard and Clara Winston. New York: Harcourt, Brace, Jovanovich, 1974.

Freidel, Frank. *FDR: Rendezvous With Destiny*. Boston: Little, Brown, 1990.

Giffen, Allison, and June Hopkins. *Jewish First Wife, Divorced: The Correspondence of Ethel Gross and Harry Hopkins*. Lanham, Md.: Lexington Books, 2003.

Gilbert, Martin. *Churchill and America*. New York: Free Press, 2005.

_____. *The Churchill War Papers*. Vol. 1, *At the Admiralty*. New York: Norton, 1993.

_____. *Winston S. Churchill.* Vol. 6, *Finest Hour, 1939-1941.* Boston: Houghton Mifflin, 1983.

Greer, Thomas H. *What Roosevelt Thought.* East Lansing: Michigan State University Press, 1958.

Gunther, John. *Procession.* New York: Harper & Row, 1965.

_____. *Roosevelt in Retrospect.* New York: Harper, 1950.

Hamby, Alonzo L. *For the Survival of Democracy: Franklin Roosevelt and the World Crisis of the 1930s.* New York: Free Press, 2004.

Harriman, W. Averell, and Elie Abel. *Special Envoy to Churchill and Stalin 1941-1946.* New York: Random House, 1975.

Heinrichs, Waldo. *Threshold of War.* New York: Oxford University Press, 1988.

Herring, George C. *Aid to Russia, 1941-1946.* New York: Columbia University Press, 1973.

Hinsley, Francis Harry, with E. E. Thomas, C. F. G. Ransom, and R. C. Knight. *British Intelligence in the Second World War.* 5 vols. New York: Cambridge University Press, 1979-88.

Hixson, Walter L. *Charles A. Lindbergh, Lone Eagle.* 2nd ed. New York: Longman, 2002.

Hopkins, Robert. *Witness to History.* Seattle, Wash.: Castle Pacific Publishing, 2002.

Hunt, John Gabriel, ed. *The Essential Franklin Delano Roosevelt.* New York: Gramercy Books, 1995.

Ickes, Harold L. *The Secret Diary of Harold L. Ickes.* Vol. 3, *The Lowering Clouds, 1939–1941.* New York: Simon & Schuster, 1954.

Ismay, General Lord. *Memoirs.* New York: Viking, 1960.

Jackson, Robert H. *That Man: An Insider's Portrait of Franklin D. Roosevelt.* New York: Oxford University Press, 2003.

James, Robert Rhodes. *Churchill: A Study in Failure.* New York: World, 1970.

Jenkins, Roy. *Churchill.* New York: Farrar, Straus & Giroux, 2001.

Johnson, Alan Campbell. *Viscount Halifax.* New York: Ives Washburn, 1941.

Josephson, Matthew. *The Robber Barons: The Great American Capitalists, 1861–1901.* New York: Harcourt Brace, 1934.

Keegan, John. *The Second World War.* New York: Viking, 1990.

Kelen, Emery. *Peace in Their Time.* New York: Alfred A. Knopf, 1963.

Kendrick, Alexander. *Prime Time: The Life of Edward R. Murrow.* Boston:

Little, Brown, 1969; paperback ed., Avon Books, 1970.

Kennan, George F. *American Diplomacy 1900–1950.* Chicago: University of Chicago Press, 1951.

Kershaw, Ian. *Fateful Choices.* New York: Penguin, 2008.

_____. *Hitler, 1936-1945: Nemesis.* New York: Norton, 2000.

Ketchum, Richard M. *The Borrowed Years, 1938–1941.* New York: Random House, 1989; Doubleday Anchor ed., 1991.

Keynes, John Maynard. *Essays in Persuasion.* New York: Norton, 1963 [original pub., 1931].

Kimball, Warren. *The Juggler: Franklin Roosevelt as Wartime Statesman.* Princeton, N.J.: Princeton University Press, 1991.

_____. *The Most Unsordid Act: Lend-Lease, 1939–1941.* Baltimore, Md.: Johns Hopkins University Press, 1969.

Klingaman, William K. *1941.* New York: Harper & Row, 1988.

Langer, William L., and S. Everett Gleason. *The Challenge to Isolation, 1937-1940.* New York: Harper, 1952.

_____. *The Undeclared War.* New York: Harper, 1953.

Lash, Joseph P. *Eleanor and Franklin.* New York: Norton, 1971.

Lawlor, Sheila. *Churchill and the Politics of War, 1940–1941.* Cambridge, England: Cambridge University Press, 1994.

Leuchtenburg, William R. *The Supreme Court Reborn: The Constitutional Revolution in the Age of Roosevelt.* New York: Oxford University Press, 1995; paperback ed., 1996.

Leutze, James, ed. *The London Journal of General Raymond E. Lee, 1940–1941.* Boston: Little, Brown, 1971.

Lippmann, Walter. *Interpretations, 1933-1935.* New York: Macmillan, 1936.

Lochner, Louis P. *Always the Unexpected.* New York: Macmillan, 1956.

Loewenheim, Francis L., Harold D. Langley, and Manfred Jonas. *Roosevelt and Churchill: Their Secret Wartime Correspondence.* New York: Da Capo, 1990.

Love, Robert W., Jr. *History of the U.S. Navy.* Vol. 1, 1775-1941. Harrisburg, Pa.: Stackpole, 1992.

Lysaght, Charles Edward. *Brendan Bracken.* London: Allen Lane, 1979.

McElwee, William. *Britain's Locust Years, 1918-1940.* London: Faber and Faber, 1962.

McJimsey, George. *Harry Hopkins.* Cambridge, Mass.: Harvard University Press, 1987.

_____. *The Presidency of Franklin Delano Roosevelt.* Lawrence: University of Kansas Press, 2000.

Matloff, Maurice, and Edwin M. Snell. *Strategic Planning for Coalition Warfare, 1941-1942.* Washington, D.C.: Office of the Chief of Military History, 1953.

Mearsheimer, John J. *Liddell Hart and the Weight of History.* Ithaca, N.Y.: Cornell University Press, 1988.

Miller, Nathan. *FDR: An Intimate History.* New York: Doubleday, 1983; New American Library ed., 1984.

Milton, Joyce. *Loss of Eden: A Biography of Charles and Anne Morrow Lindbergh.* New York: HarperCollins, 1993.

Moggridge, Donald. *Maynard Keynes: An Economist's Biography.* New York: Routledge, 1992.

Monnet, Jean. *Memoirs.* Trans. from the French by Richard Mayne. Garden City, N.Y.: Doubleday, 1978.

Morison, Samuel Eliot. *The Two-Ocean War.* Boston: Little, Brown, 1963.

Mowat, Charles L. *Britain Between the Wars, 1918-1940.* Chicago: University of Chicago Press, 1961.

Mowrer, Edgar Ansel. *Triumph and Turmoil: A Personal History of Our Time.* New York: Weybright and Talley, 1968.

Murray, Williamson, and Allan R. Millett. *A War to Be Won: Fighting the Second World War.* Cambridge, Mass.: Belknap Press of Harvard University Press, 2000.

Nicolson, Harold. *Why Britain Is at War.* Harmondsworth, England: Penguin Books, 1939.

Nicolson, Nigel, ed. *Harold Nicolson: Diaries and Letters 1930-1939.* New York: Atheneum, 1966.

Ogden, Christopher. *Life of the Party: The Biography of Pamela Digby Churchill Hayward Harriman.* New York: Little, Brown, 1994; Warner Books ed., 1995.

Olson, Lynne. *Troublesome Young Men.* New York: Farrar, Straus & Giroux, 2007.

Overy, R. J. *Dictators: Hitler's Germany and Stalin's Russia.* New York: Norton, 2004.

Parkinson, Roger. *Peace for Our Time.* New York: David McKay, 1971.

Parks, Lillian Rogers. *My Thirty Years Backstairs at the White House.* New York: Fleet, 1961.

———. *The Roosevelts: A Family in Turmoil.* Englewood Cliffs, N.J.: Prentice-Hall, 1981.

Parrish, Thomas. *Roosevelt and Marshall: Partners in Politics and War.* New York: William Morrow, 1989.

———, ed. *The Simon & Schuster Encyclopedia of World War II.* New York: Simon & Schuster, 1978.

———. *The Submarine: A History.* New York: Viking, 2004; Penguin ed., 2005.

———. *The Ultra Americans.* New York: Stein and Day, 1986; paperback ed., *The American Codebreakers: The U.S. Role in Ultra,* Scarborough House, 1991.

Pawle, Gerald. *The War and Colonel Warden.* New York: Alfred A. Knopf, 1963.

Percy, Eustace. *Some Memories.* London: Eyre & Spottiswoode, 1958.

Perkins, Frances. *The Roosevelt I Knew.* New York: Viking Press, 1946; Harper Colophon ed., 1964.

Persico, Joseph E. *Edward R. Murrow: An American Original.* New York: McGraw-Hill, 1988; Dell paperback ed., 1990.

Pogue, Forrest C. *George C. Marshall: Ordeal and Hope, 1939–42.* New York: Viking, 1966.

Ponting, Clive. *1940: Myth and Reality.* Chicago: Ivan R. Dee, 1991; paperback ed., 1993.

Rauch, Basil. *Roosevelt: From Munich to Pearl Harbor.* New York: Creative Age Press, 1950.

———, ed. *The Roosevelt Reader: Selected Speeches, Messages, Press Conferences, and Letters.* New York: Holt, Rinehart & Winston, 1957.

Raymond, John, ed. *The Baldwin Age.* London: Eyre & Spottiswoode, 1960.

Reed, Douglas. *Disgrace Abounding.* London: Jonathan Cape, 1939.

———. *Insanity Fair: A European Cavalcade.* New York: Random House, 1939.

Renwick, Robin. *Fighting with Allies.* New York: New York Times Books, 1996.

Reynolds, David. *The Creation of the Anglo-American Alliance, 1937-41.* Chapel Hill: University of North Carolina Press, 1982.

———. *From Munich to Pearl Harbor.* Chicago: Ivan R. Dee, 2001.

———. *In Command of History: Churchill Fighting and Writing the Second World War.* New York: Basic Books, 2005.

Robertson, Ben. *I Saw England*. New York: Alfred A. Knopf, 1941.

Rock, Stephen R. *Appeasement in International Politics*. Lexington: University Press of Kentucky, 2000.

Rodengen, Jeffrey L. *The Legend of Cornelius Vanderbilt Whitney*. Fort Lauderdale, Fla.: Write Stuff Enterprises, 2000.

Rollins, Alfred B., Jr. *Franklin D. Roosevelt and the Age of Action*. New York: Dell, 1960.

Romasco, Albert U. *The Politics of Recovery: Roosevelt's New Deal*. New York: Oxford University Press, 1983.

Roosevelt, Eleanor. *This I Remember*. New York: Harper, 1949.

Roosevelt, Elliott. *As He Saw It*. New York: Duell, Sloan and Pearce, 1946.

Rubin, Gretchen. *Forty Ways to Look at Winston Churchill*. New York: Ballantine Books, 2003.

Saint-Jean, Robert de. *France Speaking*. Trans. from the French by Anne Green. New York: Dutton, 1941.

Savage, Sean J. *Roosevelt: The Party Leader*. Lexington: University Press of Kentucky, 1991.

Sherwood, Robert E. *Roosevelt and Hopkins: An Intimate History*. New York: Harper, 1948.

Shirer, William L. *Berlin Diary*. New York: Alfred A. Knopf, 1941.

Shogan, Robert. *Hard Bargain*. New York: Scribner, 1995.

Simone, André. *Men of Europe*. New York: Modern Age Books, 1941.

Smith, Amanda, ed. *Hostage to Fortune: The Letters of Joseph P. Kennedy*. New York: Viking, 2001.

Smith, Jean Edward. *FDR*. New York: Random House, 2007.

Smith, Sally Bedell. *Reflected Glory: The Life of Pamela Churchill Harriman*. New York: Simon & Schuster, 1996.

Soames, Mary. *Clementine Churchill*. Boston: Houghton Mifflin, 1979.

_____. *Winston and Clementine*. Boston: Houghton Mifflin, 1998; Mariner ed., 2001.

Spears, Sir Edward. *Assignment to Catastrophe*. Vol. 1, *Prelude to Dunkirk*. Vol. 2, *The Fall of France, June 1940*. New York: A. A. Wynn, 1954–55.

Sperber, A. M. *Murrow, His Life and Times*. New York: Freundlich Books, 1968; paperback ed., Fordham University Press, 1998.

Stafford, David. *Roosevelt and Churchill: Men of Secrets*. Woodstock, N.Y.: Overlook Press, 2000.

Stettinius, Edward R., Jr. *Lend-Lease, Weapon for Victory*. New York: Macmillan, 1944.

Stimson, Henry L., and McGeorge Bundy. *On Active Service in Peace and War*. New York: Harper, 1948.

Strawson, John. *Hitler as Military Commander*. London: B. T. Batsford, 1971.

Swift, Will. *The Kennedys: Amidst the Gathering Storm*. New York: Smithsonian Books, 2008.

Swinton, Earl of, with James D. Margack. *Sixty Years of Power*. New York: James H. Heineman, 1966.

Thorne, Christopher. *Allies of a Kind*. New York: Oxford University Press, 1978; paperback ed., 1979.

Tree, Ronald. *When the Moon Was High*. London: Macmillan, 1975.

Tully, Grace. *FDR Was My Boss*. New York: Scribner, 1949.

Volkogonov, Dmitri. *Stalin: Triumph and Tragedy*. Ed. and trans. from the Russian by Harold Shukman. New York: Grove Weidenfeld, 1991.

Ward, Geoffrey C., ed. *Closest Companion*. Boston: Houghton Mifflin, 1995.

Watson, Mark Skinner. *Chief of Staff: Prewar Plans and Preparations*. Washington, D.C.: Historical Division, Department of the Army, 1950.

Wheeler-Bennett, Sir John, ed. *Action This Day: Working with Churchill*. New York: St. Martin's Press, 1969.

Wiltz, John E. *From Isolation to War. 1931-1941*. Arlington Heights, Ill.: Harlan Davidson, Inc., 1968.

Winant, John Gilbert. *Letter from Grosvenor Square*. Boston: Houghton Mifflin, 1947.

Wingate, Sir Ronald. *Lord Ismay*. London: Hutchinson, 1970.

Young, Kenneth. *Churchill and Beaverbrook*. London: Eyre & Spottiswoode, 1966.

Zevin, B. D. *Nothing to Fear: The Selected Addresses of Franklin Delano Roosevelt 1932–1945*. Boston: Houghton Mifflin, 1946.

ACKNOWLEDGMENTS

As I have had occasion to say a number of times before, a book is a collaborative enterprise and I am deeply grateful to everybody who provided help with this one. I also apologize to anyone whose contribution I may have inadvertently overlooked in the following expressions of thanks.

For his many services I am, as always, indebted to my efficient and devoted agent, Stuart Krichevsky. I also appreciate the involvement of my editor, Elisabeth Kallick Dyssegaard, who had the commendable discernment to see the merit of the idea from the outset and who, in our continuing dialectic, made valuable contributions to its development.

Since much of the book is based on information from archival sources, I wish to express my thanks to the staff of the Franklin D. Roosevelt Library at Hyde Park, N.Y., for their cooperation and in particular to Mark Renovitch for help with photographs. I am also grateful to Allen Packwood, director of the Churchill Archives Centre, Churchill College, Cambridge, for his cordially given advice and help, and I thank his staff as well. Thanks are also due to the archival staff of King's College, London, and to the cheery folks at the Oral History Office, Columbia University Libraries. I also wish to pay my awed respect to the staffs of two notable Paris institutions, the Bibliothèque Nationale and the Bibliothèque Historique de la Ville de Paris.

As always, I am happy to give special thanks to the hardworking and highly cooperative staff members of the libraries at Berea College, Eastern Kentucky University, and the University of Kentucky, all of whom have, through the years, extended every courtesy to me. I thank Carol Thomas for help with research and thanks also to my diligent Washington researcher, Mark Tacyn, for his contributions. I am indebted to Professor Lawrence K. Lynch for his critical reading of portions of the manuscript and also to my good friend and fellow author Charles Bracelen Flood for his continuing advice and encouragement.

For field help in France, particularly with respect to a memorable visit to the Maginot Line, I thank Ruth-Christine Knutson-Beveraggi. For overall help in both archival and field research at home and abroad, I thank Nancy Coleman Wolsk of Transylvania University, Lexington, Kentucky.

More personally, I am, as always grateful to Nancy for her continuing encouragement and advice, for sharing varied experiences in research, and, indeed, for her full participation in the adventure of making a book.

One more—and unique—acknowledgment: In 1992 my good friend Rudy Abramson published *Spanning the Century*, a biography of Averell Harriman, which immediately became recognized as the authoritative work on its subject. During the 1980s, in creating the book, Rudy conducted more than 150 interviews with persons who had been involved with Harriman and with his associates, the latter group including (notably) Harry Hopkins, and with public events during his time. Much of this priceless archive, containing the ideas and memories of persons many of whom left us two decades ago and more, was made available to me by Rudy, and my access to these transcripts enabled me to give the book a kind of immediacy and currency it could not have possessed otherwise. Unfortunately, fate intervened before I could show Rudy the results of my labors; to the shock of his many friends and admirers, this public-spirited and generous man died in February 2008. I deeply regret it.

INDEX

Duncan, Barbara. *See* Hopkins, Barbara
Dunkirk, 4, 92–93, 95

Early, Steve, 119, 122, 123, 193, 218
Eden, Anthony, 48, 83, 91, 135–36, 145, 159, 230, 272
England. *See* Britain
Europe, 56, 74. *See also* German European conquests
American isolationism and turbulence in, 71–72
Americans and prewar, 42, 71
Chamberlain and, 46–47
FDR and prewar, 41, 42, 44–45, 48–49, 63
European war, 90
American views of, 1, 2, 91, 93, 94, 101, 125
FDR and, 74–80, 86–89, 118–19
Hopkins, Harry, and, 86–87
Neutrality Act and, 78, 79, 80, 81
U.S. neutrality toward, 91, 93–94

FDR. *See* Roosevelt, Franklin D.
Federal Emergency Relief, 15–16
France, 1, 41, 42, 57, 104. *See also* Allies; Britain; Europe
FDR and, 63–64, 89
German conflict with, 75, 81–82, 89, 92–95, 152
German conquest of, 4, 5, 6, 85, 89, 125
German European conquests and, 2–4, 75, 80–81, 85
Monnet and, 63–64
Munich agreement and, 60, 61
U.S. aircraft and, 58, 63–65, 82, 88
U.S. supplies and, 81, 82, 94
French occupation
Britain and, 95–97, 99–100

U.S. and, 89, 95–96, 104

George VI, 177–79
German air assault on Britain, 102–3, 111, 133–35, 137, 144, 147, 156, 175, 179–80, 188, 214–16, 225, 236–39. *See also* blitz; Luftwaffe
German air power, 61
British air power and, 62–63, 99
Churchill, W., and, 62, 99, 144
German defeat without U.S. war, 118–19
German European conquests, 1, 56–57, 78
Allies and, 2–6, 75, 80–82, 85, 125
Britain and, 4–6, 75, 80–82, 85
Chamberlain and, 70–71, 75, 84, 85
France and, 2–4, 75, 80–81, 85
U.S. and, 4, 6, 74–76, 81, 85, 93–95
German invasion of Britain, possibility of, 180–81, 188–89, 197, 254, 258, 259
German invasion of Russia, 254–59, 264, 268, 272
German U-boats, 212, 229, 272
Germany, 1, 19, 181. *See also* British-German conflict; French occupation; Hitler, Adolf; Nazis; Russian-German conflict
British conflict with, 75, 81–82, 90–96, 99–100, 102–3, 111–13
Chamberlain and conquests by, 70–71, 75
Churchill, W., and, 109–10
Czech crisis and, 56, 57, 58–59
French conflict with, 75, 81–82, 89, 92, 93, 94, 95, 152
French conquest by, 4, 5, 6, 85, 89, 125